D0872354

#Parasha
Weekly Insights from a Leading Israeli Journalist

MENORAH

Sivan Rahav-Meir

#PARASHA

Weekly Insights from a
Leading Israeli Journalist

TRANSLATED BY:
Chava Wilschanski

Menorah Books

#Parasha
Weekly Insights from a Leading Israeli Journalist

First English Edition, 2017

Menorah Books
An imprint of Koren Publishers Jerusalem Ltd.

POB 8531, New Milford, CT 06776-8531, USA
& POB 4044, Jerusalem 9104001, Israel
www.menorah-books.com

Original Hebrew Edition © Sivan Rahav-Meir 2016

© Sivan Rahav-Meir 2017

All rights reserved. No part of this publication may be reproduced,
stored in a retrieval system, or transmitted in any form or by
any means, electronic, mechanical, photocopying or otherwise,
without the prior permission of the publisher, except in the case
of brief quotations embodied in critical articles or reviews.

ISBN 978-1-59264-480-3, *hardcover*

A CIP catalogue record for this title is
available from the British Library

Printed and bound in the United States

To my father and mother

Contents

Contents

Introduction

Thinking about the place of the Torah in our lives, I often feel it is the topic we talk about least. We skirt around it but do not engage it directly. Here in Israel, we view Torah through the prism of politics, whether arguing about budgets or holding demonstrations. We listen to rabbis and politicians discuss controversial issues, such as legislation on religious matters, and we get angry. And sometimes we are so preoccupied with the issues of the day that we do not even begin to fathom the hidden treasures of the Torah.

For thousands of years, the weekly *parasha* has been the pulse of our lives. We read it every Shabbat in the synagogue and it inspires us throughout the week, giving us food for thought and meaning for our existence. A famous hasidic saying tells us to "live with the times," meaning we should live with the weekly *parasha*, looking to see how its ideas meet us in our day-to-day lives. As a journalist, I have spent many years reporting on politics, the courts, the religious sector, and government ministries, and I feel that our attitude to Judaism has become very predictable as we move from one scandal, apology, protest, court intervention or legislation to the next. Structuring our lives around the *parasha* rather than the news cycle could go a long way toward improving our discourse.

In this book, I have made a modest attempt to bring the Torah into our daily conversation, to show its relevance to our lives, and to add new voices to the ones we are used to hearing. Throughout the generations, commentators on the Torah have given us pearls of wisdom and I want to make them accessible to the general public. They have plenty to say about money, relationships, education, jealousy, publicity, and anger. As we delve into the treasures contained in the Torah, it is difficult to believe how Torah has become a source of friction between us, instead of uniting us. The Jewish nation may have returned to its homeland with great joy but here in our own country, the People of the Book is not proud of its own Book, the source of our culture and identity. It seems to me that when we left exile and returned home, we left Rashi, Rashbam, the Baal Shem Tov, the Vilna Gaon, and many other sages behind.

About two years ago, I began sending out on social media a short daily idea from the weekly *parasha*, and was surprised by the scope of reactions I received. As a journalist, audience feedback is not new to me, but with these posts I felt something different. Now I was sharing a common cultural bond with my audience, a bond that brought us much closer together and made the connection more relevant.

The idea of collecting these posts and publishing them in a book came from my readers. Their positive reactions to the posts, and their requests to gather all the WhatsApp messages into one book, were the driving force behind this book. They also started asking me for ideas for speeches: "What can I say to a bar mitzva boy on *Bemidbar*?" "My brother is joining the IDF on *Bereshit*. Do you have an appropriate blessing?" "We are adopting a dog on *Korah* and need an idea for a speech."

So here it is. I chose the best posts and edited them and also wrote many new ones. I wish to emphasize that the book does not contain any new ideas. The Torah has seventy faces and I have no desire to invent the seventy-first. In fact, my personal aim is quite the opposite. I want to become more familiar with the treasure trove of existing commentaries, to search for valuable explanations that have been forgotten, and to uncover pearls of wisdom that lie gathering dust in obscure volumes.

Yet, now that I think about it, this book does indeed offer something new. Every time we meet the Torah, a new reality is formed that did not exist previously. Thus, each reader joins me in creating something new when he or she discovers how the Torah has a place in their life.

CB CB CB

Three ideas, from three different commentators, each explaining what happens to us when we engage with the Torah, were my inspiration while writing the book. I want to acquaint my readers with these commentators and their thoughts before they begin reading.

The first is Hakham Abraham Azoulay, a rabbi and kabbalist from Morocco. He compares the Torah to a mirror and teaches us that each person is reflected in it and can see himself in the Torah: "The Torah is like an illuminating mirror. Whatever shape or size stands in front of it will be reflected back. Similarly, the soul of each and every person will find an explanation in the Torah personally tailored to him."

The second is Rabbi Mordechai Yosef Leiner, who was a hasidic rebbe and author of the *Mei HaShiloah*. He wrote that the Torah helps us overcome our faults and shortcomings. Just as we use a filter to enhance a picture and hide the blemishes, so the Torah is meant to make us better people: "The Torah was only given to complete what is lacking. Whatever was lacking from the day one was created is completed by the Torah."

The third is Professor Nehama Leibowitz, one of the greatest teachers of Tanakh in contemporary times. She would sit in the university library, surrounded by piles of books. When her students once asked her why she looked so excited and curious as she sat in front of these books, she replied: "Just think about a love letter. When a lover writes a letter to his beloved, she reads every word and every punctuation mark with great excitement. She wonders why he used this particular word in one place and not elsewhere, why this sentence ends in a question mark, and why he uses that word twice. For me, the Torah is God's love letter to us and that is how we should read it." She then went back to her love letter to examine more messages from her Lover.

I hope that you will feel that the Torah is a mirror that reflects to us who we are, that balances our shortcomings, and is a love letter addressed to us.

ACKNOWLEDGMENTS

I would like to thank the many, many commentators who wrote books on the Torah. They are the basis for this book. In many cases, I only quoted from them partially, shortening their words and omitting certain sections.

Thanks to my husband Yedidya. It feels a bit strange to me to thank him because he is really an inseparable part of every word I wrote. (Rest assured, this sentence, like all the others, will be approved by him before it goes to print.)

Thank you to my children who are constantly teaching me so much. I thank them for understanding, more or less, that their mom is sitting in her office, working on her book. And of course, thanks to the army of babysitters who help.

Thank you to my dear grandma Rachel, to my in-laws Rabbi Eliav and Ziva Meir for their *divrei Torah* and their life of Torah, to my brother Matan, and to my brothers- and sisters-in-law.

Thank you to Matthew Miller, Yehoshua Miller, and Rabbi Reuven Ziegler of Menorah's parent imprint, Koren Publishers Jerusalem, for believing in this project and moving it forward with such professionalism.

Thank you to Chava Wilschanski for her excellent translation, and to the dedicated editorial staff, Rabbi Shlomo Zuckier, Nechama Unterman, and Tomi Mager, for seeing the project to completion. Thank you to marketing director Yehudit Singer for bringing it to a whole new audience of English-language readers, and to Yehudit Cohen for her valuable suggestions.

Thank you to Margalit Cooper for her unending help. Thank you to composer Yossi Green who added a dose of harmony to this book. Thank you to my first American readers – Eli and Adina Reismann. Thank you to Shoshana Silber, to my agent Benayahu Yom Tov, to my international agent Hillel Sommer, and of course to Rabbi Moshe Weiss for his enthusiasm.

Thank you to my employers at the various media outlets where I work, who gave me a small amount of free time to work on the book and who support me in my new "craze."

Thank you to editor Tsuriel Gavison, without whom the original Hebrew edition of this work would not have been possible, and to Rabbi Yosef Eliyahu, who reviewed the primary texts and saved me from embarrassing errors. If any mistakes remain in the book, they are entirely my fault and I welcome any corrections or comments.

And finally, thank you to the Creator of the World, who gave us His Torah.

Sivan Rahav-Meir
May 2017/Iyar 5777

Genesis

Genesis is a book of beginnings – the first book of the Pentateuch, the creation of the world and humanity, along with stories of the Patriarchs and Matriarchs. It is no exaggeration to state that the foundations of human life, culture, and behavior are laid down in this book. The twelve *parashot* of Genesis span a two thousand-year period, during which great nations rose and fell. However, instead of giving the broad view, the Torah zooms in on the small details: Abraham welcoming his guests into his tent, Rebecca drawing water from the well to feed camels, and Jacob blessing his children before he dies.

Nobel Prize laureate Isaac Bashevis Singer was quoted as saying that he learned the art of writing from the Book of Genesis: "Whenever I start reading it, I can't put it down. I always find new facts, events, or dramatic tension that I hadn't noticed before. I sometimes imagine that a scribe sneaks into my home when I am asleep or walking and adds new *parashot*, episodes, and names to this wonderful book."

"Let's start at the very beginning
A very good place to start."

Bereshit

Congratulations on Creation

בְּרֵאשִׁית בָּרָא אֱלֹהִים אֵת הַשָּׁמַיִם וְאֵת הָאָרֶץ.

In the beginning God created the heaven and the earth.
(Gen. 1:1)

A special name is given to the Shabbat on which we read this first *parasha*, *Shabbat Bereshit*. The Lubavitcher Rebbe said that this Shabbat influences the entire year: "All the days of the year – weekdays, Shabbatot, and festivals, as well as events in the life of an individual, all receive light and vitality from *Shabbat Bereshit*."

In this first *parasha*, we read how everything was created: the world, the solar system, the animal kingdom, human beings, and the weekly day of rest – Shabbat.

In October 2015, a few days before *Shabbat Bereshit*, Rabbi Eitam Henkin and his wife Naama were murdered in a drive-by terror shooting. She was a graphic artist and also a poet. In her poem "Miracle," she describes the atmosphere of the tranquility of Shabbat entering the world as being miraculous. These special moments are first described in this *parasha* and recur every week.

> And every week
> the sun sets behind the trees

darkness falls, and a great light miraculously appears
finding us, a herd of lost souls
standing in line to receive
our additional portion of spirituality.

And every week
Shabbat descends and gathers us to her breast
accepts our souls
marked by the travails of six days of toil
to separate the holy from the mundane.

ෆ ෆ ෆ

The Tree Should Also Be Tasty

וַיֹּאמֶר אֱלֹהִים תַּדְשֵׁא הָאָרֶץ דֶּשֶׁא עֵשֶׂב מַזְרִיעַ זֶרַע עֵץ פְּרִי עֹשֶׂה פְּרִי
לְמִינוֹ אֲשֶׁר זַרְעוֹ בוֹ עַל הָאָרֶץ וַיְהִי כֵן. וַתּוֹצֵא הָאָרֶץ דֶּשֶׁא עֵשֶׂב מַזְרִיעַ
זֶרַע לְמִינֵהוּ וְעֵץ עֹשֶׂה פְּרִי.

And God said, "Let the earth sprout vegetation, seed-yielding
herbs and **fruit trees producing fruit** according to its kind in
which its seed is found, on the earth," and it was so. And the
earth gave forth vegetation, seed-yielding herbs according to
its kind, and **trees producing fruit**, in which its seed is found,
according to its kind.

(Gen. 1:11–12)

We tend to concentrate on achieving goals and belittle the means used
to achieve them. If after having plowed his field, sown the seeds, and
worked the land for an entire year a farmer receives a low yield on his
investment because of a drought, he will consider the year to have been
unsuccessful. Our sages point out a shift in the wording in the above
verses. God first wishes to create "fruit trees producing fruit" but the
earth only gave forth "trees producing fruit." The tree is just a tree, and
not a fruit. Since Creation, there has always been a distinction between

working and the fruits of one's achievement, between toiling and the sweet fruits of success.

Rabbi Abraham Isaac HaKohen Kook explains:

> At the beginning of Creation it was intended that the tree should have the same taste as the fruit. But the earthly existence brought it about that only the taste of the fruit, the final coming to fruition, the primary goal, is experienced in its pleasure and splendor. The earth sinned, denied its essence, limited its strength, followed trends and purposes, did not give all its hidden strength so that the taste of the tree could be like the taste of its fruit.

In an ideal world, the tree would be as tasty as the fruit. Yet in our physical world, the tree itself has no taste, and we only enjoy the fruit. Although we plant a tree for the fruit it will eventually produce, the means for achieving this goal are found in the roots, trunk, branches, and leaves, which make up the major part of this organism. A large part of our lives can be compared to a tree preparing to produce fruit. We study for a degree in order to work in our profession, in order to make a living, in order to buy food, in order to live. We spend most of our time working, eating, and sleeping. The creation of the world presents us with a utopian existence in which the sweet taste of hard work and effort reminds us that the means also serve a purpose.

ଔ ଔ ଔ

Build a Relationship

וַיֹּאמֶר הָאָדָם זֹאת הַפַּעַם עֶצֶם מֵעֲצָמַי וּבָשָׂר מִבְּשָׂרִי לְזֹאת יִקָּרֵא אִשָּׁה
כִּי מֵאִישׁ לֻקֳחָה זֹאת.

And the man said, "This time is now bone of my bones, and flesh of my flesh; **she shall be called Woman**, because she was taken out of Man."

(Gen. 2:23)

We all know that *Parashat Bereshit* tells of the creation of heaven and earth, animals and man. But we are less aware that the relationship between husband and wife was also created at the dawn of the world. The following is the text that Rabbi Netanel Elyashiv, a teacher at a pre-army academy, reads out when officiating at a wedding. In honor of the first couple in the world, you are invited to read it.

> Discussing the marital relationship, the sages note: "If they are worthy – the Divine Spirit resides between them." Is it really so good that something or someone comes between man and wife? Wouldn't it better if the only thing between them is love? No, because even romantic love requires a context. No less important than the partner with whom we choose to spend the rest of our life is how we view that relationship. When husband and wife know there is more to their marriage than being nice to each other, when they have a shared mission and purpose, then their entire relationship is put into context.
>
> Compare this to army life. The soldiers in a military unit all have different views and personalities, yet ongoing disagreements between them are rare. However, if those same people were to meet in a civilian setting, chances are that they would soon end up arguing. In the army, they share a joint purpose which automatically reduces the potential for discord.
>
> Antoine de Saint-Exupéry, author of *The Little Prince*, wrote: "Love does not consist of gazing at each other, but in looking outward together in the same direction." A relationship based on feelings alone will have a very rocky foundation since emotions change. Obviously, feelings are vital and without them there is no relationship. However, a spiritual basis is also necessary. Then one thinks twice about hurling a hurtful insult and makes peace more quickly because the two partners are working together throughout their relationship for the same purpose. When you bring God into your relationship, you are really making more space for both of you.

෬ ෬ ෬

The Motive Was Unclear

וַיָּקָם קַיִן אֶל הֶבֶל אָחִיו וַיַּהַרְגֵהוּ.

Cain rose up against Abel his brother **and slew him**.
(Gen. 4:8)

What was the motive?

The brand-new world is all wrapped up ready for its opening festivities. Then the first murder in history occurs. The first civil war was literally a war between two biological brothers – Cain and Abel.

The Torah does not give the reason why Cain murdered his brother; it simply describes the event. We are not explicitly told what Cain said and what happened in the field. A famous midrash looks for his motives. The sages first suggest the brothers were arguing about land, money, and clothes, i.e. property, even though the entire world belonged to just the two of them! Then they suggest the brothers were arguing about the location of the Temple – in whose territory it would be built – at a time when hardly anyone else inhabited the entire world. Another suggestion is that they were arguing about a woman who was born together with them. These three motives – money, religious beliefs, and relationships between men and women – have been the reasons for outbreaks of violence ever since.

We are often told that romantic, criminal, or nationalistic reasons were the motives for murder, as if to justify the act. There is probably good reason why the Torah is vague about the first murder, why no context or motive is given. Whatever the reason may have been, no motive ever justifies murder. What was true regarding the first murder in history is equally valid to this very day.

Noah

The Animals Went in Two by Two

וַיֹּאמֶר ה' לְנֹחַ בֹּא אַתָּה וְכָל בֵּיתְךָ אֶל הַתֵּבָה.

And the Lord said to Noah, "Come **into the ark**, you and all your household."

(Gen. 7:1)

We can read the Torah on different levels. There is the wonderful children's story about a man called Noah who lived thousands of years ago. He built an ark and all the animals went in two by two. But there are many more levels to this story and the Torah is also telling us something relevant to us today. One of the many commentators who tried to explain this relevancy was Rabbi Shalom Noah Berezovsky, better known as the *Netivot Shalom*, the title of a book he wrote: "Noah's ark teaches a lesson for all generations. Even when everything seems bleak and a storm rages outside, there is an ark to save us. In our generation there are three Noah's arks: Torah, Shabbat, and unity. These are the three forces of good that will enable us to conquer the forces of evil in our world."

The *Netivot Shalom* explains that in times of difficulty, when the floodwaters threaten to engulf us, we are able to escape to the safety of learning Torah, which has the power to save us. We can escape to the weekly Noah's ark of Shabbat to be our salvation and we can turn to unity and "be together with worthy people."

This *parasha* was written not only for that generation, but for all generations. However bad the situation is, there is always some place to escape to, and even in the worst possible scenario, we can cling to the good.

CB CB CB

The Power of Words

מִכֹּל הַבְּהֵמָה הַטְּהוֹרָה תִּקַּח לְךָ שִׁבְעָה שִׁבְעָה אִישׁ וְאִשְׁתּוֹ וּמִן הַבְּהֵמָה
אֲשֶׁר לֹא טְהֹרָה הִוא שְׁנַיִם אִישׁ וְאִשְׁתּוֹ.

Of all the clean animals you shall take for yourself seven pairs, a male and its mate, and **of the animals that are not clean**, two, a male and its mate.

(Gen. 7:2)

Reading online comments on the internet can be very unsettling. Obscene, insulting, violent, and frightening language is commonly used. I am constantly amazed that people don't even bother to hide behind a pseudonym but use their own name and display their own cover photo when using such foul language.

In the *Parashat Noah*, we encounter a completely different use of language. Noah is commanded to bring every living species into the ark: seven pairs of clean animals and one pair of not clean animals. The Torah usually uses precise language, yet in this instance the text – "the animals that are not clean" instead of "impure animals" – seems unnecessarily verbose and there must be a reason why the animal species are not defined as being impure, but rather as "not clean." Every effort is made, and cumbersome language is used, to avoid labeling an animal as impure. The Torah chooses to use the more refined term "not clean." (Similarly, describing a person as "not so good-looking" is more delicate than "ugly.")

We learn from the Torah that the words we use reflect on our inner state of mind and that each word has great influence. Using the above verse as an example, the sages state: "One should never allow something disgusting to come out of one's mouth." Why are they so insistent? Because the Torah itself uses seemingly superfluous words to avoid labeling an animal as impure.

It is well worth the time and effort to speak in a more respectful manner. Before you hit the keyboard and call someone a "traitor" or "a piece of trash," take a second to think how if reflects on you and how it affects others.

ೞ ೞ ೞ

Welcome to the Family

כָּל הַחַיָּה כָּל הָרֶמֶשׂ וְכָל הָעוֹף כֹּל רוֹמֵשׂ עַל הָאָרֶץ לְמִשְׁפְּחֹתֵיהֶם יָצְאוּ מִן הַתֵּבָה.

Every beast, every creeping thing, and all fowl, **everything that moves upon the earth, according to their families** they went out of the ark.

(Gen. 8:19)

The word "family" appears for the first time in the Torah in this *parasha*. Civilization was destroyed during the Flood because of moral bankruptcy and infidelity. As they prepare to leave the ark, the inhabitants are commanded to leave in family groups. After the great storm, at the dawn of a new order, we meet the family unit. Since then, civilization has been built upon this start-up. Welcome!

Since then and until today, the family is here to stay. When your mom calls and you are busy doing something else, when your grandma needs help, when your siblings annoy you, they are still your family. The family unit is the new Noah's ark that has been with us ever since the Flood. Our parents, spouse, and children help us refine our personal characteristics, teaching us to be tolerant and respectful. The family unit gives us a backbone, strength, and meaning.

A wise person told me the following about the family: "Putting another person's wishes ahead of mine is the only way to build my own character."

CR CR CR

Our Tower of Babel

וַיֹּאמְרוּ הָבָה נִבְנֶה לָּנוּ עִיר וּמִגְדָּל וְרֹאשׁוֹ בַשָּׁמַיִם וְנַעֲשֶׂה לָּנוּ שֵׁם פֶּן נָפוּץ עַל פְּנֵי כָל הָאָרֶץ.

And they said, "Come, let us build ourselves **a city and a tower with its top in the heavens, and let us make ourselves a name**, lest we be scattered upon the face of the entire earth."

(Gen. 11:4)

I recently read that in a certain year more people died attempting to take selfies than as victims of shark attacks. Twelve people found their death looking for a creative angle to take their selfie, whereas only eight people were mauled to death by a frenzied shark. How is this piece of information connected to the *parasha*? Because in addition to the story of the ark, the Torah also tells about the Tower of Babel.

After the Flood, people began to take advantage of the latest technology which, in that era, was stones and rocks for building. "Let us build ourselves a city and a tower with its top in the heavens." What did they wish to perpetuate by building this grand tower? The Flood and the lessons learned from it? Would it be used to house families or as a school to educate children? No! The sole purpose of the tower was self-perpetuation, "Let us make ourselves a name." For them, technology was an end, not a means.

The Midrash vividly describes how building the tower became the supreme task of that generation, overruling any other concerns: "If a person fell to his death, they didn't notice. But if one brick fell, they cried out, despairing of how to replace it." A person falling from the tower to his death did not bother them at all, but they bitterly mourned the loss of a precious brick that fell to the earth.

According to Professor Nehama Leibowitz, building a tower to reach the heavens is not merely a historical anecdote. She claims that every generation builds its own Tower of Babel and that there is always the danger of becoming enslaved to the latest technology and worshiping new ideas: "Man uses the wisdom given to him by God to make all kinds of other gods for himself and mainly to make himself into a god and to perpetuate his own greatness."

Leibowitz wrote this telling sentence before people died on the altar of the selfie.

Lekh Lekha

Go for Yourself!

וַיֹּאמֶר ה' אֶל אַבְרָם לֶךְ לְךָ מֵאַרְצְךָ וּמִמּוֹלַדְתְּךָ וּמִבֵּית אָבִיךָ אֶל הָאָרֶץ
אֲשֶׁר אַרְאֶךָּ.

And the Lord said to Abram, "**Go forth from your land and
from your birthplace** and from your father's house, to the land
that I will show you."

(Gen. 12:1)

The command to "Go forth" was not only given to Abraham, but to
everyone who reads this verse. Rabbi Shalom Noah Berezovsky expands
on this idea in his book *Netivot Shalom*. It may seem oversimplified and
overused, but it fills me with renewed energy every time I read it.

> Go for yourself. Everything a person encounters in his spiritual
> and material life, the bad and the good, is given to him so that
> he will correct his purpose in life. Therefore the verse says, "Go
> for yourself," to your purpose, to correct your soul, and to what
> you are supposed to improve in this world. So if a Jewish person
> learns Torah, and prays and does good deeds, but does not fulfill
> the purpose for which he is placed in this world, then after he
> passes away and goes up to Heaven, he will be asked, "What did
> you do in this world? You did not fulfill the main thing which

was your purpose in the world." This is the instruction given to all of the Jewish people, the sons of Abraham: "Go for yourself," go and reach the correction of your personal soul, and achieve the purpose intended just for you. The Torah chooses the word "go" to tell us that this is our purpose, to go and progress constantly toward our purpose in life. This is the difference between spiritual and material matters. In material matters, it is fine to stay at the same place without moving forward. However, in spiritual matters, we must always be moving forward, because staying still means going backwards.

ೞ ೞ ೞ

Happy Week Begins

וַיֵּלֶךְ אַבְרָם כַּאֲשֶׁר דִּבֶּר אֵלָיו ה'.

And Abram went, as **the Lord had spoken to him**.
(Gen. 12:4)

The *HaYom Yom* is an anthology of thoughts and quotes applicable for every day of the year which is studied by Chabad followers. In this book, the week in which we read *Parashat Lekh Lekha* is called the "really happy week." God commands Abraham, "Go out from your land and from your birthplace and from your father's house, to the land that I will show you," and the great journey begins.

This command is actually mankind's third test. Adam and Eve sinned in *Parashat Bereshit,* civilization was destroyed in the Flood in *Parashat Noah,* and Abraham had now been chosen as the new leader of the world. During the week of *Lekh Lekha* we learn about him and his journey.

The explanation for calling it a happy week is given in the *HaYom Yom* book:

> *Bereshit* is a cheerful *parasha,* even though its ending is not all that pleasant. *Noah* has the Flood, but the week ends on a happy note

with the birth of our father Abraham. The really joyous week is that of *Parashat Lekh Lekha*. We live every day of the week with Abraham, the first to dedicate his very life to spreading Godliness in the world. And Abraham bequeathed his self-sacrifice as an inheritance to all Jews.

Cß Cß Cß

The Neighbor's Field

וַיְהִי רִיב בֵּין רֹעֵי מִקְנֵה אַבְרָם וּבֵין רֹעֵי מִקְנֵה לוֹט.

And there was a quarrel between the herdsmen of Abram's cattle and between the herdsmen of Lot's cattle.

(Gen. 13:7)

I rely on my children's nursery school teachers. They do not have the time to tell all the details of the weekly *parasha*, so they choose the salient points. One of my children brought home a summary of what they had discussed that week and there were two topics, one very large and the other small.

The first had a historical, dramatic theme: "For all the land that you see I will give to you and to your seed to eternity.... Rise, walk in the land, to its length and to its breadth, for I will give it to you." After the universal themes of the first two *parashot* (*Bereshit* and *Noah*) we now read for the first time about the special connection between the Jewish people and the Land of Israel.

However, the nursery school teacher taught her pupils an additional, seemingly insignificant detail. She asked why Abraham and his descendants (us!) will merit living in the Land of Israel and told her young pupils about the quarrel between the herdsmen. Abraham and Lot originally shared the same land but were forced to separate after the quarrel. Our sages say that Lot's herdsmen allowed their cattle to graze freely in neighboring fields and Abraham's workers would accuse them of stealing. Abraham instructed his herdsmen to muzzle their cattle so that they would not eat even a single blade of grass belonging to people who already dwelled in the land. Lot's behavior was inappropriate for someone living in Israel and he chose to move elsewhere to Sodom. How very unsurprising!

We can all learn an important lesson from the nursery school teacher. If you want to inherit the Land of Israel, to speak in abstract terms about your right to the land, then begin with the small details. Make sure your cattle don't graze in your neighbor's field.

CR CR CR

Going Against the Norm

וַיֵּרָא ה' אֶל אַבְרָם וַיֹּאמֶר אֵלָיו אֲנִי אֵל שַׁדַּי הִתְהַלֵּךְ לְפָנַי וֶהְיֵה תָמִים.

And God appeared to Abram, and He said to him, "I am the Almighty God; walk before Me **and be perfect**."

(Gen. 17:1)

I once heard a young man dressed in the latest fashion ask another young man who was wearing traditional hasidic garb: "Do you really think that our forefather Abraham dressed like you in black and white and wore a hat like yours?" The Hasid replied: "I am absolutely certain that he didn't dress like me. And I am sure that he looked around to see the latest fashion trends in his day and then chose to wear the exact opposite."

We are not commanded to wear outdated, unfashionable clothes. However, in his time, Abraham was considered to be an outsider and a fighter for his beliefs, even though we now look up to him as a model for inspiration. In his commentary on the various episodes narrated in this *parasha*, Rabbi Samson Raphael Hirsch notes that Abraham is meant to instill within us the strength to stand as an alternative to the dominant culture and not be absorbed by it. This goes for both worldwide culture and for norms among the Jewish people:

> The isolation imposed upon Abraham in his day placed him in total opposition to the prevailing *zeitgeist*. His values were the polar opposite of those of his day. No person is permitted to declare "I

am righteous and honest" according to currently acceptable standards. Everyone is responsible for himself toward God. If you have to do something, and the way the majority do so is not true, then you must serve God, even if it places you in the minority. Had we not inherited from Abraham the courage to be in the minority, how would we have been able to exist in the past and continue to do so in the present? Some people promote a "Judaism that keeps up with the spirit of the times." The strongest opposition to this idea comes from the first commandment given to Abraham to "Go forth." We can be sure that Abraham's first appearance on the world's stage did not fit into the spirit of the times in Babylon, Assyria, Sidon, or Egypt. Just like Abraham, we are required to be courageous and have complete faith in our inner truth.

Vayera

Call Waiting

וַיֵּרָא אֵלָיו ה' בְּאֵלֹנֵי מַמְרֵא וְהוּא יֹשֵׁב פֶּתַח הָאֹהֶל כְּחֹם הַיּוֹם. וַיִּשָּׂא
עֵינָיו וַיַּרְא וְהִנֵּה שְׁלֹשָׁה אֲנָשִׁים נִצָּבִים עָלָיו וַיַּרְא וַיָּרָץ לִקְרָאתָם מִפֶּתַח
הָאֹהֶל וַיִּשְׁתַּחוּ אָרְצָה.

Now the Lord appeared to him in the plains of Mamre, and
he was sitting at the entrance of the tent when the day was
hot. **And he lifted his eyes and saw, and behold, three men
were standing beside him**, and he saw and he ran toward
them from the entrance of the tent, and he prostrated himself
to the ground.

(Gen. 18:1–2)

Sitting at the entrance to his tent, deep in conversation with God
Himself, Abraham notices three men approaching. What does he
do? He interrupts his conversation with God, who created the entire
world, and goes to extend his hospitality. He abandons the spiritual
experience of prophecy in order to help others. Abraham's actions are
recorded in the Torah so that all future generations will learn a lesson
in prioritizing. Helping those in need was passed on by Abraham into
the Jewish DNA.

Rabbi Israel Salanter, the founder of the *Musar* movement, taught that "someone else's material needs are my spiritual

responsibility" and also that "spiritual life is superior to physical life in my own life, but the physical life of another is an obligation of my spiritual life."

We can learn further from Abraham's hospitality: "He ran toward them from the entrance of the tent," "and Abraham hastened to the tent to Sarah, and he said, hurry," "and to the cattle did Abraham run," "and he hastened to prepare it." The common thread in all these quotes is haste and speed. Not only is Abraham helping others, he does so with the utmost alacrity. He is not simply fulfilling an obligation but is doing so wholeheartedly.

ଔ ଔ ଔ

The Essence of Sodom

וַיֹּאמֶר ה' זַעֲקַת סְדֹם וַעֲמֹרָה כִּי רָבָּה וְחַטָּאתָם כִּי כָבְדָה מְאֹד.

And the Lord said, "**The cry of Sodom and Gomorrah has become great**, and their sin has become very grave."

(Gen. 18:20)

Sodom and Gomorrah are not just the symbol of evil; they were actual cities! In *Parashat Lekh Lekha* we read that God decided to destroy them because of the unethical and morally depraved behavior of their inhabitants. Our sages give a thought-provoking example of their actions: "The thoughtful Sodomites provided guest houses in their city, each with beds of a single standard size. When a guest came looking for lodgings, they would make sure that the bed fit perfectly. If he was shorter than the bed, his hosts would stretch him out until he fit. Should he be too tall for the bed, they would hack off his feet." This is the source of the Hebrew expression *mitat Sedom* (lit. "bed of Sodom") as a symbol of evil.

What a stark contrast to Abraham's hospitality, as described at the beginning of the *parasha*. This small example of the beds typifies an entire philosophy. "We are all equal" may seem like a positive mindset but in fact it can lead to apathy, hardheartedness, and cruelty. The people of Sodom wanted life to be organized and that everyone would fit into the same mold. They could not understand the need for giving space for each person's individuality.

CR CR CR

Why Is Abraham Called Our Forefather?

וַיִּגַּשׁ אַבְרָהָם וַיֹּאמַר הַאַף תִּסְפֶּה צַדִּיק עִם רָשָׁע.

And Abraham approached and said, "**Will You even destroy the righteous with the wicked?**"

(Gen. 18:23)

Does being a believer mean that one must be passive and subservient? In the *parasha* Abraham is told that Sodom is about to be destroyed. Let us compare his reaction to that of Noah when he was told about the Flood. Noah does not argue with God about the evil decree to destroy the world. He builds the ark to save himself and his family. Contrast this with Abraham, who is told about the impending destruction of Sodom and protests to God against His decision.

This is one of the reasons why Abraham, and not Noah, is considered the first of the Patriarchs (*Avraham Avinu*). Abraham's reaction is that of a spiritual leader. Note how he argues with God: "Will You even destroy the righteous with the wicked?" "Will the Judge of the entire earth not perform justice?" The negotiations continue. Abraham demands that if fifty righteous people are found in the city, then the city must not be destroyed; then if only forty-five, forty, thirty, twenty, or even ten righteous people.

Abraham was the first person to believe in God. Belief in God, the Creator of the world, entails getting involved, praying, requesting, begging, initiating, and taking responsibility.

CR CR CR

23

The Fearful Believer

וַיֹּאמֶר אַבְרָהָם אֶל שָׂרָה אִשְׁתּוֹ **אֲחֹתִי הִוא** וַיִּשְׁלַח אֲבִימֶלֶךְ מֶלֶךְ גְּרָר וַיִּקַּח אֶת שָׂרָה.

And Abraham said of Sarah his wife, "**She is my sister**," and Abimelech the king of Gerar sent and took Sarah.

(Gen. 20:2)

Why did Abraham fear what would happen to his wife Sarah at the hands of Abimelech? In his famous answer to Abimelech, he openly voices his concern that the locals, who had no fear of the Lord, would kill him: "Surely, there is no fear of God in this place, and they will kill me because of my wife."

This same expression, "fear of God," is also used to describe the Egyptian midwives who feared God and therefore did not kill the Jewish newborns nor did they throw them into the river as they had been commanded by Pharaoh. In both instances, "fear of God" is used to describe the strong attitude taken by a foreigner in a weak position on the basis of an inner fear of God.

Rabbi Abraham Isaac HaKohen Kook writes about human and divine ethics in *Lights of Holiness* (*Orot HaKodesh*) in the section "Ethics of Holiness" (*"Musar HaKodesh"*) He says that human ethics are important and good but do not have the power to stand up against the swirling winds of various human desires, when they powerfully arise. He continues that fear of God is necessary to educate an entire nation throughout the generations: "Certainly ethics in its weakness is not able to lead broadly, human society in its depth and vastness, to penetrate the depths of the soul, and to turn the heart of stone into the heart of flesh for both humankind and the individual person. There is no alternative, other than one should be directed based on divine ethics."

This is Abraham's message to us in his reply to Abimelech.

CB CB CB

Sarah Too Was a Prophetess

וַיֹּאמֶר אֱלֹהִים אֶל אַבְרָהָם אַל יֵרַע בְּעֵינֶיךָ עַל הַנַּעַר וְעַל אֲמָתֶךָ כֹּל
אֲשֶׁר תֹּאמַר אֵלֶיךָ שָׂרָה שְׁמַע בְּקֹלָהּ כִּי בְיִצְחָק יִקָּרֵא לְךָ זָרַע.

And God said to Abraham, "Do not be displeased concerning the
lad and concerning your handmaid; **whatever Sarah tells you,
listen to her voice**, for in Isaac will be your seed."

(Gen. 21:12)

"Abraham was inferior to Sarah in prophecy!!!"

The exclamation marks are my addition to this remarkable and
surprising comment by our sages. Abraham is normally the main focus of
our attention and yet we are told that Sarah should have the central role
since her spiritual level as a prophetess was higher than her husband's.
God instructs him: "Whatever Sarah tells you, listen to her."

Sarah occupies a prominent place in the Torah, both in her life
and death. Rabbi Shabtai Sabato explains the above statement: since
Abraham spoke to God more often than she did, the sages were talking about quality, not quantity. Sarah had a greater understanding of
the significance of the prophecies, and what their divine task entailed.
Together they were charged with leading the process of a new nation, a
new land, and a new Torah.

Another fascinating aspect of Abraham and Sarah's prophecies is
that there is no mention of Abraham talking to God after Sarah's death.
It is as if God's regular revelation to Abraham could no longer occur
once she had departed. Regardless of who was on a higher spiritual
level, the togetherness they shared had disappeared and with it Abraham's ability to prophesy. Rabbi Sabato notes that this is an example of
one of the rules governing prophecy: "The Divine Spirit does not rest
upon one who is sad." Since Abraham grieved after his wife's death, he
was not able to reach the level of joy and completeness necessary to
receive the word of God.

Hayei Sara

Forever Young

וַיִּהְיוּ חַיֵּי שָׂרָה מֵאָה שָׁנָה וְעֶשְׂרִים שָׁנָה וְשֶׁבַע שָׁנִים שְׁנֵי חַיֵּי שָׂרָה.

And the life of Sarah was one hundred years and twenty years and seven years; [these were] the years of the life of Sarah.

(Gen. 23:1)

Why does the opening verse of *Parashat Hayei Sara* describe the age at which Sarah died in such a detailed manner instead of simply telling us that she was 127 years old? Our sages teach us that at the age of one hundred she was like twenty, and at the age of twenty she was like seven. She was always young, always free of sin, and always had the fresh outlook of a person turning a new page in the chapter of her life.

Rabbi Nahman of Breslov offers an uplifting commentary on this verse:

> This is the main purpose in life – to begin life anew every day. Even when he becomes old, he should consider himself to be an infant who has not started living and serving God. Thus, each day he should begin worshiping God anew. Like our Matriarch Sarah, whenever a righteous person gets old, he should still consider himself to be an infant. Thus, each day he will add to his worship of God so all the days and years of his life will really be

years full of life, adding holiness and vitality every single day. This is the true meaning of a long life.

A long life means that every single minute is a new beginning. A Breslov Hasid once summed it up by telling me that one should have a hundred new beginnings every day.

❧ ❧ ❧

Be Kind!

וְהָיָה הַנַּעֲרָ אֲשֶׁר אֹמַר אֵלֶיהָ הַטִּי נָא כַדֵּךְ וְאֶשְׁתֶּה וְאָמְרָה **שְׁתֵה וְגַם גְּמַלֶּיךָ אַשְׁקֶה** אֹתָהּ הֹכַחְתָּ לְעַבְדְּךָ לְיִצְחָק וּבָהּ אֵדַע כִּי עָשִׂיתָ חֶסֶד עִם אֲדֹנִי.

And it will be, that the maiden to whom I will say, "Lower your pitcher and I will drink," and she will say, "**Drink, and I will also water your camels**," is the one You designated for Your servant, for Isaac, and through her may I know that You have performed loving-kindness with my master.

(Gen. 24:14)

The stage is set for the audition to find a bride for Isaac. Eliezer is responsible for picking the winning candidate and he sets details of the test. Whenever I read this story, I am struck by how mundane Eliezer's demands are and how rooted they are in the small details of real life. The girl who gives water to Eliezer and also offers to water his camels is worthy of entering Abraham's family and becoming one of the Matriarchs.

So what do you need to do to pass Eliezer's test? Be kind, think of others, and take note of their most physical needs. In this case, she not only offered to take care of a thirsty stranger, but she also thought about the thirsty camels. As soon as Rebecca had finished running back and forth to the well, Eliezer presented her with two bracelets weighing ten gold shekels.

Rashi explains that these gifts were not merely items of jewelry, but alluded to the two tablets of stone and the Ten Commandments.

Nothing is as it seems on the surface and every detail in this story is laden with symbolism. Since she passed Eliezer's test, Rebecca joins the Jewish people's Patriarchs and Matriarchs as a link in the chain that will lead to Mount Sinai. By passing this deceptively simple test, Rebecca becomes part of the eternal chain.

03 03 03

The Finer Points of Love

וַיֹּאמְרוּ נִקְרָא לַנַּעֲרָ וְנִשְׁאֲלָה אֶת פִּיהָ. וַיִּקְרְאוּ לְרִבְקָה וַיֹּאמְרוּ אֵלֶיהָ הֲתֵלְכִי עִם הָאִישׁ הַזֶּה וַתֹּאמֶר אֵלֵךְ.

And they said, "Let us call the maiden and ask her." And they summoned Rebecca, and they said to her, "Will you go with this man?" **And she said, "I will go."**

(Gen. 24:57–58)

What is love? In her answer to her family, Rebecca highlights one aspect of love in her simple but meaningful answer: "I will go!" With one Hebrew word, *elekh*, she agrees to go with Eliezer to marry Isaac and join Abraham's family. It has been said that this terse response (one word in Hebrew) is the most important word in the entire *parasha*. I will go, despite all my doubts, despite the difficulties in making the decision, despite the fact that agreeing to marry is a somewhat irrational leap of faith into the unknown. I will go!

When Rebecca first lays her eyes on Isaac, she is overwhelmed and falls off her camel when she sees him praying in the field. Rebecca had never encountered a person of such stature or observed prayer in this manner. This initial wonderment at seeing her future husband is a pivotal moment. In a marriage, we should strive to retain this feeling of excitement for our spouse.

One of the most beautiful verses in the Torah describes love: "And Isaac brought her to the tent of Sarah his mother, and he took Rebecca, and she became his wife, and he loved her. And Isaac was comforted for [the loss of] his mother." Marriage means continuity. You are not alone.

Indeed, you are a part of a bigger picture with a past and a future. When Rebecca enters the tent, the Divine Spirit returns to Abraham and Isaac's home and the loneliness they felt after Sarah's demise is lifted. Part of Sarah's blessing and spirit is now felt again in their lives.

This verse gives a timeline for love. Whereas it is often thought that relationships are primarily built before marriage, the Torah presents a different view. Love between husband and wife develops and deepens over the years, mainly after they have begun building their joint home. First Rebecca enters Isaac's tent and only then does the verse say "and he loved her."

CB CB CB

In Praise of Fools

וַיְסַפֵּר הָעֶבֶד לְיִצְחָק אֵת כָּל הַדְּבָרִים אֲשֶׁר עָשָׂה.

And the servant told Isaac **all the things that he had done**.
(Gen. 24:66)

Parashat Hayei Sara describes the first Jewish arranged marriage. We are told all the details of the search for a bride and the successful outcome. Commentators have often studied the endless details in this chapter for pointers about looking for a compatible match and setting up a new home.

Professor Nehama Leibowitz gives us an insight into a successful marriage and tells us not to be afraid to be a sucker! In her explanation on this chapter, she expands on this theme:

> The Torah does not normally give detailed descriptions of everyday life such as the view, furnishings, household goods etc., so there must be an important reason why such details are given. Take note of the following details. The Torah tells us the exact number of camels Eliezer took on his journey – no less than ten. The fact that the fountain was not close to the trough and that Rebecca had to run up and down with her pitcher to fill the trough

is narrated twice. We are told no less than three times that all the camels drank until they were full. Note that the camel is called "the ship of the desert" because of its ability to store water for days. When Eliezer and the camels reached their destination, the stock of water in their humps was gone and they needed a refill. Why are we told all these details? To emphasize that Rebecca did not make just two or three journeys with her pitcher from the well to the trough but many, many more. All the time the visitor stands silently, watching in wonder but not helping her in her task. Rebecca did not question his actions; she continued running, with diligence and patience.

The quick-witted and practical people of today are likely to call the young girl who spent hours helping strangers a misguided lass who is too innocent for her own good and mistaken in her behavior – in short, a sucker! To help understand Rebecca and the lesson that the Torah wanted to teach from Eliezer's test, let us quote Akavia ben Mehalalel: "I would rather be called a fool my entire life than be wicked in front of God even for a moment." Rebecca did not weigh the pros and cons of her actions like "smart" people do. Rather, she willingly gave water to the man and his camels. It is these "fools" who keep the world going, then and to this day.

Toledot

Warning: Cynics Ahead

וְאֵלֶּה תּוֹלְדֹת יִצְחָק בֶּן אַבְרָהָם. אַבְרָהָם הוֹלִיד אֶת יִצְחָק.

And these are the generations of Isaac the son of Abraham;
Abraham fathered Isaac.

(Gen. 25:19)

George Patton, an American army general in World War II, famously said:
"Watch what people are cynical about, and one can often discover what they
lack." Even in the most emotional and holy moments, there will always
be those who choose to ruin the atmosphere with a cynical comment.

The opening verse in *Parashat Toledot* tells us that "these are the
generations of Isaac the son of Abraham; Abraham fathered Isaac." What
does the second part of the verse, "Abraham fathered Isaac," teach us? Our
sages explain that the gossipmongers of that time claimed that Isaac was
not Abraham's son, but had a different father. Other slanderers claimed
that Abraham was indeed the father, but Sarah was not his mother. God
had to actively interfere with nature in order to convince those gossipmongers that they were mistaken. God made Isaac look exactly like his
father Abraham so that the familial connection was absolutely clear.

Rabbi Yerucham Levovitz, the legendary *mashgiah* of the Mir
yeshiva in pre-war Europe, wrote that the Torah is clear and honest for
those who want to read it in such a manner, but one may always choose

to interpret reality in a negative and mocking way: "Whoever wishes to be mistaken, there is no advice for him. The words of the Torah are certainly clear, but for whom? Only for someone who desires honesty. From this we learn to steer clear of gossipmongers and slanderers."

On the one hand, the Torah has an answer for those cynical gossipmongers proving them to be mistaken. Alternatively, maybe even so they wouldn't be convinced, and the Torah was providing an answer that was appropriate for the general public. Either way you look at it, the *parasha* begins with a warning about the dangers of being cynical. Whoever chooses to mock and be patronizing may very well find himself being cynical even about Abraham.

CR CR CR

The Temporary and the Eternal

וַיִּגְדְּלוּ הַנְּעָרִים וַיְהִי עֵשָׂו אִישׁ יֹדֵעַ צַיִד אִישׁ שָׂדֶה וְיַעֲקֹב אִישׁ תָּם יֹשֵׁב אֹהָלִים.

And the youths grew up, and Esau was **a man who understood hunting, a man of the field**, whereas Jacob was **an innocent man, dwelling in tents**.

(Gen. 25:27)

The Torah describes the struggle between Jacob and Esau about who will receive Isaac's blessing, which in fact is a struggle between two philosophies of life: living as a violent and cruel hunter or an innocent, gentle person. In each one of us is the inner tension between Esau, who represents the here and now, and Jacob, who looks ahead.

Rabbi Avigdor Nebenzahl, former rabbi of the Old City in Jerusalem, writes that the world is so full of noise and distractions that we don't have any time to contemplate when deciding between the two options. He says that if we were to have the peace and quiet to think about the two, it would become obvious that Jacob's way of looking ahead is the natural choice. He elaborates on this theme in a book of his essays, edited by Rabbi Yosef Eliyahu:

If we stop to think for a moment about which way to choose, then even if we don't think in terms of the World to Come, but only about matters of here and now in this world, such as honor and fame, it would still make sense for a person to change his ways and follow the philosophy represented by Jacob. To prove my point, you can ask if anyone still remembers Jacob who dwelt in tents. The answer is a definite yes. In our prayers, we say "the Lord of Jacob" three times a day. If we ask whether anyone still remembers Esau the hunter, the answer is also a definite yes. Those who learn the Torah of Jacob! Aside from being mentioned in the Torah, there is no remnant left of Esau, just like many other once-famous evil people. If it were not for Jacob's nation, which exists forever and still mentions them, no traces of their legacy would remain. What remains of the great empires of Sennacherib or Pharaoh?

Alas, the day-to-day world does not even allow for a person to make a calculation based on this reasoning and realize that Esau embodies the here and now, while Jacob embodies eternity.

So, in fact, even in terms of Esau's reckoning, it is better to be Jacob.

CB CB CB

Fatigue Is the Enemy

וַיֹּאמֶר עֵשָׂו אֶל יַעֲקֹב הַלְעִיטֵנִי נָא מִן הָאָדֹם הָאָדֹם הַזֶּה כִּי **עָיֵף אָנֹכִי** עַל כֵּן קָרָא שְׁמוֹ אֱדוֹם.

And Esau said to Jacob, "Pour for me some of this red, red stew, **for I am tired**"; therefore he was named Edom.

(Gen. 25:30)

Much has been written about the differences between Jacob and Esau. The sages have noted Jacob's good inclination and his decision to be an innocent and righteous man, as opposed to Esau's evil inclination and the violent and cruel choices he makes. A seemingly trivial factor which influences Esau's choices is fatigue.

Fatigue is not only a modern ailment. Thousands of years ago, in *Parashat Toledot*, the Torah warned us about its dangers. One of the most important events in this *parasha* is Esau's agreement to sell the birthright and future spiritual leadership to Jacob in exchange for a red lentil stew. What led Esau to make this choice? Why does he prefer the temporal stew to something eternal? Esau's fatigue is mentioned twice in this narrative. First we are told that he was tired when he returned from the field and again when he asked Jacob to eat the stew he said that he was tired. Fatigue is both a physical and a mental state. It causes apathy and leads to a lack of concentration and difficulty in listening. Sleep deprivation and living on a sleep deficit results in poor judgment, lack of motivation, moodiness, and anxiety. So it is not surprising that the tired Esau could not focus on delicate spiritual matters.

Rabbanit Yemima Mizrachi notes that the Code of Jewish Law opens with the instruction: "One should strengthen oneself like a lion to get up in the morning to serve his Creator." A person must make the effort and overcome temptation when getting out of bed. While this may seem obvious, Mizrachi adds that in our times we must also be diligent about going to bed on time in the evenings. It is easier to keep the midnight oil burning than to call it a day because of all the things distracting us. We feel we have to check our WhatsApp, email, Facebook once or even multiple times before we allow ourselves to go to bed. So nowadays a person has to "strengthen himself like a lion" in order to go to sleep.

CB CB CB

Whose Land Is It?

וְכָל הַבְּאֵרֹת אֲשֶׁר חָפְרוּ עַבְדֵי אָבִיו בִּימֵי אַבְרָהָם אָבִיו סִתְּמוּם פְּלִשְׁתִּים וַיְמַלְאוּם עָפָר.

And all the wells that his father's servants had dug in the days of Abraham his father **the Philistines blocked them up and filled them with earth.**

(Gen. 26:15)

A small but terrible detail caught my attention in the struggle described in this *parasha* between Isaac and the Philistine shepherds. Isaac's enemies continually stop up the wells he has dug. They are destroying the water source for both sides of this conflict. They do not care that they will have no water. The Philistines do not want the land to flourish for Isaac, and apparently not for them either. Their hate for Isaac causes them to harm themselves. Contrast their behavior with that of Isaac, who takes the exact opposite approach. He wants the Land of Israel to be plentiful for the benefit of everyone who lives there, so he wants to dig more and more wells so that everyone will enjoy fresh water.

The feud between Isaac and the Philistines reminds me of the famous judgment of King Solomon, who rules that the disputed infant be cut in two. One of the mothers agrees to this decision – she is happy as long as neither she nor the contesting mother receives the infant. The other mother is prepared to forfeit the infant, as long as it remains in one piece. From her perspective, what matters most is that the infant lives. Based on the two women's reactions, Solomon rules that the second one is the biological mother.

Perhaps we can make an analogy and say that the quarrel in this *parasha* is also a test about the right to the land. There is a struggle between those who wish to destroy the opposing side's efforts at all costs, even if it their own efforts will also be ruined, and those who want both sides to flourish.

ಣ ಣ ಣ

Faith 2.0

וַיָּשָׁב יִצְחָק וַיַּחְפֹּר אֶת בְּאֵרֹת הַמַּיִם אֲשֶׁר חָפְרוּ בִּימֵי אַבְרָהָם אָבִיו וַיְסַתְּמוּם פְּלִשְׁתִּים אַחֲרֵי מוֹת אַבְרָהָם וַיִּקְרָא לָהֶן שֵׁמוֹת כַּשֵּׁמֹת אֲשֶׁר קָרָא לָהֶן אָבִיו.

And Isaac again dug the wells of water which they had dug in the days of his father, Abraham, and the Philistines had stopped them up after Abraham's death; **and he gave them names like the names that his father had given them.**

(Gen. 26:18)

The following sentence has an internal contradiction: Isaac is supposed to continue in Abraham's ways. How is it possible to be the heir of someone who rebelled and reinvented everything? Is Isaac's life meant to be an exact replica of his father's? Or is he also expected to rebel?

It is sometimes easier to be a pioneer, the first one to plunge into the deep waters like Nahshon at the Red Sea, than to be part of the second generation of a revolution. Isaac's role is a very complex one. When we read the text we have a sense of *déjà vu* as Isaac's activities take him to the same places as his father had been; he also has to confront Abimelech, he rebuilds the exact same wells as his father had, and dubs them the same names.

According to kabbalistic tradition, Isaac is associated with bravery. Let us consider just how much bravery is required to hold yourself back, not to reinvent yourself but to continue on the path that already exists, the one your father walked along. If Isaac, the second generation, had not succeeded in this difficult task, Abraham's revolution would have come to an unceremonious end.

It is very exciting to initiate something. Continuing is far less glamorous. We should ask ourselves in all honesty who we look up to more and who is likely to attract more fame? Someone who leaves his current lifestyle, taking the dramatic step of becoming religiously observant, eager to tell everyone about his amazing new discovery? Or someone who decides to continue in the ways of his father, grandfather, and great-grandfather, keeping the Torah and observing the commandments?

Vayetze

A Lesson in History

וַיֵּצֵא יַעֲקֹב מִבְּאֵר שָׁבַע וַיֵּלֶךְ חָרָנָה.

And Jacob left Beer Sheba, **and he went to Haran.**
(Gen. 28:10)

Parashat Vayetzeh tells of Jacob and his dream: "And he dreamed, and behold, a ladder set up on the ground, its top reaching to heaven; and behold, angels of God were ascending and descending upon it. And behold, the Lord was standing over him." This famous dream can be explained on two levels.

Our sages teach that the ladder and the dream represent the essence of world history. Jacob sees the nations of the world ascending the ladder, as leaders of the world, and then descending, as they fall from power. Babylon rises and falls, followed by Greece, Edom, Egypt, Persia, Rome, and so on throughout history. After the dream, Jacob will receive the name Israel and will represent the Jewish people through the generations. Already at this stage, he learns of all the powers of evil (including Hamas and ISIS) that will rise and inflict their heinous crimes on the world, but in the end will fall.

Note the continuation of the verse: "And behold, the Lord was standing over him." There is a leader controlling world events and there is a purpose to all these upheavals. One small nation will survive, and evil will not rule forever. The people of Israel also have a role to play on the global stage of history, as stated in the subsequent verse: "And you shall burst forth westward and eastward and northward and southward; and through you all the families of the earth shall be blessed." The Jewish people are commanded to forge ahead and spread blessing throughout the world.

Other commentators explain the dream at the level of the individual and say that it symbolizes the constant relationship between God and man. The commandments we fulfill and the good deeds we do "ascend" and, at the same time, a wealth of goodness "descends" from above. According to this approach, the use of the words heaven and earth, symbolizing the spiritual and material worlds, is not coincidental. Each individual is the manifestation of "a ladder set up on the ground, its top reaching to heaven" and embodies the constant tension between the holy and the mundane. We draw encouragement from the knowledge that "the Lord was standing over him."

An additional point worth noting is the contrast between Jacob's dream and an earlier attempt to reach heaven by means of the Tower of Babel. Those who began construction of the tower saw it as a symbol of human arrogance. In this *parasha*, Jacob also connects to heaven but in a completely different manner. Importantly, he also knows how to return to earth.

03 03 03

Don't Miss Out!

וַיִּיקַץ יַעֲקֹב מִשְּׁנָתוֹ וַיֹּאמֶר אָכֵן יֵשׁ ה' בַּמָּקוֹם הַזֶּה וְאָנֹכִי לֹא יָדָעְתִּי.

And Jacob awakened from his sleep, and he said, "**Indeed, the Lord is in this place**, and I did not know."

(Gen. 28:16)

The *parasha* opens with a description of Jacob fleeing from Esau and choosing a random spot, as far as he was concerned, to spend the night. He had not planned to sleep in this spot. Awaking from his dream, Jacob discovers that he had been sleeping at a holy place. He is given some important news and then, "Jacob awakened from his sleep, and he said, 'Indeed, the Lord is in this place, and I did not know.'"

These events occurred unexpectedly. We do not always know in advance where and when we will encounter God. You do not only discover holiness when you plan to. The opposite is actually the case. We may be at work, relaxing at home, or in the middle of a seemingly banal relationship and we just don't notice how much magic and profundity there is in this situation. We live in a generation in which we turn media on and off with the flick of a switch, flitting between TV channels. We have gotten used to immediately exiting a situation if we don't enjoy it, not even remaining for one minute. When this becomes a way of life, we run the risk of missing out on many opportunities. We may be tempted to "turn off" the situation we find ourselves in, but we may very well lose out on a great deal of goodness hiding below the surface. For example, couples contemplating divorce who decide to make the effort toward reconciliation may suddenly discover love and purpose in their relationship.

"Indeed, the Lord is in this place, and I did not know." This verse tells us to be calm, relaxed, and aware of our surroundings. You never know what you might miss out on if not.

CB CB CB

The Power of the Spirit

וַיִּשָּׂא יַעֲקֹב רַגְלָיו וַיֵּלֶךְ אַרְצָה בְנֵי קֶדֶם. וַיַּרְא וְהִנֵּה בְאֵר בַּשָּׂדֶה.

Now Jacob lifted his feet and went to the land of the people of the East. And he looked, and behold, there was a well in the field.
(Gen. 29:1–2)

A good example of the mind-body relationship can be found in *Parashat Vayetzeh*. Jacob has a dream, God gives him wonderful promises about his own personal future and that of the Jewish people. Jacob gets up and sets out on his way, with the good news still ringing in his ears.

The Midrash explains the beginning of the verse, "Jacob lifted his feet and went," as follows: "Since Jacob was given good tidings, his heart lifted his legs and it became easy for him to walk." His legs did not do the walking; his heart carried him.

A further example of how the mind and soul can influence the body and give it superhuman strength is seen later on in the *parasha*. Jacob managed to single-handedly remove the large stone covering the mouth of the well, a job usually shared by many men. What gave him the strength? The divine promises he had been given and Rachel, whom he had just glimpsed for the first time. He now possessed supernatural strength.

In addition to telling us how the spiritual affects the material, these verses also teach us who can have the most influence on a person, give them strength, and "lift" them up – God and one's spouse.

ଓଓଓ

The Purpose of Life

וַתֵּרֶא רָחֵל כִּי לֹא יָלְדָה לְיַעֲקֹב וַתְּקַנֵּא רָחֵל בַּאֲחֹתָהּ וַתֹּאמֶר אֶל יַעֲקֹב
הָבָה לִּי בָנִים וְאִם אַיִן מֵתָה אָנֹכִי.

And Rachel saw that she had not borne [any children] to Jacob, and Rachel envied her sister, and she said to Jacob, "**Give me children, and if not, I am dead.**"

(Gen. 30:1)

The following is a feminist reading written six hundred years ago on the above verse. This *parasha* contains one of the most difficult verses in the Torah. During her difficult years of being childless, Rachel lashes out at Jacob: "Give me children, and if not, I am dead."

Throughout the ages, commentators have given various explanations on this emotionally charged exchange between Rachel and Jacob. Six hundred years ago, Spanish rabbi Isaac Arama wrote the following: Every woman has "two purposes in life." The first is to give birth to and bring up children and the other is "to be educated in wisdom and piety." Rabbi Arama wrote that Rachel's words were misplaced because she only focused on one of her missions but ignored the second one: to study and become educated, to learn Torah and do good deeds. That is also an integral part of a woman's mission.

Professor Nehama Leibowitz quotes Rabbi Arama's explanation in her books and explains how fundamentally important it is. She writes that Rachel is fleeing from fulfilling part of her mission; Rachel did not understand that she had additional functions in life beyond giving birth. Later in the *parasha*, we are told that Rachel gave birth to Joseph and then to Benjamin.

We can only contemplate what Professor Leibowitz herself thought of what she had written. She was highly successful in being "educated in wisdom and piety" but never merited to give birth.

Vayishlah

Don't Be Afraid to Be Afraid

בָּאנוּ אֶל אָחִיךָ אֶל עֵשָׂו וְגַם הֹלֵךְ לִקְרָאתְךָ וְאַרְבַּע מֵאוֹת אִישׁ עִמּוֹ.
וַיִּירָא יַעֲקֹב מְאֹד וַיֵּצֶר לוֹ.

We came to your brother, to Esau, and he is also coming toward you, and four hundred men are with him. **Jacob became very frightened and was distressed.**

(Gen. 32:7–9)

A hasidic friend phoned us a few years ago to protest about the words of a popular song he had heard on the radio: "One who believes is not afraid." He told us that as a believing Jew the one thing that frightened him most was to lose his belief and asked us to contact the composer and share his protest.

Our friend is right. We are supposed to be afraid. Not for no reason, but we should fear sinning. In this *parasha*, Jacob prepares to meet Esau. The Torah explicitly notes his fear: "Jacob became very frightened." The Midrash elaborates: "Jacob said, 'Woe is to me; my sin may cause God's promise not to be fulfilled.'" Jacob was not afraid of the enemy, Esau, but was frightened because of his own spiritual level.

Do these terms of fear and sin even have any place in the public discourse today? The headlines abound with defining what is a criminal offence and what is legally permitted. Has anyone ever dared to say that he is afraid of sinning? When was the last time you even heard the word "sin" mentioned in the news? Has anyone ever talked publicly about trying to steer clear of sin? The *parasha* is a contrast to the ethos of native-born Israelis, who are so cool and self-assured. We are told about one of the forefathers of the Jewish people who was afraid, and wasn't afraid to say so.

∞ ∞ ∞

I Am Unworthy

קָטֹנְתִּי מִכֹּל הַחֲסָדִים וּמִכָּל הָאֱמֶת אֲשֶׁר עָשִׂיתָ אֶת עַבְדֶּךָ כִּי בְמַקְלִי
עָבַרְתִּי אֶת הַיַּרְדֵּן הַזֶּה וְעַתָּה הָיִיתִי לִשְׁנֵי מַחֲנוֹת.

I am unworthy of all the kindnesses and of all the truth that You have shown Your servant, **for with my staff I crossed this Jordan,** and now I have become two camps.

(Gen. 32:11)

In this *parasha* we are told of Jacob's soul-searching as he returns to the Land of Israel after an absence of twenty years. He speaks to God and says: "I am unworthy of all the kindnesses and of all the truth that You have shown Your servant." He reminisces how he was empty-handed when he had previously fled and how he was returning now: "For with my staff I crossed this Jordan, and now I have become two camps." Having thanked God for his large family and for having survived, Jacob continues to pray for the future: "Please save me."

Sometimes, the music explains a text better than the lyrics. Yonatan Razel, a singer and composer, recalls listening to his grandfather relate how he had jumped from a train rolling toward a concentration camp and was thus saved, later moving to Israel. Razel's grandfather always spoke of how he felt intimately connected with the above verse. He always felt so small compared to the great kindness heaped upon him during his life. At one point he had nothing; now he is surrounded by his large family in Israel. Many years later, when Yonatan Razel's daughter made a miraculous recovery from a head injury, he discovered just how meaningful this verse was to him. Feeling unworthy of all the kindness, he also wanted to express his thanks and composed a tune to the words of the verse above.

46

There is something in Razel's composition that touches listeners and the song *Katonti* has become highly popular both in Israel and worldwide. Each and every listener, with his or her own life story, feels unworthy of all the kindness they have received and offers up a prayer for the future.

Rabbenu Bahya was a commentator living in Spain in the thirteenth century. He explains that these words form the key to all our prayers. We should first give thanks – "I am unworthy" – and only then make requests – "please save me."

> It is fitting that when a person prays he should focus on his worthlessness and the greatness of his Master whom he serves, and should focus on the abundance of kindness bestowed upon him by God.

We must first thank God for all the good He heaps upon us and only then make a request from Him.

03 03 03

Limping but Upright

וַיִּוָּתֵר יַעֲקֹב לְבַדּוֹ וַיֵּאָבֵק אִישׁ עִמּוֹ עַד עֲלוֹת הַשָּׁחַר... וַתֵּקַע כַּף יֶרֶךְ יַעֲקֹב בְּהֵאָבְקוֹ עִמּוֹ.

And Jacob was left alone, and a man wrestled with him until the break of dawn ... **and the socket of Jacob's hip became dislocated as he wrestled with him.**

(Gen. 32:25–26)

Addressing the hundreds of people who had gathered together, Henya Biegel said: "We will come to the *huppa* but we will be limping." Henya Biegel's son Ariel is married to Sara Litman. A few days before their wedding date, as they were traveling to the pre-wedding celebrations, Sara's father, Rabbi Yaakov Litman, and her younger brother Netanel were murdered in a terrorist attack. Sara and Ariel's wedding was postponed. On the original date and in the hall where the wedding was scheduled to have taken place, a memorial service was held for the terror victims. The weekly

47

parasha of that week was *Vayishlah*. We read about the struggle between Jacob and a mysterious figure that represents human evil. At the end of the nocturnal struggle, the Torah relates: "And the sun rose for him… and he was limping on his thigh." The sun does finally rise and banishes the evil of the night. Jacob continues on his journey, but he is limping. Many explanations have been given for the significance of his limping.

Henya Biegel added her personal explanation for this verse, simple in concept, but far from simple in context. This was not a scholarly, objective understanding of the verse, but one based on personal experience. She addressed the crowd at the memorial service:

> This Shabbat we will read in the Torah about Jacob who is given the name Israel and who struggles with Esau's archangel. This is a struggle in the dark, in exile, and so much is hidden. It was a difficult struggle, but in the morning everything became clear. When the light shone through it was clear that Jacob was the victor. He continued on from there, limping in pain but nevertheless going forward. This is how I feel today. We are involved in a struggle, but we will emerge. Our fellow Jews are supporting us in every possible way. We have been injured, we are limping now, but we will arise. In one week we will stand under the *huppa*, limping but upright. That is the only way forward, to show the evil murderers that the power of life is stronger than any other force.

ශ ශ ශ

Taking Our Time

יַעֲבָר נָא אֲדֹנִי לִפְנֵי עַבְדּוֹ וַאֲנִי אֶתְנָהֲלָה לְאִטִּי לְרֶגֶל הַמְּלָאכָה אֲשֶׁר לְפָנַי וּלְרֶגֶל הַיְלָדִים עַד אֲשֶׁר אָבֹא אֶל אֲדֹנִי שֵׂעִירָה.

Now, let my master go ahead before his servant, **and I will move at my own slow pace, according to the pace of the work that is ahead of me and according to the pace of the children**, until I come to my master, to Seir.

(Gen. 33:14)

We are slower. The world runs on ahead, going from one innovation to the next, from one novel ideology to its successor. The pulse of the Jewish people beats slower and deeper. Many commentators adopt this view as they try to penetrate the secret of the Jewish people as expressed in this verse. Jacob tells Esau, "I will move at my own slow pace, according to the pace of the work that is ahead of me and according to the pace of the children." Jacob tells Esau to run ahead and he will go at a slower space, citing his work and his children as the two reasons for his more deliberate gait.

The Midrash explains that "work" alludes to the break we take from our work on Shabbat and the festivals. Jacob explains that his lifestyle has a different pace. For thousands of years, Jews have stopped working on the Jewish days of rest. When the rest of the world seems to be progressing, earning money, and building, Jacob and his descendants choose to pause, to take a spiritual break, even if they risk financial loss and even if the Esau of that particular generation considers them to be old-fashioned.

The second reason for Jacob's slow rate of progress is his children. The family is one of his core principles. Every parent can identify with the phrase, "I will move at my own slow pace," and knows how applicable it is to bringing up children (and bringing ourselves up at the same time). It takes time to dress an infant in the morning, to ask a child what lunch to prepare, and help him do his homework after school. It's not a simple question of popping something into the microwave to heat it up. Parents need to take a slower pace. Jacob tells Esau and the culture he represents then and forever after, "You will always think that I am lagging behind, but in reality I will not be left behind. At my pace, and in my personal lifestyle, I will survive long after you."

CB CB CB

When Rashi Does Not Know

וַיַּעַל מֵעָלָיו אֱלֹהִים בַּמָּקוֹם אֲשֶׁר דִּבֶּר אִתּוֹ.

And God went up from him **in the place where He had spoken with him.**

(Gen. 35:13)

At the end of God's revelation to Jacob, the Torah tells us that "God went up from him in the place where He had spoken with him." In his commentary to this verse, Rashi writes, "I do not know what it is teaching us." Rashi cannot explain how the words "in the place where He had spoken with him" add to our understanding of the verse.

This is not the place to delve into the many answers that have been given over the years to Rashi's difficulty. Instead, we will focus on the language that Rashi uses. He could have simply not written anything at all on this verse. However, in his opinion, every detail in the Torah contains a message for those who study the Torah, not merely information. There is a reason behind every name, date, and description and if we haven't found the reason we should not be ashamed to say, "I don't know." (And we all know how difficult it is to utter that phrase.)

Rashi was very humble when he set about writing his monumental explanation on the Torah. Out of a sense of personal integrity and a constant search for meaning, there are several occasions when he writes that he simply does not know why certain words are written. We can learn from Rashi not to be embarrassed to say we don't know. However, there is an additional lesson we can learn from here. Rashi addresses the reader and calls on him or her to continue searching for an answer. He is suggesting to us that maybe we will be able to offer an answer to his question as we read his commentary hundreds of years later.

Vayeshev

Let's Talk It Out

וַיִּרְאוּ אֶחָיו כִּי אֹתוֹ אָהַב אֲבִיהֶם מִכָּל אֶחָיו וַיִּשְׂנְאוּ אֹתוֹ וְלֹא יָכְלוּ דַּבְּרוֹ לְשָׁלֹם.

And his brothers saw that their father loved him more than all his brothers, **so they hated him, and they could not speak with him peacefully**.

(Gen. 37:4)

The famous story of Joseph and the brothers begins in *Parashat Vayeshev*. Why did the brothers not speak to Joseph? Why didn't they tell him what was bothering them? Joseph has his dreams, wears a coat of many colors, and his brothers are jealous of him: "And they hated him, and they could not speak with him peacefully." Their deafening silence and inability to speak to Joseph led to a deterioration in their relationship. They hated him, distanced themselves from him, threw him in the pit, and he was later sold as a slave. Thus hatred led to exile and slavery in Egypt.

How did they get into such a mess? Some commentators claim that the siblings' feud with its severe outcome resulted from their silence and distance from each other. There are occasions when it is acceptable to sweep certain, small issues under the carpet and not deal with them, but when there is an increasingly serious dispute and the two sides are moving apart, there is no reason to suffer in silence. It is best to speak frankly. Both sides should air their grievances in order to ensure that the problem is not covered by a blanket of silence. Violence begets more violence. It is better to talk to the opposing side to try and understand them rather than let the negative feelings build up inside until they become blown out of all proportion and the result is a worsened relationship and continued treachery.

The same holds true for the different sectors and tribes within the Jewish people, relationships between siblings, and also between husband and wife. It is no coincidence that in his words of wisdom in Ecclesiastes, King Solomon teaches us, "a time to speak," followed immediately by "a time to love."

CB CB CB

Admit Your Guilt

הוא מוצֵאת וְהִיא שָׁלְחָה אֶל חָמִיהָ לֵאמֹר לְאִישׁ אֲשֶׁר אֵלֶּה לּוֹ אָנֹכִי הָרָה וַתֹּאמֶר הַכֶּר נָא לְמִי הַחֹתֶמֶת וְהַפְּתִילִים וְהַמַּטֶּה הָאֵלֶּה. וַיַּכֵּר יְהוּדָה וַיֹּאמֶר צָדְקָה מִמֶּנִּי.

She was taken out, and she sent to her father-in-law, saying, "I am pregnant from the man to whom these belong," and she said, "Please recognize whose signet ring, cloak, and staff these are." **Then Judah recognized them, and he said, "She is more righteous than I."**

(Gen. 38:25–26)

Judah admits his guilt, or we might say: a Jew admits his guilt. This chapter describes the relationship between Judah and Tamar. Just as she is about to be punished, Judah pulls himself together and publicly admits his guilt: "Then Judah recognized them, and he said, 'She is more righteous than I.'" Judah's greatness is demonstrated here in that he ignores all the excuses he could have given and decides not to deny his involvement. He faces the crowds and publicly admits his misdeeds. His decision led to an important development in Jewish history. Judah married Tamar and their offspring founded the Judaic dynasty leading to King David and beyond.

In his book *Tzror HaMor*, Rabbi Abraham Saba, a kabbalist who lived at the time of the expulsion from Spain, describes Judah's actions: "He lives up to the meaning of his name." Judah's name in the Torah is *Yehuda* which comes from the root "*modeh*," to admit. Judah became the symbol of publicly admitting one's guilt.

The Jewish people are called *Yehudim*, meaning the sons of Judah – not the sons of Reuben or the sons of Zebulun. Out of all the Twelve Tribes, we are named after Judah, the person who knew how to admit. According to Rabbi David Kimhi, the Radak, we are called *Yehudim* not despite Judah's behavior, but because of it. We are always supposed to remember who we are named after and not become arrogant. "God had the reason for this, that the kings of the kingdom of Judah should not behave haughtily to the people of Israel … that they should be humble and rule the people with humility and good faith."

ꞔꞢ ꞔꞢ ꞔꞢ

Father, You Are Always Here

וַתִּתְפְּשֵׂהוּ בְּבִגְדוֹ לֵאמֹר שִׁכְבָה עִמִּי וַיַּעֲזֹב בִּגְדוֹ בְּיָדָהּ וַיָּנָס וַיֵּצֵא הַחוּצָה.

And she grabbed him by his garment, saying, "Sleep with me." **But he left his garment in her hand and fled** outside.

(Gen. 39:12)

Joseph had every excuse to sin with Potiphar's wife. His brothers had thrown him into the pit, he had been living in Egyptian society for many years, and he had no assurances that he would ever be reunited with his father Jacob or the rest of his family. And yet, Joseph resisted the temptation. Our sages explain: "At that moment, his father's image appeared to him in the window." Out of the blue, Jacob's face appeared in front of him and Joseph was unable to deviate from his father's ways. In a lesser-known midrash, the sages add that "he also saw his mother Rachel's image."

Facing his parents' images, Joseph confronts his past and is reminded of the future and flees Potiphar's home. A person's parents, teachers, and rabbis are supposed to be a role model and a moral compass. When they look after you and give you direction you will follow their course. The success of their educational investment is realized at times when they are not around. Will you still be influenced by what your parents taught you even if they are not there to tell you what to do?

I venture to add my personal explanation to this midrash. I believe that not only do the parents' images influence their children, but, in addition, our children's image has a bearing on our behavior as parents. Children are like a moral compass that affects our parenting style and conscience. From the moment we become parents, we look at things differently. When we have to make a choice on a certain matter, the expected reaction of our children will influence our decision. In my work as a television journalist I have to decide whether to show violent and hard-to-see footage from the scene of a terror attack or scenes from a certain reality show. My calculations are often influenced by the fact that I am now a mother. I have also found this to be the case with my colleagues. Not only are we influenced by our parents, but also by parenthood.

ෙ ෙ ෙ

What's New Today?

וַיְהִי אַחַר הַדְּבָרִים הָאֵלֶּה חָטְאוּ מַשְׁקֵה מֶלֶךְ מִצְרַיִם וְהָאֹפֶה לַאֲדֹנֵיהֶם לְמֶלֶךְ מִצְרָיִם.

Now it was after these events that the cupbearer of the king of Egypt and the baker sinned against their master, against the king of Egypt.

(Gen. 40:1)

Following the incident involving Joseph and Potiphar's wife, the Torah states, "Now it was after these events," and continues with the story of Pharaoh's two ministers who were sent to jail. Why connect these two fascinating stories? The first narrative involves a young Jewish man named Joseph who flees from the wife of Potiphar, a senior minister, while the second is a story about two ministers to Pharaoh who were derelict in their duties and thrown into jail.

Rashi's answer to this question teaches us a lesson about the media, shaming, and public opinion: "Because that cursed woman [Potiphar's wife] had accustomed the people to speak badly about the righteous [Joseph], God brought to the Egyptians the sin of these men, so that they would turn their attention to them and not to him [Joseph]." Rashi is telling us that people have a constant craving for a juicy scandal. They need something – or usually, someone – to talk about. For a few days, Joseph and Potiphar's wife was the most talked-about news item; everyone was thirsty for more details. To divert attention away from this story and make the people focus on the next scandal, God brought them a new piece of gossip from the royal court. As if by chance, two ministers were thrown into jail, where they just happened to meet Joseph, who was able to explain their dreams; he was then taken out of prison. One minister was thrown into jail because a fly was found in Pharaoh's goblet, and another because of a pebble found in the king's bread. What an exciting piece of news! Just imagine the online posts, comments, tweets, and office gossip that started flying around when this new story broke.

What can we learn from this? That we are predisposed to move from one drama to the next, from one "high" to another, and we would be well advised to take things in proportion. But there is another point to note: headlines don't tell us everything. They describe only the visible layer of the story. By chance, the two ministers were thrown into jail, where they just happened to meet Joseph, who was able to explain their dreams; he was then taken out of prison to explain Pharaoh's dreams and thus rose to prominence. But behind the scenes, the reality is quite different. Amid these scandals, coming one on the heels of the other, and evading the expert analysts who seem to know everything, historical developments with great purpose and significance can unfold.

Miketz

The Solution Starts with Me

וַיְהִי בַבֹּקֶר וַתִּפָּעֶם רוּחוֹ וַיִּשְׁלַח וַיִּקְרָא אֶת כָּל חַרְטֻמֵּי מִצְרַיִם וְאֶת כָּל חֲכָמֶיהָ וַיְסַפֵּר פַּרְעֹה לָהֶם אֶת חֲלֹמוֹ וְאֵין פּוֹתֵר אוֹתָם לְפַרְעֹה.

Now it came to pass in the morning that his spirit was troubled; so he sent and called all the magicians of Egypt and all its wise men, and Pharaoh told them his dream, **but no one interpreted them for Pharaoh.**

(Gen. 41:8)

Pharaoh dreams first about fat and lean cows and again about healthy and thin ears of corn. He feels that he is twice being told a message through these dreams but cannot work out the exact explanation for these dreams. To help him unravel the mystery, Pharaoh summons his many advisors, but they are unable to help him: "no one interpreted them for Pharaoh."

Our sages explain the meaning of that phrase: "They solved the dreams – but not for Pharaoh. Their voice was not heard by him, and he was not satisfied with their solutions." The Midrash relates that the magicians suggested a variety of explanations (Pharaoh will have seven daughters and they will all die, he will capture seven kingdoms which will then rebel against him) but he didn't accept any of them: "no one interpreted them – for Pharaoh."

When we are looking for the answer to a question, we may not be sure of the exact solution we want, but we have an "inner sense" of what is not the answer and we recoil from bad solutions. By process of elimination, we home in on the correct answer, intuitively knowing what is most appropriate.

Pharaoh's dream is eventually explained by Joseph (derisively nicknamed "the dreamer" by his brothers). Joseph listens intently and, with Pharaoh's cooperation, provides an interpretation, which addresses Pharaoh on a national level rather than a personal one. Joseph suggests that during the seven good years, Pharaoh should store food in preparation for the seven lean years that will follow. As soon as Joseph gives this explanation, Pharaoh instinctively recognizes it to be the correct solution.

Rabbi Isaac Abrabanel was a commentator and statesman at the time of the expulsion from Spain. He comments on the solution to the dreams and notes: "When a person solves the veracity and correctness of the dream, then it will strike a chord of truth in the dreamer's heart and he will accept the solution."

Although we may require help and advice from spiritual guides, deep down we ourselves know what is best.

ষ ষ ষ

Language Creates Reality

וַיֹּאמֶר פַּרְעֹה אֶל עֲבָדָיו הֲנִמְצָא כָזֶה אִישׁ אֲשֶׁר רוּחַ אֱלֹהִים בּוֹ.

So Pharaoh said to his servants, "**Can we find anyone like this,** a man who has the spirit of God in him?"

(Gen. 41:38)

Are we influenced by the language spoken by those around us? Do we have any chance of changing the style and manner of discourse in our surrounding culture? *Parashat Miketz* relates that not only was Joseph not conversely affected by Egyptian culture, but he somehow managed to positively influence it. Throughout the *parasha*, Joseph does not say much but when he does, there is a central theme running through his conversations. He tells Potiphar's wife, "How can I commit this great evil, and sin against God?" When Pharaoh's butler and baker turn to Joseph to solve their dreams he asks them, "Don't interpretations belong to God?" And when Pharaoh himself requests an explanation for his dreams, Joseph replies, "It is not I; God will give an answer that will bring peace to Pharaoh." Giving Pharaoh a detailed explanation of the dreams, Joseph continues, "What God is doing He has told Pharaoh." And then, "It is because the thing is established by God, and God will shortly bring it about."

In a world of idolatry, Joseph constantly mentions God. When a person sins, it is against God. He solves dreams. He is above us. It is quite amazing to note how even Pharaoh is influenced by Joseph's manner of speech. The language spoken in our surroundings enters our consciousness and causes us to speak in a different manner, and this is true even for Pharaoh. He listens intently to Joseph's words, accepts them, and decides that he needs someone to oversee the years of plenty and of famine in his country. Pharaoh demonstrates the extent to which Joseph's vocabulary influenced him in the following statement (unedited version): "Can we find anyone like this, a man who has the spirit of God in him?"

୧୫ ୧୫ ୧୫

Don't Be Right, Be Patient

וַיָּבֹאוּ אֲחֵי יוֹסֵף וַיִּשְׁתַּחֲווּ לוֹ אַפַּיִם אָרְצָה. וַיַּרְא יוֹסֵף אֶת אֶחָיו וַיַּכִּרֵם וַיִּתְנַכֵּר אֲלֵיהֶם וַיְדַבֵּר אִתָּם קָשׁוֹת ... וַיַּכֵּר יוֹסֵף אֶת אֶחָיו וְהֵם לֹא הִכִּרֻהוּ.

And Joseph's brothers came and prostrated themselves to him, with their faces to the ground. And Joseph saw his brothers, and he recognized them, **but he made himself a stranger to them, and he spoke to them harshly**.... Now Joseph recognized his brothers, but they did not recognize him.

(Gen. 42:6–8)

If we are correct, shouldn't we let everyone know? Broadcast it for all to hear? In this *parasha*, Joseph comes face-to-face with his brothers. Many years have elapsed since he last saw them. He now holds a senior position in Pharaoh's household, whereas they have been suffering from famine in the Land of Israel and have come to Egypt to request food. This could have been a very emotional reunion. So why doesn't he reveal his true identity to them and say, "I am Joseph"?

There is more to this initial encounter than meets the eye. If he would have revealed himself immediately, there could very well have been great excitement, but that emotion would quickly pass to be replaced by anger, frustration, and embarrassment. After all, the brothers had thrown Joseph into a pit. How could they now look him in the eye, and how could he look them in the eye? Why does Joseph draw out the course of events and test his brothers? The emotional reunion will only occur in the following *parasha*, only once the brothers have proved that they have fully repented of their wrongdoing and undergone a complete change. Only then will they be able to meet their long-lost brother.

Joseph's behavior is a lesson to teach us to think before we act. Even if we are correct, we should consider whether what we wish to say is appropriate and, if so, under what circumstances. There may be a family or a value which is of greater importance and we should carefully weigh our words before impulsively saying something which may be hurtful to others. From Joseph we learn that sometimes we have to be smart when trying to manage a sensitive and complicated situation so that the outcome does not damage anyone. In the present example, Joseph would have had every right and reason to reveal himself. Yet his behavior teaches us not to get bogged down in being right. Instead, be smart and think how you can get everyone out of this crisis in one piece and united.

Vayigash

You Cannot Erase the Past, but You Can Correct It

וְלֹא יָכֹל יוֹסֵף לְהִתְאַפֵּק לְכֹל הַנִּצָּבִים עָלָיו וַיִּקְרָא הוֹצִיאוּ כָל אִישׁ מֵעָלָי
וְלֹא עָמַד אִישׁ אִתּוֹ בְּהִתְוַדַּע יוֹסֵף אֶל אֶחָיו.

And Joseph could not control himself in front of the people
beside him, and he called out, "Take everyone away from me!"
**So no one stood with him when Joseph made himself known
to his brothers.**

(Gen. 45:1)

The previous *parasha* ended in a cliff-hanger. What will happen next?
Will it be possible for Joseph and his brothers to reconnect? Joseph
could have revealed himself much earlier in the story and informed
his brothers that the Egyptian ruler is none other than their long-lost
brother. However, they would have been embarrassed and so would
he. The family would have disintegrated instead of growing into
the Jewish nation. It is impossible to erase the fact that they threw
Joseph into the pit, abandoning him to be sold into slavery, yet it is
possible to make amends and correct past misdeeds. This is called
repentance, and *Parashat Vayigash* relates how the brothers went
through the process.

First, they are remorseful: "Indeed, we are guilty about our
brother, that we witnessed the distress of his soul when he begged us,

and we did not listen." However, regret alone is insufficient. In the next stage of repentance, they prove that they have indeed changed their ways. Joseph plans to imprison Benjamin, the youngest brother, only for Judah to jump forward begging that Joseph take him instead.

This is a demonstration of collective responsibility at the highest level and it corrects the error of abandoning Joseph. By showing unity and solidarity, the brothers prove that they have learned their lesson. Now, and only now, is the setting right for the emotional scene: "And Joseph could not control himself.... And he wept out loud.... And Joseph said to his brothers, 'I am Joseph. Is my father still alive?'"

Now is the right time for the brothers to be reunited and call for their father Jacob to come from the Land of Israel. The sin of selling Joseph will always be there, lurking in the background, but once the brothers have successfully passed the test Joseph set for them, they can now look at one another squarely in the eye.

ભ ભ ભ

The Vaccine

וַיֹּאמֶר אֲנִי יוֹסֵף אֲחִיכֶם אֲשֶׁר מְכַרְתֶּם אֹתִי מִצְרָיְמָה. וְעַתָּה אַל תֵּעָצְבוּ
וְאַל יִחַר בְּעֵינֵיכֶם כִּי מְכַרְתֶּם אֹתִי הֵנָּה כִּי לְמִחְיָה שְׁלָחַנִי אֱלֹהִים
לִפְנֵיכֶם.

And he said, "I am your brother Joseph, whom you sold into Egypt. And now **do not be sad, and let it not trouble you that you sold me** here, because God sent me before you to preserve life."

(Gen. 45:4–5)

The very emotional reunion between Joseph and his brothers is not only a familial reconciliation, but also a formative national moment in which a family begins to develop into a nation. For that reason, every detail and nuance has future significance. The course of events describing how one brother is sold into slavery, rises to prominence, and is reunited with his brothers is far more than a gripping soap opera. It is no less than the creation of the Jewish people.

According to Rabbi Hanan Porat, the lesson to be learned from this family feud is that it leads to exile. On this occasion the exile was to Egypt, but throughout our history, whenever we wanted to throw a brother into a pit or when we were afflicted by infighting and jealousy there was a tragic outcome. Porat views the reunion between Joseph and his brothers as a vaccine given to the Jews to protect them and enable them to survive in the future. The family did not break up and Joseph and his brothers taught us a lesson for the future at the very beginning of our nation.

> As we embark on the long journey of nationhood, God initiates an immunization program and gives Jacob's family a shot of the "collective responsibility" vaccine. This vaccine contains strains of various germs: jealousy, hatred, arrogance, and divisiveness. By giving us a shot, God is strengthening the antibodies of our national collective to help us overcome all the crises and internal divisions that we will have to confront in the future. Only after Jacob's family has been given this extra boost and has successfully passed the trial of taking responsibility for each other can the brothers face the darkness of any future exile knowing that they have the strength to overcome anything without danger of the nation breaking apart.

CB CB CB

The First *Aliya*

וַיֹּאמֶר אָנֹכִי הָאֵל אֱלֹהֵי אָבִיךָ אַל תִּירָא מֵרְדָה מִצְרַיְמָה כִּי לְגוֹי גָּדוֹל אֲשִׂימְךָ שָׁם. אָנֹכִי אֵרֵד עִמְּךָ מִצְרַיְמָה וְאָנֹכִי אַעַלְךָ גַם עָלֹה וְיוֹסֵף יָשִׁית יָדוֹ עַל עֵינֶיךָ.

And He said, "I am God, the God of your father. Do not be afraid of going down to Egypt, for there I will make you into a great nation. I will go down with you to Egypt, and I will also bring you up, and Joseph will place his hand on your eyes."

(Gen. 46:3–4)

Yitzhak Rabin once caused a furor when he called those who move away from Israel "the dregs of the weaklings." This negative view of people who leave the Land of Israel has its roots in this *parasha*. Although the Torah does not use such harsh words to describe those who leave, it certainly does praise those who move to the Land of Israel. In between the two dramatic incidents of Joseph revealing himself to his brothers and Jacob's reunion with his son, the Torah goes off on a tangent and provides a detailed description of Jacob leaving the Land of Israel and setting off for Egypt.

The Torah is telling us something about the essence of the attitude and connection to the land. Leaving and returning to Israel is not a national population transfer from one country to the next, nor is it like emigration and immigration for an individual. The Torah simply uses the terms going up and down. When Joseph sends his brothers back from Egypt to their home in order to bring Jacob back, he says, "Go up to my father." Rashi asks why Joseph doesn't simply use the verb "travel" and answers that "the Land of Israel is higher than any other land."

Even when God appears before Jacob, He Himself talks of going up and down: "I will go down with you to Egypt, and I will also bring you up." We know that Jacob was forced to leave the Land of Israel because of the famine, but nevertheless it was still a descent.

A person who moves to a new country is called an immigrant. However, a Jew who returns to Israel is always called an *oleh* – one who goes up – from the time that Jacob went up to this very day when a Jew leaves France and moves to Israel. The verse also tells us that everyone who comes up to Israel is not coming alone: "I will go down with you to Egypt, and I will also bring you up."

CB CB CB

"Hear O Israel," Here and Now

וַיֶּאְסֹר יוֹסֵף מֶרְכַּבְתּוֹ וַיַּעַל לִקְרַאת יִשְׂרָאֵל אָבִיו גֹּשְׁנָה וַיֵּרָא אֵלָיו וַיִּפֹּל
עַל צַוָּארָיו וַיֵּבְךְּ עַל צַוָּארָיו עוֹד.

And Joseph harnessed his chariot, and he went up to meet Israel
his father, to Goshen, **and he appeared to him, and he fell on
his neck, and he wept on his neck for a long time.**

(Gen. 46:29)

This is almost superhuman behavior. Joseph and Jacob meet after
twenty-two years. Joseph hugs his father and weeps, but, according to
Jewish tradition, Jacob calls out, "Hear O Israel: the Lord is our God,
the Lord is one." What made him say this particular sentence at such
an emotional moment?

Some commentators explain Jacob's behavior by saying that he
was merely sticking to a timetable. When father and son met, it was
the proper time of day for saying the *Shema* prayer. Others explain that
Jacob felt that the appropriate behavior on this particular occasion was
to hold himself back and not let his emotions rule his behavior. He felt
that at this precise time and place, the right thing to do was to proclaim
the Jewish people's most basic tenet of faith.

Most of us would not react like him and we are probably not even
expected to. Jacob's behavior was certainly superhuman and can serve as
an inspiration to us. He teaches us self-control and also self-confidence.

Vayehi

The Good Life

וַיְחִי יַעֲקֹב בְּאֶרֶץ מִצְרַיִם שְׁבַע עֶשְׂרֵה שָׁנָה וַיְהִי יְמֵי יַעֲקֹב שְׁנֵי חַיָּיו שֶׁבַע שָׁנִים וְאַרְבָּעִים וּמְאַת שָׁנָה.

And Jacob lived in the land of Egypt for seventeen years, and Jacob's days, the years of his life, were a hundred and forty-seven years.

(Gen. 47:28)

This *parasha* is called *Vayehi*, which means, "And he lived." Yet we are told how Jacob separated from his sons prior to his death and are given details of the funeral procession. The Lubavitcher Rebbe explains the seeming contradiction between the title and contents of the *parasha*:

A true life is one of dedication, of studying the Torah and of keeping the commandments, and Jacob obviously lived such a lifestyle. However, if we consider our sages' statement, "Do not believe in yourself until the day you die," then the Torah cannot sum up Jacob's life and write "and Jacob lived" while he was still alive. Even with Jacob, who was definitely considered "alive" and continued to be dedicated to God after all the trials and sorrow he went through, we must apply the sages' statement. Therefore, the Torah only sums up Jacob's life shortly before his death, when it

67

was proven beyond any doubt that he had remained a righteous person throughout his entire life, even when living in Egypt. The final verdict: "And Jacob lived."

We can all think of politicians, public figures, and spiritual leaders who were once considered very successful, yet ended their lives as failures. If we were to present a positive mid-life assessment of their careers, and they were later convicted and sent to prison or forced to resign because of a scandal, then we would be considered fools. No one is ever immune, not even Jacob. Only as he is about to die can one really see what kind of life a person has led and declare, "And he lived."

∽ ∽ ∽

A Blessing for Our Children

וַיְבָרֲכֵם בַּיּוֹם הַהוּא לֵאמוֹר בְּךָ יְבָרֵךְ יִשְׂרָאֵל לֵאמֹר יְשִׂמְךָ אֱלֹהִים
כְּאֶפְרַיִם וְכִמְנַשֶּׁה.

And he blessed them on that day, saying: "With you, Israel will bless, saying, '**May God make you like Ephraim and like Manasseh.**'"

(Gen. 48:20)

What is the greatest blessing we can bestow on our children? We would obviously wish that they be granted an easy and comfortable life. And if we only could, we would try and cushion their whole life and shield them from any difficulties. Yet, as we all know, we do face trials and challenges during our lives. Precisely for that reason, Jacob formulates the special text of his blessing that has become such a common phrase for Jews throughout the generations. Jacob places his hands on Joseph's sons Ephraim and Manasseh and blesses them. The opening words of his blessing, "May God make you like Ephraim and like Manasseh," are said by many Jewish parents on Friday night before making Kiddush.

Why were these two grandchildren chosen among all of Jacob's children who had grown up in his household to become the model and symbol to be emulated? As we know from Jewish history, from the time of Jacob to our current situation there have been many periods of exile and unceasing struggles against foreign cultures, some still ongoing. Growing up in Egypt, in a culture diametrically opposed to their own, Ephraim and Manasseh still managed to hold on to their independent culture. The sons of the vizier, who grew up in the Egyptian palace, remained Jacob's grandchildren. Jacob blesses all his children, grandchildren, great-grandchildren, and all future generations that we should pass the test as successfully as Ephraim and Manasseh in every age and in every place: in Egypt, New York, Yemen, Russia, and Israel.

CB CB CB

Rebuke Is a Blessing

וְזֹאת אֲשֶׁר דִּבֶּר לָהֶם אֲבִיהֶם וַיְבָרֶךְ אוֹתָם אִישׁ אֲשֶׁר כְּבִרְכָתוֹ בֵּרַךְ
אֹתָם.

And this is what their father spoke to them **and blessed them; each one, according to his blessing,** he blessed them.
(Gen. 49:28)

What comprises a blessing? It is known that Jacob blessed his sons in his final days on earth. Yet not all of them received a blessing; some were reprimanded. For example, Reuben was told off about his impulsivity and Simeon and Levi were criticized for their violent acts. What kind of blessings are these? They are certainly not ordinary ones, and their purpose is therapeutic rather than simply wishing good on someone. What greater blessing can someone be given than an honest assessment of what his good and bad points are? It will enable him to work on correcting his negative characteristics. Rabbi Shlomo Wolbe talks about this special occasion when Jacob blesses his sons:

> Their father revealed their bad characteristics to them so that they would know to steer clear of them, and this is considered a blessing. If someone is told about bad features he should avoid,

it would put him on the right path for the rest of his life. After all, a person's characteristics are his innermost self. If you know your shortcomings, then you know what to avoid. A person can go through his entire life without ever knowing his good and bad points. Jacob gave his sons an immeasurable blessing by revealing to each one their characteristics, by telling each tribe what its essence, the source of its soul, is.

൙ ൙ ൙

What the Pale Child Taught Max Nordau

וַאֲנִי בְּבֹאִי מִפַּדָּן מֵתָה עָלַי רָחֵל בְּאֶרֶץ כְּנַעַן בַּדֶּרֶךְ בְּעוֹד כִּבְרַת אֶרֶץ לָבֹא אֶפְרָתָה וָאֶקְבְּרֶהָ שָּׁם בְּדֶרֶךְ אֶפְרָת הִוא בֵּית לָחֶם.

As for me, when I came from Padan, Rachel died in front of me in the land of Canaan on the way, when there was still a stretch of land to come to Efrat, and I buried her there on the way to Efrat, which is Bethlehem.

(Gen. 48:7)

Jacob gives an overview of his entire life, and one of the most important points for him is the death of his wife: "As for me, when I came from Padan, Rachel died in front of me." Rashi gives the reason why she was buried on the roadside: When the Jewish people would go into exile, they would pass her grave and pray, and Rachel would weep and wait throughout all the exiles until her children would return to the Land of Israel. The prophet Jeremiah tells her, "There is reward for your work … and the children shall return to their border."

Rachel's story greatly influenced Max Nordau, an assimilated Jew who became one of the founders of the Zionist movement. The following is a moving testimony to how he changed.

On the second night of the First Zionist Congress in Basel, Nordau spoke in German, giving a long speech. Several times, he quoted three Hebrew words from Jeremiah, using them as a motto: "The children shall return to their border." When asked by a young representative at the congress how he found this verse, and especially in Hebrew, for this did not fit Nordau's educational background, he replied:

I know these words from the person to whom I am obliged for all my Judaism and Zionism. A person whose name I don't even know. A person who was actually only a little boy of eight or ten. And this is what happened.

I have a children's clinic in Paris. A woman, an immigrant from Poland, her hair covered with a scarf, came in with a pale boy, eight or ten, who had been sick for three weeks. Someone recommended that she bring him to me. I took out the form for new patients and tried to speak to him in our local language, but he could hardly understand French. I asked his mother, who was also very poor at French, and she said, "No – he doesn't go to a regular school, he goes to a *heder*, a Jewish religious school." I scolded her harshly: "This only causes anti-Semitism. We have opened the door for you, the gates to the country, to refugees from Poland. Why doesn't your child learn the national language here?" She apologized and said that he is still young and that her husband is from the "old generation," but that he will grow and study in the "gymnasium" [modern school], and will learn the language. In anger, I asked the child, "In *heder*, what did you learn?" His eyes lit up, and in Yiddish, which I understood because of my German, told me what he had last studied in *heder*.

"Jacob," he said, "was dying and he invited Joseph and commanded him, swore him, pleaded before him, 'Please, don't bury me in Egypt. There is the Cave of Machpela – Abraham, Isaac, Jacob, Sarah, Rebecca – and there I buried Leah. Take me from Egypt and bury me with them. And when I came from Padan, Rachel died in the land of Canaan, on the way to Efrat, and I buried her there, on the way, in Bethlehem.' Why, in the middle of Jacob's request, does he tell the story of the Tomb of Rachel? Rashi says," – and this is all the child talks about, eight or ten years old, speaking about the "sages" – "that Jacob felt a necessity to apologize to Joseph and say, 'I bother you like this, to take me from Egypt to Hebron, and I, myself, didn't bother to take your mother Rachel. And despite the fact that I was very close, next to Bethlehem, I didn't even take her into the city, I buried her on the way. But I am not guilty and didn't act wrongly. God wanted it this way. He knew: the murderer Nebuchadnezzar would, in the future, exile the sons of Rachel, her sons, during the destruction of the First Temple, and then she would leave her grave and weep and wail and her voice would be heard: Rachel weeps for her children. But the Lord responds to her: Stop your voice from weeping, and your eyes from tears, because there is a reward for your actions, and a hope for the future, and the children will return to their borders.'"

And I, I didn't know what to do with myself. I turned away toward the window so that the mother and child wouldn't see the tears rolling down my cheeks, and I said to myself, "Max, aren't you ashamed of yourself? You are an educated man, known as an intellectual, with a medical degree, but you don't know anything about the history of your people. Nothing about the holy scriptures. And here, this sick child, weak, an immigrant, a refugee, he speaks of Jacob and Joseph and Jeremiah, and Rachel, as if it was yesterday, it all lives in front of his eyes." I wiped the tears from my cheeks and turned to them and said, in my heart, "A people, with children like this, that actually live their past, they will have a sparkling future."

In the weekend newspaper I saw an advertisement, "Whoever believes that the fate of the Jewish people is important to them, whoever is pained by anti-Semitism, and whoever is looking for a solution, please call to help find an answer. Dr. Theodor Herzl." I called immediately. When we founded the first Zionist Congress I was honored to give a speech. The image of that little boy, whose name I don't even remember, stood in front of my eyes. But I will never forget those words because they are the foundation of Zionism, they are the pillars of Judaism: "and the children will return to their borders."

Exodus

The Book of Genesis is called the "Book of Creation" because it tells of the creation of the world and all living life, and then of the Patriarchs and Matriarchs of the Jewish nation. The Book of Exodus is called the "Book of Exile and Redemption" because it tells of the journey from slavery to freedom, from Egypt to the wilderness on the way to the Land of Israel.

Rabbi Shlomo Wolbe tells us what we will encounter when we read the "Book of Exile and Redemption." He says that this is not a history textbook but a timeless book, telling not only the story of a nation, but also of individuals. "Exile is a state in which a person does not live in his natural place. Redemption is when a person returns there."

The journey begins in the Book of Exodus.

Shemot

Moses: Salvation in a Name

וַיִגְדַּל הַיֶּלֶד וַתְּבִאֵהוּ לְבַת פַּרְעֹה וַיְהִי לָהּ לְבֵן וַתִּקְרָא שְׁמוֹ מֹשֶׁה וַתֹּאמֶר
כִּי מִן הַמַּיִם מְשִׁיתִהוּ.

The child grew up, and she brought him to Pharaoh's daughter,
and he became like her son and she named him Moses, and she
said, "**Because I drew him from the water.**"

(Ex. 2:10)

One of the most common names in this *parasha*, and indeed in the
whole Torah, is Moses or *Moshe*. He is given his name by Pharaoh's
daughter, who found him in the river and drew him out. If that were
the reason for his name, she should have used the passive form of the
verb and not the participle, *Mashuy* (drawn) and not *Moshe* (drawing).
His name tells us that Moses is destined to draw others away from
danger and save them. Long before he becomes the leader of the Jewish people and leads them out of Egypt, he is already involved in saving others. The Midrash relates that a youthful Moses demonstrated
his tenderness while shepherding a weak kid goat that had run away
from the flock.

A person's name is the word one hears most throughout one's life.
The message Moses heard from the day he was named was: Save, Draw

75

Out, Save, Draw Out. Just as Pharaoh's daughter saved you, you should be sensitive to other people's difficulties. Draw them out!

ଔ ଔ ଔ

Do Not Use Your Hands

וַיֵּצֵא בַּיּוֹם הַשֵּׁנִי וְהִנֵּה שְׁנֵי אֲנָשִׁים עִבְרִים נִצִּים וַיֹּאמֶר לָרָשָׁע לָמָּה תַכֶּה רֵעֶךָ.

And he went out on the second day and two Hebrew men were quarreling, **and he said to the wicked one, "Why are you hitting your friend?"**

(Ex. 2:13)

I always assumed that the expression "do not raise your hand against your friend" was one of those sayings invented by nursery school teachers. In fact, the source for this saying is from this *parasha*. Moses leaves the Egyptian palace and sees two Jews quarreling. He reacts by saying "to the wicked one, 'Why are you hitting your friend?'" Rashi explains why he calls him a wicked person: "Even though he did not hit him, he is called wicked because he raised his hand."

This comment requires further explanation. Why is someone who merely raised his hand, but did not actually hit anyone, called a wicked person? Hasidic thought gives one possible reason. Every limb in our body is created with a purpose. For example, a hand is meant to be used for giving charity to the poor and needy. The hand is meant to help others, and when it is used for the opposite purpose, it is a sin.

Thus, the very act of raising your hand to hit another person (even if you do not actually hit him) is already in violation of the purpose of that limb's creation and therefore the sin begins at the very instant when the hand "betrays" its destiny and is raised in the air.

ଔ ଔ ଔ

Holy Is Here

וַיֹּאמֶר אַל תִּקְרַב הֲלֹם שַׁל נְעָלֶיךָ מֵעַל רַגְלֶיךָ כִּי הַמָּקוֹם אֲשֶׁר אַתָּה עוֹמֵד עָלָיו אַדְמַת קֹדֶשׁ הוּא.

And He said, "Do not draw near here. Take your shoes off your feet, because **the place upon which you stand is holy soil**."

(Ex. 3:5)

Moses sees the Burning Bush and hears the famous sentence, "Take your shoes off your feet, because the place upon which you stand is holy soil." As Rabbi Michi Yosefi explains, this sentence teaches us that **we do not need to travel to faraway holy sites in order to undergo a process of change. This verse shows that the opposite is true.**

> "Take off your shoes" – remove whatever is restraining you,
> "From your feet" – from your habits.
> "Because the place upon which you stand is holy soil" – you do not always need to look for a new place, to change residence, to search for a special place to study, or to travel to an isolated island. The place that you are standing on at this moment can become holy.

All you need to do is to remove the restraints and habits that are holding you back.

og og og

The Antihero Hero

לֹא אִישׁ דְּבָרִים אָנֹכִי גַּם מִתְּמוֹל גַּם מִשִּׁלְשֹׁם גַּם מֵאָז דַּבֶּרְךָ אֶל עַבְדֶּךָ כִּי כְבַד פֶּה וּכְבַד לָשׁוֹן אָנֹכִי.

I am not a man of words, neither from yesterday nor from the day before yesterday, nor from the time You have spoken to Your servant, for I **am heavy of mouth and heavy of tongue**.

(Ex. 4:10)

Moses argues with God for seven (!) days at the Burning Bush, because he is not prepared to accept the task God has assigned to him. Among the various arguments he puts forth, one is particularly compelling: "I am not a man of words, neither from yesterday, nor from the day before yesterday, nor from the time You have spoken to Your servant, for I am heavy of mouth and heavy of tongue."

When I was young, I imagined Moses as a Hollywood-type personality who leads his people through the Red Sea, who descends from Mount Sinai with the tablets, a charismatic leader who leads his people to freedom. It is easy to forget that the Torah tells us that he had a stutter, a far cry from one of those superstar leaders that we have become accustomed to today. He probably did not proclaim "Let my people go" with the pathos that we might imagine him to.

Political commentators repeatedly tell us that our past leaders would not have been elected under Israel's current system of open primary elections within the various political parties. Would Moses have been electable? An eighty-year-old stutterer who expressed no desire whatsoever to be a leader? Moses is more than happy for Aaron to carry out the task, but God insists. God specifically wants a leader like Moses.

Before Moses departs to meet Pharaoh, the Torah tells us something else. It will not be possible to carry out a grandiose operation like the Exodus from Egypt if there is any jealousy between Moses and Aaron. God tells Moses that his brother Aaron will "come forth toward you, and when he sees you, he will rejoice in his heart." Your brother will not be angry that you are going to do great things; he will be extremely happy for you. You will be partners in this important task, and you will work together in harmony.

To sum up, we are presented with an elderly, non-charismatic leader who is aware of – and afraid of – the weight of responsibility on him, and who works in tandem with others.

We should be so lucky today.

Va'era

A Leader, Not a Talent

הוּא אַהֲרֹן וּמֹשֶׁה אֲשֶׁר אָמַר ה' לָהֶם הוֹצִיאוּ אֶת בְּנֵי יִשְׂרָאֵל מֵאֶרֶץ מִצְרַיִם עַל צִבְאֹתָם: הֵם הַמְדַבְּרִים אֶל פַּרְעֹה מֶלֶךְ מִצְרַיִם לְהוֹצִיא אֶת בְּנֵי יִשְׂרָאֵל מִמִּצְרָיִם הוּא מֹשֶׁה וְאַהֲרֹן.

These are Aaron and Moses, to whom the Lord said, "Take the Children of Israel out of the land of Egypt with their legions." They are the ones who spoke to Pharaoh, the king of Egypt, to let the Children of Israel out of Egypt; **these are Moses and Aaron.**
(Ex. 6:26–27)

When I used to present a morning television show, I interviewed participants in a reality show throughout the show's season. These were youngsters who came to audition for the Israeli version of *American Idol.* Each week, a large number of participants were dismissed, until the final round. My co-presenter and I had a real challenge. From week to week, we could observe whether the participants were changing. When they first came to the studio to be interviewed, they were excited and true to themselves. Slowly but surely, some of them became more snobby and abrasive, and acted as it they were the best "talent stars," while other competitors remained exactly the same and some even become nicer people. This expressed itself in how they treated the journalists, the camera people and make-up artists, the other interviewees, and their behavior in general. It was a fascinating experiment to see how fame and success influence people and change them.

In this connection, let us read the following verses and make an interesting observation. "These are Aaron and Moses, to whom the Lord said, 'Take the Children of Israel out of the land of Egypt.' They are the ones who spoke to Pharaoh, the king of Egypt, to let the Children of Israel out of Egypt; these are Moses and Aaron." Why are they first introduced as Aaron and Moses and later as Moses and Aaron? One explanation given by our sages is that "they were considered equal." They worked together in harmony without competition between them. So it did not matter who was mentioned first – sometimes it was Aaron and other times it was Moses.

Another explanation is that Moses and Aaron "remained the same in their mission and in their greatness from the beginning to the end." They did not change at all. Moses did not become a different person as he rose to greatness from the baby in the cradle to the leader of the Jewish people, and Aaron did not change when he became the High Priest. Their rise to greatness did not damage their good character.

ॐ ॐ ॐ

Exile of the Soul

לָכֵן אֱמֹר לִבְנֵי יִשְׂרָאֵל אֲנִי ה' וְהוֹצֵאתִי אֶתְכֶם מִתַּחַת סִבְלֹת מִצְרָיִם.

Therefore, say to the Children of Israel, "**I am the Lord, and I will take you out from under the burdens of the Egyptians.**"
(Ex. 6:6)

In a certain sense, the Exodus from Egypt is not yet over. When Pharaoh hears the demand to send the Jews free from slavery, he reacts by imposing additional work. Not only does he refuse to free them, he also adds to the slaves' burden. Why does he react in such a manner? Pharaoh understood something fundamental about human nature. If the Children of Israel are completely engrossed in their physical slavery and have no time to think about spiritual matters, ideas about freedom and deliverance will disappear. If all their time is taken up building pyramids, they will not have a spare second to think in peace. This truth is always valid.

Rabbi Nahman of Breslov writes a wonderful essay, in my opinion, about the national and individual exodus from Egypt in which he explains that we are all in exile. An exile of the soul. In order to go out of this exile, we have to reach a state of tranquility:

> Everything that happened to the Children of Israel during the Exodus from Egypt happens to everyone who wishes to achieve everlasting life. At the time of the Exodus, Moses, a truly righteous person, comes and wants to take the Hebrew person out of the exile of his soul. Then the *sitra ahra*, the Devil, becomes stronger and stronger and makes his burden in this world even harder with desires and livelihood until he finds it difficult to move from his current situation and return to God. And this is exactly what every person goes through all the time, and everyone can understand all this for himself according to his understanding the ups and downs that he goes through several times throughout his life, which can be compared to the exile in Egypt because the main part of the exile is the exile of the soul. A person who is aware of this will see this in whatever occurs in his life, both the good and the bad.

Events that enslave and confuse us, that distract us from our main purpose in life, were not one-off events that occurred in Egypt; they are with us at all times in our life, even now.

೫ ೫ ೫

A Good Age to Begin

וּמֹשֶׁה בֶּן שְׁמֹנִים שָׁנָה וְאַהֲרֹן בֶּן שָׁלֹשׁ וּשְׁמֹנִים שָׁנָה בְּדַבְּרָם אֶל פַּרְעֹה.

And Moses was eighty years old and Aaron was eighty-three years old when they spoke to Pharaoh.

(Ex. 7:7)

Ageism is defined as discrimination against the elderly, based on holding preconceived opinions about people based on their age. Stereotypical views of the elderly are usually negative.

The Exodus from Egypt is meant to teach us to stand up against preconceived views and reconsider our belief system on many matters, including ageism. As the whole process of the Exodus is about to begin, the Torah tells us that "Moses was eighty years old and Aaron was eighty-three years old when they spoke to Pharaoh." This is not a mere technicality, it represents a way of thinking. Eighty is the best possible age to begin speaking to Pharaoh, to become a leader, and change the world. The world belongs to those with experience or, maybe, the world belongs to the elderly who are young at heart.

CB CB CB

Thank You, Thank You, and Thank You Again

וַיֹּאמֶר ה' אֶל מֹשֶׁה אֱמֹר אֶל אַהֲרֹן קַח מַטְּךָ וּנְטֵה יָדְךָ עַל מֵימֵי מִצְרַיִם...
וְיִהְיוּ דָם וְהָיָה דָם בְּכָל אֶרֶץ מִצְרַיִם וּבָעֵצִים וּבָאֲבָנִים.

> And the Lord said to Moses, "**Say to Aaron: Take your staff and stretch forth your hand over the waters of Egypt**... and they will become blood, and there will be blood throughout the entire land of Egypt, even in wood and in stone."
>
> (Ex. 7:19)

As the Plagues of Egypt are about to begin, the Torah relates that God tells Moses to tell Aaron to stretch out his hand over the river. It seems strange that Moses does not do it himself!

Our sages offer a powerful explanation. Since the river sheltered him in his basket when he was an infant, Moses is not allowed to hit the river now, and instead Aaron is given the job. The reasoning seems somewhat odd. What difference does it make that the river once "helped" Moses? Will it be "insulted" if Moses hits it now? Since when do rivers have feelings? And why is it better that Aaron hit the river?

Rabbi Avigdor Nebenzahl discusses this question in his book *Talks on the Book of Exodus* (*Sihot LeSefer Shemot*) and says that we are concerned about Moses and his soul, rather than about the river's feelings:

> The Torah teaches us about showing gratitude toward the world as a whole. Moses is not showing gratitude for the sake of the river, but for his own virtue and self-education. Showing gratitude is a skill that needs to be practiced every day, by demonstrating appreciation to your Creator, your spouse, children, friends, and yes, even to inanimate objects. One needs a profound awareness about the importance of showing gratitude, as it is very difficult to avoid being tainted by ungratefulness. People should set aside fixed times to exercise this important trait.

At the start of the great miracles of the Exodus, the Torah emphasizes the basics, the need to show gratitude. Before Moses actually leads the Children of Israel out of slavery, he teaches them to take note of even the small actions, and to say "Thank you."

03 03 03

Do Not Add Fuel to the Fire

וַיֵּט אַהֲרֹן אֶת יָדוֹ עַל מֵימֵי מִצְרָיִם וַתַּעַל הַצְּפַרְדֵּעַ וַתְּכַס אֶת אֶרֶץ מִצְרָיִם.

And Aaron stretched forth his hand over the waters of Egypt, **and the frogs came up and covered the land of Egypt**.

(Ex. 8:2)

After the plague of blood comes the second plague of the frogs. The Midrash tells us that the plague began with just one frog which the Egyptians hit again and again, causing it to multiply into many frogs. Each time they hit a frog, it multiplied into two frogs.

Rabbi Yaakov Yisrael Kanievski (or as he is better known, the *Steipler*) asks in his book *Birkat Peretz* why the Egyptians continued hitting the frogs? After all, once they had hit one or two frogs, they should have realized that this only made them grow in number and they ought to have stopped! He explains that this behavior is typical of people who get angry and cannot stop. The anger eats them up, they try to take revenge, even though that will only bring more evil into the world, and the vicious cycle continues.

> If one is insulted and does not respond in kind, the incident slowly fades away. However, when one reacts to the person insulting him, the latter will respond even more harshly. The vice of anger tries to persuade a person to react to a provocation. However, if we think rationally, it is better to ignore it and let it pass until he has calmed down. When he reacts to the person facing him, things spin out of control and the other person will also react back angrily. Logic therefore dictates that it is best not to lash out against the one who makes you angry and to let it pass. But the voice of anger says, "What, I should let him get away with this!?" and begins to take revenge or hit back and then the other person fights back and so on and so forth, and the end is like the plague of the frogs in Egypt.

The *Steipler* is giving us a tool for dealing with anger. If you see a frog, or if people make you angry, move on and try to ignore it, to prevent the episode from getting blown out of proportion.

Bo

All or Nothing

וַיֹּאמֶר מֹשֶׁה בִּנְעָרֵינוּ וּבִזְקֵנֵינוּ נֵלֵךְ בְּבָנֵינוּ וּבִבְנוֹתֵנוּ בְּצֹאנֵנוּ וּבִבְקָרֵנוּ
נֵלֵךְ כִּי חַג ה' לָנוּ.

And Moses said, "**With our youth and with our elders we will
go, with our sons and with our daughters, with our flocks
and with our cattle** we will go, for it is a festival of the Lord
for us."

(Ex. 10:9)

It was a head-to-head challenge between Moses and Pharaoh. The
Torah describes a confrontation between Jewish and Egyptian values.
In this *parasha* Pharaoh allows the Jewish nation to leave Egypt to go
and worship their God and then to return. He asks Moses, "Who will
be going?" but adds that he will only allow the males to go. Contrast
this with Moses' reply: "With our youth and with our elders we will
go, with our sons and with our daughters, with our flocks and with
our cattle we will go, for it is a festival of the Lord for us." Moses does
not beat around the bush but is quite forthright in his reply: every
single person is included.

Judah Leib Gordon is considered one of the most important
poets of the *Haskala* period. He was very critical of Jewish traditional

practice and coined the phrase "Be a man in the street and a Jew in your home." Yet, despite his aversion to keeping the Torah, in one of his most famous poems, entitled *With Our Youth and with Our Elders,* his words echo Moses' reply to Pharaoh. Below are two stanzas:

We are one people, for we have one God
For we were dug out from the hole of one pit
Also one Torah with its special language
And we were tied to it with golden bonds
With this three-stranded cord that ties us to it
We will go with our youth and with our elders

We will cling to God, we will not abandon His religion
And let His holy tongue not be forgotten by us
We have seen evil, we will still see good
We have yet to live in our land where we once lived
If God has decided, we will once again hold a spindle
We will go with our youth and with our elders.

ଓ ଓ ଓ

We Are Not Robots

וַיֹּאמֶר מֹשֶׁה גַּם אַתָּה תִּתֵּן בְּיָדֵנוּ זְבָחִים וְעֹלוֹת...וְגַם מִקְנֵנוּ יֵלֵךְ עִמָּנוּ לֹא תִשָּׁאֵר פַּרְסָה כִּי מִמֶּנּוּ נִקַּח לַעֲבֹד אֶת ה' אֱלֹהֵינוּ וַאֲנַחְנוּ לֹא נֵדַע מַה נַּעֲבֹד אֶת ה' עַד בֹּאֵנוּ שָׁמָּה.

And Moses said, "You too shall give sacrifices and burnt offerings into our hands…. And also our cattle will go with us; not a hoof will remain, for we will take from it to worship the Lord our God, **and we do not know how we will worship the Lord until we arrive there.**"

(Ex. 10:25–26)

Does religious life operate on autopilot? Do religious Jews live in accordance with an exact set of written instructions? In this *parasha* Moses continues to plead before Pharaoh to release the slaves to go to the wilderness to worship God. He tells Pharaoh, "And we do not know how we will worship the Lord until we arrive there." Commenting on this verse, Professor Pinchas Peli writes:

> Moses' words, which sound like a declaration of intent during diplomatic negotiations, also reflect a profound theological truth. They teach us that there is no fixed, preordained formula for worshiping God. True worship entails constant searching and discovery, agonizing trial and error, one step forward and two steps back, bold decisions, and strengthening one's belief. Faith is not a bed of roses which awaits us at the end of the path. And we do not know how we will worship the Lord – until we arrive there.

The following hasidic story illustrates why there is no fixed, preordained formula in spiritual matters and why we need to constantly search and discover, progress and then regress, experience ups and downs, and arrive at new horizons.

A Rebbe asked one of his followers what he would do if he found a wallet full of money on Shabbat. "Would you pick it up?" The Hasid replied that of course he would not touch it because handling money on Shabbat is forbidden. The Rebbe called him a fool and immediately posed the same question to a second follower. Having heard the Rebbe get angry with the first response, he replied that of course he would pick it up. The Rebbe told him off and called him a sinner. He then asked a third follower, who replied, "I do not know what I would do. I would have an inner turmoil and hopefully would reach the correct decision." The Rebbe was pleased that he had finally received a proper answer to his question. "And we do not know how we will worship the Lord until we arrive there."

C3 C3 C3

Free Will

וּמֹשֶׁה וְאַהֲרֹן עָשׂוּ אֶת כָּל הַמֹּפְתִים הָאֵלֶּה לִפְנֵי פַרְעֹה וַיְחַזֵּק ה' אֶת
לֵב פַּרְעֹה וְלֹא שִׁלַּח אֶת בְּנֵי יִשְׂרָאֵל מֵאַרְצוֹ.

And Moses and Aaron performed all these miracles before Pharaoh, **and the Lord hardened Pharaoh's heart**, and he did not
let the Children of Israel out of his land.

(Ex. 11:10)

In addition to the many open miracles described in this *parasha*, we find
another, more subtle one: free will. One of the central themes in *Bo* is
what goes on in Pharaoh's heart, as the Torah describes his vacillations
in great detail: one minute he agrees to let the Jewish people go and the
next moment he changes his mind. Generations of philosophers have
discussed whether Pharaoh even had free choice, and if he did, why does
it say that God hardened his heart?

One of the answers that I like says that the more you choose evil,
the less free will you have. At first, everyone is free to choose, but after
enough bad decisions, one's ability to shift to a better path decreases
over time. One descends toward corruption, losing any and all sensitivity and compassion. One's conscience is no longer struggling against his
evil vices like it once did.

The more Pharaoh clung to his evil and cruel ways, the further
away he moved from showing mercy. The same applies to a drug addict
or an alcoholic. The deeper one sinks into addiction, the harder it is to
call it quits. (The same may apply to all of us, regarding any of our bad
habits.) We do have choice, but when we insist on going along a path
leading the wrong way, then the correct path becomes more and more
remote. The opposite is also true. The more we choose to do good, the
further we move away from evil.

CB CB CB

What Exactly Are We Talking About?

וַיֹּאמֶר ה׳ אֶל מֹשֶׁה וְאֶל אַהֲרֹן בְּאֶרֶץ מִצְרַיִם לֵאמֹר: הַחֹדֶשׁ הַזֶּה לָכֶם
רֹאשׁ חֳדָשִׁים רִאשׁוֹן הוּא לָכֶם לְחָדְשֵׁי הַשָּׁנָה.

And the Lord spoke to Moses and to Aaron in the land of Egypt,
saying, "This month shall be to you the beginning of months;
it shall be the first month of the year to you."

(Ex. 12:1–2)

Mazal Tov! The Children of Israel have received their first commandment from God, and told to fix the first day of every month as Rosh
Hodesh. From this point and forward, we will be given all 613 commandments.

Public discourse does not usually deal with the commandments;
we prefer to argue about political parties, legislation, and crises. So what
are the mitzvot really all about? And how are they part of the Jewish
experience (not the political, economic, or public one)?

Ori Melamed lives in Tel Aviv; he is a restaurant critic, standup
comedian, musician, and the son of a respected journalist. Another fact
about him is that he became religious after having grown up in a non-
religious home. After his friends and colleagues questioned his choice,
he decided to put in writing what Judaism means to him, not just what
one might find on social media. He writes about three terms and what
they mean to him: prayer, language, and holiness.

> To pray – but not in the borrowed sense like when I used to say,
> "I pray that the opposing team will lose the game," which really
> meant that I hoped that something good will happen. Now,
> when I say to pray, I mean to stand and concentrate on meeting
> the Master of the World and to let the words of the prayers flow
> over me. To feel that I am not here. To breathe. To be one with
> the words. To go back three steps at the start of the *Amida* and
> to find myself out of this world, out of the universe, out of the

rat race. I find myself saying ancient words, my spirit and soul suddenly in the center, my body resting on the sidelines.

Language – words and expressions such as holiness, humility, modesty, blessings, God's Name, the *Hallel* prayer, soul, and Hasidism were once irrelevant and orphaned to me. Now they are part of my lexicon and life.

Holiness – we need to have both a holy realm and a profane one. Not everything can be profane. Just like we cannot have the Shabbat lights burning for seven days, so we cannot have the stores open for seven days. Because there is a holy time, a holy place, holy words, holy actions. There are words we say on Shabbat and words for weekdays. There are actions we do when we perform a mitzva and we have religious articles we use when perform a mitzva. We have high and low, this world and the World to Come, pure and impure, Paradise or the unmentionable alternative, Shabbat and Motza'ei Shabbat.

ೞ ೞ ೞ

Midday, Midnight

וַיְהִי בַּחֲצִי הַלַּיְלָה וַה׳ הִכָּה כָל בְּכוֹר בְּאֶרֶץ מִצְרַיִם מִבְּכֹר פַּרְעֹה הַיֹּשֵׁב עַל כִּסְאוֹ עַד בְּכוֹר הַשְּׁבִי אֲשֶׁר בְּבֵית הַבּוֹר וְכֹל בְּכוֹר בְּהֵמָה.

And it came to pass at midnight, and the Lord hit every firstborn in the land of Egypt, from the firstborn of Pharaoh who sits on his throne to the firstborn of the captive who is in the dungeon, and every firstborn animal.

(Ex. 12:29)

The stage is set, the Exodus from Egypt is about to begin. "And it came to pass at midnight, and the Lord hit every firstborn in the land of Egypt." The plague of the firstborns occurs at midnight, the last of the Ten Plagues, after which Pharaoh agrees to let the people go. The Torah then relates another highlight, which occurs twelve hours later, at midday: "And it came to pass on that very day, that the Lord took the

Children of Israel out of the land of Egypt with their legions." After the dramatic night, the Children of Israel left Egypt in broad daylight, with their heads held up high, not like thieves at night.

The Lubavitcher Rebbe explains how the two expressions of midday and midnight are connected to a perpetual movement going from slavery to freedom:

> And it came to pass at midnight – the darkest moment in the daily cycle symbolizes a situation in which a person is stuck in the darkness of the world. Even such a person has the strength to "go out of Egypt" and continue on. It is possible to leave the darkest situation and become a free person.
>
> In contrast, midday is the brightest moment of the daily cycle and symbolizes the brightest parts of a person's life. However, such people also have to "go out of Egypt" and realize that their current situation is considered to be slavery when compared to even higher levels which they should still be striving to reach.

CG CG CG

Freeze the Emotion

וְהָיָה לְךָ לְאוֹת עַל יָדְךָ וּלְזִכָּרוֹן בֵּין עֵינֶיךָ לְמַעַן תִּהְיֶה תּוֹרַת ה' בְּפִיךָ כִּי בְּיָד חֲזָקָה הוֹצִאֲךָ ה' מִמִּצְרָיִם.

And it shall be to you as a sign upon your hand and as a remembrance between your eyes, in order that the law of the Lord shall be in your mouth, for with a mighty hand the Lord took you out of Egypt.

(Ex. 13:9)

Our nephew began to lay tefillin the week we read *Parashat Bo* and the entire family commemorated this great occasion at the Western Wall. His father blessed him by wishing that the excitement he feels today when putting on his tefillin for the first time would remain the same for the rest of his life. I wonder whether that is possible. How does one retain that same sense of excitement after the first time? The commandment of tefillin is mentioned for the first time in this *parasha*. How are we supposed to take the monumental event of the Exodus and "reduce" it to a daily ritual which involves both the heart and the hand?

Professor Nehama Leibowitz has a creative way of explaining the connection between the onetime event of the Exodus and the daily routine of laying tefillin and compares it to a dormant volcano, adorned with dried lava.

> The miracle of the departure from Egypt bears the same relationship to tefillin as the effervescent living liquid to its congealed and solidified counterpart. The mystic intensity of divine love, revealed to the contemporaries of the Exodus in the form of the unprecedented, supernatural miracles associated with that event, was permanently reproduced in the shape of the tefillin adorning the arm (next to the heart) and the head (next to the mind) of the Jew, who thereby relives that historic experience and resurrects it every day.

Her explanation is applicable not only to tefillin but to many commandments in which we take exceptional events and "freeze" them in time for eternity.

Beshallah

Majority Rules?

וַיַּסֵּב אֱלֹהִים אֶת הָעָם דֶּרֶךְ הַמִּדְבָּר יַם סוּף וַחֲמֻשִׁים עָלוּ בְנֵי יִשְׂרָאֵל מֵאֶרֶץ מִצְרָיִם.

So God led the people around by way of the desert to the Red Sea, and the **Children of Israel were armed when they went out of Egypt**.

(Ex. 13:18)

This verse tells us that the Children of Israel were armed (*hamushim*) when they left Egypt. Rashi suggests two meanings for this word, the first being the literal translation of being armed when setting out on an arduous journey to the wilderness. His second suggestion comes from a play on the word for five (*hamesh*), as he suggests that only one in five of the Children of Israel actually left Egypt. This claim is mind-blowing, that only one fifth of the Jews went out of Egypt, while the remaining four-fifths died in the plague of darkness because they did not want to take part in the Exodus. They did not believe in this idea and wanted no part of it. The vast majority of the Jews, eighty percent, were left behind. Who were they and why did they take a pass on the Exodus? And most importantly, what do they teach us about the relationship between a majority and minority population?

While it is true that "democracy is the worst form of government, except for all the others" and the majority vote always decides, does this mean that the majority is always right? Does the majority know how to distinguish between right and wrong, not just when it comes to elections but concerning issues such as culture, values, and spiritual matters? History is full of examples in which the majority view was wrong. How often do we do something or think a certain way just because "everyone" does?

I have no answers and I raise these questions as food for thought. Pharaoh was not the only one who heard the message "Let my people go" and rejected their passage from slavery to freedom. Eighty percent of the Jews reacted likewise.

ଔ ଔ ଔ

Shout Out

וּפַרְעֹה הִקְרִיב וַיִּשְׂאוּ בְנֵי יִשְׂרָאֵל אֶת עֵינֵיהֶם וְהִנֵּה מִצְרַיִם נֹסֵעַ אַחֲרֵיהֶם וַיִּירְאוּ מְאֹד וַיִּצְעֲקוּ בְנֵי יִשְׂרָאֵל אֶל ה'.

And Pharaoh drew near, and the Children of Israel lifted up their eyes, and behold, the Egyptians were advancing after them and **they were very frightened, and the Children of Israel cried out to the Lord.**

(Ex. 14:10)

Is prayer a practical proposition? It seems so old-fashioned, unrealistic, and primitive. When a terrorist attack occurs, God forbid, we have become accustomed to hearing condemnation, words of condolence to the bereaved families, and a whole slew of suggestions about how to improve security to prevent such tragedies. We have become used to the predictable arguments between right- and left-wing thinkers.

When we read this verse, we see another option, prayer, which has been part of the Jewish ethos from time immemorial. Prayer is definitely not a substitute for a determined and persistent war against terror, nor can it replace any other practical actions that need to be taken. Yet, when Pharaoh drew close to the Children of Israel and they felt trapped between the Egyptians and the Red Sea they "cried out to God." Rashi explains that they "grabbed hold of their ancestors' practices," referring to the practice of our Forefathers and Foremothers to pray. "Above all I pray" preempts "First of all I condemn." Prayer may sound old-fashioned and impractical, but it has been part of our tradition and heritage for thousands of years. When we experience trying times, we shout out for help. Instead of merely shouting at each other and at our political leaders, consider crying out to God for help!

C8 C8 C8

Complaining During the Miracle

וַיָּבֹאוּ בְנֵי יִשְׂרָאֵל בְּתוֹךְ הַיָּם בַּיַּבָּשָׁה וְהַמַּיִם לָהֶם חוֹמָה מִימִינָם וּמִשְּׂמֹאלָם.

And the Children of Israel came into the middle of the sea on dry land, and **the water was for them as a wall on their right and on their left.**

(Ex. 14:22)

One of the most incredible texts I have ever come across is written about this verse. *Parashat Beshallah* relates the miraculous and exalted scenes at the Splitting of the Sea, but the Midrash tells of a conversation between two Jews, Reuben and Simeon, as they walked on the land in the middle of the sea during this historic event: "In Egypt we were immersed in mortar and at the Red Sea we are immersed in mortar. In Egypt we had the mortar that accompanied the bricks and here at the Red Sea we have the mud caused by the splitting waters."

Reuben is questioning what the difference is between the Exodus and slavery. In the middle of this miraculous event, he looks around and all he sees is mud and dirt. As far as he is concerned, mortar is mortar, just this time it is in a different place. He is unable to comprehend the greatness of the moment, indeed lacking clarity and perspective. He cannot see past his muddy shoes to look up and see the amazing events taking place around him.

We learn from this midrash that perspective is what counts. You can be living a dream existence and not realize it, not appreciate it, not even understand it. How to view a situation, whatever it might be, is almost completely subjective. We decide how to view the world around us. This midrash, while short, is of great significance. A person may be walking through the Split Sea, and all does is complain.

Cහ
 Cහ
 Cහ

Peace and Security

וַיָּבֹאוּ מָרָתָה וְלֹא יָכְלוּ לִשְׁתֹּת מַיִם מִמָּרָה... וַיִּלֹּנוּ הָעָם עַל מֹשֶׁה לֵאמֹר
מַה נִּשְׁתֶּה.

And they came to Marah, but they could not drink water from
Marah... **and the people complained against Moses saying,
"What shall we drink?"**

(Ex. 15:23–24)

In addition to the miracle of the Splitting of the Sea, this *parasha* contains a number of complaints made by the Children of Israel. Right at the start of their journey, they ask Moses, "Is it because there are no graves in Egypt that you have taken us to die in the desert?"

A short time later, they complain about being thirsty, "The people complained against Moses, saying, 'What shall we drink?'"; and then they grumble about longing for the fleshpots of Egypt and accuse Moses and Aaron of bringing them to the wilderness in order "to starve this entire congregation to death."

This is not the end of the litany of complaints. On another occasion, they complain about being thirsty and ask, "Why have you brought us up from Egypt to make me and my children and my livestock die of thirst?" No wonder that now, even Moses despairs: "And Moses cried out to the Lord, saying, 'What shall I do for this people? In a short time they will stone me.'"

The consequences of their actions are not really surprising: "And Amalek came and fought with Israel." When the people are tired, agitated, skeptical, lacking in faith, and angry, Amalek seizes the opportunity and attacks. Ever since then, our enemies have known when the time is right to fight us. A common identity and vision are not simply nice slogans, they are essential to our security.

೦೩ ೦೩ ೦೩

Ups and Downs

וַיֹּאמְרוּ אֲלֵהֶם בְּנֵי יִשְׂרָאֵל מִי יִתֵּן מוּתֵנוּ בְיַד ה' בְּאֶרֶץ מִצְרַיִם בְּשִׁבְתֵּנוּ עַל סִיר הַבָּשָׂר בְּאָכְלֵנוּ לֶחֶם לָשֹׂבַע כִּי הוֹצֵאתֶם אֹתָנוּ אֶל הַמִּדְבָּר הַזֶּה לְהָמִית אֶת כָּל הַקָּהָל הַזֶּה בָּרָעָב.

And the Children of Israel said to them, "**If only we had died at the hand of the Lord in the land of Egypt, when we sat by the fleshpots**, when we ate bread to our fill! For you have brought us out into this desert, to starve this entire congregation to death."

(Ex. 16:3)

The miraculous Splitting of the Sea and the ensuing uplifting Song of the Sea are the high points of this *parasha*. The Children of Israel leave Egypt for the wilderness, going from slavery to freedom, from bondage to redemption, at the beginning of a new era in history. However, all too soon, they descend from these great heights and hit the ground with a painful and disappointing thud. They complain to Moses and Aaron, "If only we had died at the hand of the Lord in the land of Egypt, when we sat by the fleshpots, when we ate bread to our fill! For you have brought us out into this desert, to starve this entire congregation to death."

Euphoria and depression – the pendulum swings swiftly back and forth. One day they are full of enthusiasm for their miraculous deliverance, and the next they are disappointed, full of misplaced nostalgia about slavery and talking about death.

The human tendency to swing between "highs" and "lows" accompanies the Children of Israel on their journey in the wilderness and, indeed, throughout our history. Just think of the difference in reaction to the Six Day War and a few years later to the Yom Kippur War.

These mood swings occur at breakneck speed. Just eight verses separate the Song of the Sea and this harsh complaint. However, we can look at the bright side. The "highs" beat the "lows" in the end: every day, in the morning prayers we say the Song of the Sea and not the verses of complaint.

ભ ભ ભ

Open Your Eyes

רְאוּ כִּי ה' נָתַן לָכֶם הַשַּׁבָּת עַל כֵּן הוּא נֹתֵן לָכֶם בַּיּוֹם הַשִּׁשִּׁי לֶחֶם
יוֹמָיִם שְׁבוּ אִישׁ תַּחְתָּיו אַל יֵצֵא אִישׁ מִמְּקֹמוֹ בַּיּוֹם הַשְּׁבִיעִי.

See that the Lord has given you the Sabbath. **Therefore, on the sixth day He gives you bread for two days.** Let each man remain in his place; let no man leave his place on the seventh day.

(Ex. 16:29)

The Children of Israel complain of hunger and God sends them food in the form of manna that falls from heaven. Every day they received the same amount, and on Fridays they would receive a double portion so that they would not need to gather it on the Shabbat day. It is easy to become accustomed to this way of life and even to denigrate it.

Maybe this is the reason why Moses feels a need to emphasize the uniqueness of their situation: "See that the Lord has given you the Sabbath. Therefore, on the sixth day He gives you bread for two days. Let each man remain in his place; let no man leave his place on the seventh day."

The verse opens with the unique word "See." Take a good look, or in the words of Rabbi Ovadia Seforno, "Understand that God has given you the Sabbath and this is not just a commandment, but also a gift." In the wilderness, the Jewish people merited to experience the blessing inherent in Shabbat first-hand. (I wonder if it is like getting double one's usual salary every Friday.) However, there is the immediate danger that they will ignore the blessing, so Moses instructs them to take a special look and internalize the nature of this gift.

Many years have passed, and we take the wonderful gift of Shabbat, which helps us "restart" our lives once every week, for granted. In the 1950s, Naomi Shemer composed a poem, *The Eighth Day of the Week* (*Yom Het BaShavua*).

> It will be a weekday
> Like today, like yesterday
> It will be the eighth day of the week
> Then we will open our eyes
> To a crisp morning.

When reading her poem, we ask ourselves: What would happen if we did not have the Shabbat? Would there be an eighth, a ninth, and a tenth day of the week? Maybe we would count days to infinity instead of having the cyclical counting which affords us a weekly day of rest after six days of work? Moses thus urges us to "see" that we have been given a wonderful gift.

Yitro

We Will Hear and We Will Do

וַיִּשְׁמַע יִתְרוֹ כֹהֵן מִדְיָן חֹתֵן מֹשֶׁה אֵת כָּל אֲשֶׁר עָשָׂה אֱלֹהִים לְמֹשֶׁה
וּלְיִשְׂרָאֵל עַמּוֹ כִּי הוֹצִיא ה' אֶת יִשְׂרָאֵל מִמִּצְרָיִם.

**Now Yitro, the priest of Midian, Moses' father-in-law, heard
all that God had done** for Moses, and for Israel His people, how
the Lord had taken Israel out of Egypt.

(Ex. 18:1)

Yitro leaves his home to join the Jewish nation as it is making history.
Rashi asks, "What news did he hear that he came? The Splitting of the
Sea and the war with Amalek." Sitting in the comfort of his own home,
Yitro hears the tremendous story of the Jewish people. Not satisfied with
just hearing the news, he gets up and goes to join them.

In this Yitro was unique. Many had heard about the phenomenon
of a nation going from slavery to freedom, but he was the only one who
joined them. While others ignored the news, and Amalek even went out
to fight them, Yitro took these unique events to heart. With his act, he
teaches that it is not sufficient to hear about impressive and great events;
they must motivate us to positive action.

Interestingly, Yitro was the high priest of the Midianites who
actively practiced idol worship. And yet, despite his senior position
and his advanced age, when he hears of a new belief which seems to

him to be more correct, he is not ashamed to admit that he had been mistaken and that he is now going to change his life and join the Jewish nation.

Rabbi Hayim ben Attar, the *Or HaHayim,* says that the Evil Inclination stands guard at a person's ear and prevents the words he hears from penetrating his soul. We may hear ideas that open new vistas and offer a new way of thinking, but not change our way of life. Yitro heard and immediately decided to act on what he had heard. In doing so, he teaches us not to be satisfied with just hearing the news. Rashi's explanation, "he heard, he came," is a paradigm for us to emulate.

 og og og

Adjudicate Everything

וַיִּשְׁמַע מֹשֶׁה לְקוֹל חֹתְנוֹ **וַיַּעַשׂ כֹּל אֲשֶׁר אָמָר.**

So Moses listened to his father-in-law, **and did all that he said.**
(Ex. 18:24)

Yitro gives sound advice to Moses about delegating authority and proposes that he appoint judges to help cope with the burden of cases coming to him. The Torah spends three whole verses giving a detailed explanation of how Moses implemented Yitro's proposal. Why was it so important for the Torah to repeat the plan that had been mentioned just a few verses earlier? I have two answers to this question:

1. It is easy for a leader to hire an external consultant to prepare a report on an important issue and then put it away in a drawer to gather dust. It is very easy to hear an excellent piece of advice and then put it aside and wait. Moses heard and immediately implemented, as the Torah states explicitly, "Moses listened to his father-in-law, and did all that he said."
2. Despite the overall similarity, there is nevertheless one difference between Yitro's proposal and Moses' implementation.

Yitro suggests that Moses only deal with cases involving large sums of money – "the big thing" – whereas Moses has another idea and decides that he will deal with the complex cases – "the difficult thing" – and not the expensive ones. The deciding factor is not the sum of money involved, but the importance of the matter at hand. The Talmud says, "You should treat a case involving one coin with the same care and mind as you would treat a case involving one hundred coins." So if a case was of particular importance, even if it only involved one shekel, Moses would deal with it.

C8 C8 CS

What Did *You* Hear at Sinai?

וַיְהִי בַיּוֹם הַשְּׁלִישִׁי בִּהְיֹת הַבֹּקֶר וַיְהִי קֹלֹת וּבְרָקִים וְעָנָן כָּבֵד עַל הָהָר וְקֹל שֹׁפָר חָזָק מְאֹד וַיֶּחֱרַד כָּל הָעָם אֲשֶׁר בַּמַּחֲנֶה.

And it was on the third day in the morning that there were thunderclaps and lightning flashes and a thick cloud on the mountain, and a very powerful blast of a shofar, **and the entire nation in the camp trembled**.

(Ex. 19:16)

The Ten Commandments, the thunderclaps, the lightning flashes, and the shofar blast. Amidst this incredible collective experience Rabbi Shlomo Wolbe focuses on the individual. His message speaks to the balance between the individual and the group at such times.

> Was there such mass excitement that even if someone did not really agree with what he saw, he went along with the crowd and shouted with them? No. Every person made the decision in his own heart that he wished to receive the Torah. All of them as one, and at the same time, each one on his own, accepted it. We find it difficult that such a massive event could take place in our nation, among all of its divisions and disagreement. Yet this is the

true nature of the people of Israel. On one hand we have overall unity and, on the other hand, every single individual agrees of his own accord. If there had been even one dissenting voice, the Torah could not have been given.

Rabbi Wolbe adds that, in addition to the miracle of the Torah descending from heaven, the other miracle was the ability to create total unity while simultaneously discovering the individualism of each person.

Unity among us is important, but that does not mean that, within the parameters of halakha, the individual's privacy is erased and each person accepted the Torah in the same way. After the Ten Commandments were given, the people obviously talked among themselves about what they had heard. At that point they realized that, although they had all heard the same words, each one interpreted it differently according to what suited his soul. No one's individuality was taken away; to the contrary, when the Torah was given, each person received his independent identity.

Myriads of people stood at Mount Sinai and each individual received his or her own identity.

Mishpatim

The God of the Small Details

וְאֵלֶּה הַמִּשְׁפָּטִים אֲשֶׁר תָּשִׂים לִפְנֵיהֶם.

And these are the laws that you shall set before them.
(Ex. 21:1)

In the previous *parasha* of *Yitro*, we read about the unique and historic event of the Revelation at Mount Sinai when we were given the Torah. *Parashat Mishpatim* (laws) certainly lives up to its name because it contains fifty-three of the 613 commandments of the Torah. The long list of laws deals with violence, murder, damages, false testimony, bribery, returning lost property, the prohibition to eat meat and milk together, the laws of Shabbat, the festivals, and many more.

What a contrast! We just experienced the life-altering event of the Jewish people in which we heard God Himself speak, and now we have to deal with the nitty-gritty of life, with legal and administrative matters. Why do we have to descend to the most minute details and read the fine print?

We are being told to exchange the spiritual highs of Mount Sinai for an organized system of laws that will enable us to preserve what we heard there. We must set aside our ecstasy and excitement and learn how to preserve the lofty ideas we heard at Mount Sinai by applying them to our everyday lives. The formula that God gives us is the laws mentioned in *Mishpatim*.

Throughout the generations, some have feared placing too much emphasis on the Ten Commandments. Therefore, they opposed the custom of standing up in synagogue when they are read out from the Torah. Judaism does not have a Top Ten list of commandments. All the others are equally holy and important, and the Ten Commandments are merely the headlines, introducing all the laws and legislation to follow.

The continuation of the Revelation at Mount Sinai starts here with the laws in *Mishpatim*, accompanying our daily lives ever since.

ભ ભ ભ

The Truth About "An Eye for an Eye"

עַיִן תַּחַת עַיִן שֵׁן תַּחַת שֵׁן יָד תַּחַת יָד רֶגֶל תַּחַת רָגֶל.

An eye for an eye, a tooth for a tooth, a hand for a hand, a foot for a foot

(Ex. 21:24)

Wouldn't you be surprised if I told you that "an eye for an eye" is one of my favorite expressions in the Torah? The reason why these words are so meaningful to me is that they contain a mega-principle. The Torah does not really mean that we should take an eye for an eye, or a tooth for a tooth, or one life for another. People who understand the Torah as such (and maybe even enjoy poking fun at it) are treading on dangerous ground because the Written Law, the Tanakh, cannot be understood without the Oral Law which includes the Mishna, Talmud, Midrash, and every book on halakha that has ever been published until this very day. This is the chain of tradition that is passed down from one generation to the next and it is the only way to interpret and understand the Torah and live a Jewish life.

This verse is a perfect example. The Torah says, "an eye for an eye," and the Oral Law explains that this means monetary compensation. If a person loses his eyesight, he needs to be compensated for the damage caused to him. This expression reminds us to always look up the halakhic interpretation and not rely on what we think the Torah is saying. Someone who reads the Torah on this shallow level runs the risk of losing an eye or a tooth and, more importantly, the Torah itself.

CS CS CS

God's VIPs

כָּל אַלְמָנָה וְיָתוֹם לֹא תְעַנּוּן.

You shall not oppress any widow or orphan.
(Ex. 22:21)

We normally associate VIPs and celebrities with success, money, and glamor. In this *parasha* we are told about God's VIPs: the poor man, the stranger, the widow, and the orphan. "You shall not oppress any widow or orphan. If you oppress him, beware, for if he cries out to Me, I will surely hear his cry."

These are God's celebrities to whom He is especially attentive and gives preferential treatment. The *Sefer HaHinukh* expands on this list and says that every one of us is sometimes a bit of an outsider who feels vulnerable and alone:

> We should learn from this cherished commandment to have pity on a person who moves away from the country of his birth and that of his ancestors to a new place. We see that the Torah warned us to take care of anyone who needs assistance. The Torah hints at the reason for this commandment in the verse, "because you were strangers in the land of Egypt," and reminds us that we have already been hurt once with that great sorrow of a people who feel themselves to be among strangers in a strange country.

We can easily add to the list of people who "feel themselves to be among strangers in a strange country." A recent immigrant or a child starting a new school are just two examples of people who deserve extra special and positive care from us.

CRICRICRI

Don't Jump to Conclusions

וְדָל לֹא תֶהְדַּר בְּרִיבוֹ.

You shall not favor **a poor man** in his lawsuit.
(Ex. 23:3)

Among the many laws in this *parasha*, we are told not to favor a poor man in a lawsuit. There is a profound psychological truth behind this instruction. In a court case between a poor and rich person, the judges are obviously not allowed to favor the rich person, yet note how the Torah warns us not to automatically take the side of the poor person, because the underdog is not always right. Just because he is dressed in rags, it does not necessarily mean that justice is on his side, and sometimes the person dressed in a designer suit just may be in the right.

Although this verse refers to a judge or a *dayan*, in reality it is an important message for all of us. The Torah is hinting to us that in many cases public opinion unwittingly favors the underdog. This might be due to populism or the influence of Hollywood movies, but it is a given. Television cameras will be quick to film someone standing outside a welfare office complaining about injustice and publicize his story, even if moments earlier he had burst into the office and threatened to hit one of the workers. A soldier who feels he has been mistreated will get more public sympathy than his commanding officer, and a parent who organizes a petition against the school principal will be considered a hero who fights against the corrupt and indifferent establishment.

It is true that a poor person will often be in the right and that he often lacks connections with the legal establishment, but that does not mean justice is always on his side. "You shall not favor a poor man in

his lawsuit" is a reminder to check the facts before automatically deciding who to side with.

෯ ෯ ෯

Help Yourself

כִּי תִרְאֶה חֲמוֹר שֹׂנַאֲךָ רֹבֵץ תַּחַת מַשָּׂאוֹ וְחָדַלְתָּ מֵעֲזֹב לוֹ **עָזֹב תַּעֲזֹב עִמּוֹ.**

If you see your enemy's donkey lying under its burden, you shall
not ignore him. **You shall surely help along with him.**
(Ex. 23:5)

Rabbi Nahman of Breslov offers an insightful point on how a person
has to help himself based on this verse. We are commanded to help
someone in distress. For example, if you see his mule struggling with
its heavy burden you must help the owner take off the burden to ease
its discomfort. The Torah tells us, "You shall surely help along with him"
in doing this task.

Rabbi Nahman writes quite emphatically that whenever you
help someone, he needs to assist in the process. You must work "with
him," not without him. You cannot save someone who does not want to
save himself. This is an important piece of practical advice but it applies
equally in spiritual matters. There are some believing people who rely
solely on the *tzaddik* and do not do anything at all for themselves. In
Rabbi Nahman's words:

> If he wants to take himself completely out of the picture and
> does not work to mend his soul at all, if he only wants the *tzad-
> dik* to do everything on his behalf and he will not make any
> effort, then the *tzaddik* should definitely not do anything for
> him. For it is impossible to help him when he does not want to
> do anything at all to correct himself. A person has free will and
> one cannot rise to a higher level unless the awakening comes
> from within him.

109

Teruma

Giving Leads to Loving

דַּבֵּר אֶל בְּנֵי יִשְׂרָאֵל וְיִקְחוּ לִי תְּרוּמָה מֵאֵת כָּל אִישׁ אֲשֶׁר יִדְּבֶנּוּ לִבּוֹ תִּקְחוּ אֶת תְּרוּמָתִי.

Speak to the Children of Israel, and have them take for Me a contribution; **from every person whose heart inspires him to generosity, you shall take My contribution.**

(Ex. 25:2)

How does one create love? God has just split the Red Sea and given us the Torah at Mount Sinai; does He really need our contribution in order to build the *Mishkan*? Why does the Torah give all the technical specifications and building instructions? Why does God instruct us to bring all the fabrics, precious stones, and planks of wood and work so hard to build the *Mishkan*? Surely He does not need our assistance!

Of course not. But He wants us to be partners, a committed and involved party to this project. God does not want us to passively stand by, merely reciting, "We will do and we will hear." No, God wants us to prove our words with actions. When a person contributes money or other resources to a project he or she becomes a partner. Even if we only hold a few shares in a company, we follow its fortunes as if we are the actual owners.

Giving leads to loving. This holds true for a relationship: the more we invest in it, the more we feel connected. And all the hard work involved in looking after our young children binds us to them. The more we invest in studying the Torah, the more it belongs to us and we feel part of it. The more we contribute to the *Mishkan*, the more we become active partners.

Rabbi Eliyahu Dessler makes this point succinctly: "We might think that giving is the consequence of loving, but in fact loving is the consequence of giving."

CB CB CB

The Heart and the *Mishkan*

וְעָשׂוּ לִי מִקְדָּשׁ וְשָׁכַנְתִּי בְּתוֹכָם.

And they shall make Me a sanctuary and **I will dwell in their midst**.

(Ex. 25:8)

Parashat Teruma opens with the technical instructions for building the *Mishkan* in the wilderness, followed by this verse which has been the source of endless discussions throughout the ages about the where holiness belongs. God says, "And they shall make Me a sanctuary and I will dwell in their midst."

We are given the blueprint of the building with the exact specifications, but God does not intend to dwell in it. He says, "I will dwell in *their* midst," and not, "I will dwell in *it*." So where do we find holiness, in the *Mishkan* or in our midst? In our hearts, that is the fitting place for holiness. Rabbi Yaakov Hayim Sofer explains this answer in his book *Kaf HaHayim*.

> The Torah does not say, "I will dwell in it," teaching us that the main point of building the *Mishkan* was not to have a home for the Divine Presence, the *Shekhina*, to dwell in, but that they should mend their ways and follow God's instructions and their hearts should be open to God, and thus He will dwell in everyone's

heart. This is why it says, "and they shall make Me a sanctuary and I will dwell in their midst." Even though He commanded them to build the *Mishkan*, the most important thing is that they make themselves holy so that I can dwell among them, meaning within each one of them.

CB CB CB

What Takes Up More Space?

כְּכֹל אֲשֶׁר אֲנִי מַרְאֶה אוֹתְךָ אֵת תַּבְנִית הַמִּשְׁכָּן וְאֵת תַּבְנִית כָּל כֵּלָיו וְכֵן תַּעֲשׂוּ.

According to all that I show you, the pattern of the *Mishkan* and the pattern of all its vessels; **and so you shall do.**

(Ex. 25:9)

There are those who see all the technicalities in these *parashot* as the most important part of the Torah. After all, the entire Creation, including the creation of man, the entire animal and plant kingdoms, Shabbat, and the universe, is described in little more than forty verses at the start of the Book of Genesis. Yet the details of building the *Mishkan* take up more than four hundred verses. Why is the height of the building and the fabrics used to cover it described in such detail whereas the creation of the world is glossed over?

The Torah is neither a science book nor a history book. If you want to read about the world and its wondrous features, look up that information in an encyclopedia. The Torah expects man to be action-oriented. It demands that we work and keep the commandments. The focus of the Torah is not information about the world, but on why man is placed in the world and what his purpose in life is. The Creation is given so little space because it relates what God did, but when the *Mishkan* is set up, we are the ones who are commanded to act.

CB CB CB

Symbols of Hope

וְעָשׂוּ אֲרוֹן עֲצֵי שִׁטִּים אַמָּתַיִם וָחֵצִי אָרְכּוֹ וְאַמָּה וָחֵצִי רָחְבּוֹ וְאַמָּה וָחֵצִי
קֹמָתוֹ.

And they shall make an ark of acacia wood, two and a half
cubits its length, a cubit and a half its width, and a cubit and a
half its height.

(Ex. 25:10)

A person needs to have hope. Cedar wood was used to build the *Mishkan*,
and our sages tell us that Jacob brought these trees when he moved from
the Land of Israel to Egypt. He told his sons, "My children, in the future
you will be redeemed from this land and God will command you to build
the *Mishkan*. Plant trees now so that when God will instruct you to build
it, the trees will be ready." Why could they not simply buy the wood from
the local population where the trees were already growing? Why did
Jacob need the inconvenience of bringing them from the Land of Israel?

We are meant to learn something from this. Jacob wanted to
raise the spirits of the Jewish slaves in Egypt and give them a symbol of
hope and optimism. Whenever they would see the cedar trees during
the long, dark years of slavery, they would be reminded of Jacob, of their
destiny, and of the promise that they would be redeemed. Lofty ideas
about the future are fine, but a person needs to see something tangible
with his own eyes as well.

A modern-day illustration of this point can be seen from Natan
Sharansky. He was the most famous Prisoner of Zion and was let out of
the Soviet Union and allowed to move to Israel in 1986. Sharansky was
the symbol of the struggle for freedom who spent many years incarcer-
ated in jail, often in solitary confinement, under the most trying conditions. He would often go on hunger strikes as part of his protest for
freedom – he fasted for a total of four hundred days throughout his incar-
ceration. When asked what gave him strength, Sharansky replied, "My
small book of Psalms. It was not me who carried it, the Psalms carried me."

ൣ ൣ ൣ

114

With Distinction!

וְנָתַתָּה אֶת הַפָּרֹכֶת תַּחַת הַקְּרָסִים וְהֵבֵאתָ שָׁמָּה מִבֵּית לַפָּרֹכֶת אֵת אֲרוֹן
הָעֵדוּת וְהִבְדִּילָה הַפָּרֹכֶת לָכֶם בֵּין הַקֹּדֶשׁ וּבֵין קֹדֶשׁ הַקֳּדָשִׁים.

And you shall place the dividing curtain beneath the clasps. You
shall bring there on the inner side of the dividing curtain the Ark
of the Testimony, **and the dividing curtain shall separate for
you between the Holy and the Holy of Holies.**

(Ex. 26:33)

The *Mishkan* had a separating curtain, just as we have to make separa-
tions in real life. There were degrees of holiness, with the outer section
called the Holy, and the inner part the Holy of Holies. In real life we can't
simply bifurcate everything into good and evil, pure and impure, but
there are varying intermediate shades, with internal subdivisions. Reality is complex; if we choose to do bad, then there are differing degrees
of how low we stoop. If we choose to do good, we can go up one step
at a time, always striving to be better.

It is easier and more simplistic to see life as a dichotomy, but our
sages have taught us that "if you do not have the knowledge, how can
you separate?" Knowledge is necessary in order to make distinctions –
between good and evil, and also *within* good and evil, to know that there
are varying levels and shades.

Tetzaveh

Our Shabbat Clothes

וְעָשִׂיתָ בִגְדֵי קֹדֶשׁ לְאַהֲרֹן אָחִיךָ לְכָבוֹד וּלְתִפְאָרֶת.

And you shall make holy garments for your brother Aaron, for honor and glory.

(Ex. 28:2)

Long before *haute-couture* designers and stylists ruled the world of fashion, the Torah had a lot to say about clothing. Most of *Tetzaveh* deals with the High Priest's garments, and the commentators repeatedly tell us about the essence of these garments, how we should relate to them, and how to design them. The Torah calls them "holy garments."

Rabbi Shalom Noah Berezovsky, the *Netivot Shalom*, asks what can be considered "holy garments" now that we no longer have a High Priest. Before answering, he explains the wondrous system whereby the High Priest would atone for the sins of the entire Jewish people, by wearing the special clothes which would erase their wrongdoings. Our sages say that each garment atoned for a specific sin: "The turban atoned for the haughty people, the tunic atoned for speaking *lashon hara*," etc. This is a difficult concept to grasp – how can one person's garments atone for another person's sins? Is it possible that the leader of a nation is so connected to each and every member that his deeds have an influence over an entire nation?

The *Netivot Shalom* continues his explanation by saying that we still have holy garments in our times, namely our Shabbat clothes. He says that the Shabbat finery we wear once a week has the power to repair any misdemeanors we may have done during the previous six days. This is a certainly a mind-boggling statement.

> The essence of Shabbat clothes is that they are holy garments that purify all the limbs of a Jewish person, in order for him to enter Shabbat and absorb its light and holiness. By wearing Shabbat clothes, we have a chance to purify our limbs and bring holiness into ourselves.

C3 C3 C3

Appreciating Clothing

וְאַתָּה תְּדַבֵּר אֶל כָּל חַכְמֵי לֵב אֲשֶׁר מִלֵּאתִיו רוּחַ חָכְמָה וְעָשׂוּ **אֶת בִּגְדֵי** אַהֲרֹן **לְקַדְּשׁוֹ** לְכַהֲנוֹ לִי.

And you shall speak to all the wise hearted, whom I have filled with the spirit of wisdom, and they shall **make Aaron's garments to sanctify him**, so he may be a priest to Me.

(Ex. 28:3)

Tetzaveh deals extensively with clothing. Are we supposed to make a blessing when putting on clothing?

Every morning, right at the start of our morning prayers we say, "Blessed are You, Lord our God, King of the universe, who clothes the naked." Rabbi Abraham Isaac HaKohen Kook wrote a commentary on the siddur and explained this blessing by saying that we are giving our thanks to God for two reasons. First, for the very fact that we even have clothes to wear and that they are not completely worn out. Second, for the fact that we are humans rather than animals, and understand the need for clothing. Rabbi Kook explains that, as opposed to animals, man is blessed with a moral sensitivity and a refined soul, and he give thanks to

God for the understanding that he can live a life more honorable than that of animals. Man has to wear clothes, animals do not.

Rabbi Kook writes that we thank God for the "refined spiritual sense that God planted in our souls that causes us to wear honorable garments."

ɔʒ ɔʒ ɔʒ

The Divine Presence Dwells Between Them

וְזֶה הַדָּבָר אֲשֶׁר תַּעֲשֶׂה לָהֶם לְקַדֵּשׁ אֹתָם לְכַהֵן לִי.

And this is the thing that you shall do for them **to sanctify them to serve Me as priests.**

(Ex. 29:1)

My husband's brother got married the week that *Tetzaveh* was read in the Torah, so all the speeches and blessings during the wedding ceremonies and ensuing festivities focused on the one word that is so common in this *parasha* – holiness: "When he enters the Holy," "holy garments," "to serve in the Holy."

Many of the speakers compared the *Mishkan* in the wilderness to the new home that the young couple were setting up. Rabbi Katz, who conducted the wedding ceremony, quoted the well-known saying of our sages: "If a man and woman are worthy, then the Divine Presence, the *Shekhina*, dwells between them." He asked what the sages are adding to our understanding, since the Divine Presence is always present, as it says in the Zohar, "There is no location that the Divine Presence is not found." If so, why do the sages say that it will only dwell between the married couple if they are worthy? Rabbi Katz answered that holiness is always to be found in the home, but the couple will only feel it if they are worthy. When both husband and wife make the effort to have a home worthy of the Divine Presence, they will know that holiness indeed dwells among them.

Ki Tissa

Is Money Good or Bad?

זֶה יִתְּנוּ כָּל הָעֹבֵר עַל הַפְּקֻדִים מַחֲצִית הַשֶּׁקֶל בְּשֶׁקֶל הַקֹּדֶשׁ עֶשְׂרִים
גֵּרָה הַשֶּׁקֶל **מַחֲצִית הַשֶּׁקֶל תְּרוּמָה לַה'**.

Everyone who goes through the counting shall give half a shekel
according to the holy shekel. Twenty gerahs equal one shekel;
half of one shekel shall be an offering to the Lord.

(Ex. 30:13)

A midrash tells us how God told Moses that the people were to give
half a shekel. "He showed him a coin of fire and said to him, this is what
they should give."

Rabbi Elimelekh of Lizhensk, better known by the name of his
famous book, the *Noam Elimelekh*, writes that this text hints that money
is like fire. Just as fire can be beneficial for heating and cooking, but
can also destroy and burn, so money can also be used either for giving
tzedaka and other productive ends or it can be used to destroy the world.
This complex relationship to money is no less true today. Words such
as cash, profit, livelihood, dollars, and business are neutral terms, neither good nor bad. Money is a tool and the way we use it determines
whether it is used well or badly. We decide whether we use it to help
and be helped, or whether we become enslaved to it.

The Hebrew language has several words to describe money. Here are a few of our sages' pearls which use a play on words to teach us that money is not the most important thing, but rather it is temporary and transient:

> Why is it called property (*nekhasim*)? Because they are hidden (*nikhsim*) from one person and revealed to another.
> Why are they called coins (*zuzim*)? Because they move (*zazim*) from one person and are given to another.
> Why is it called money (*mamon*)? Because what you count (*moneh*) is not really anything.
> Why is it called small change (*maot*)? Because they come and go from time to time (*me'et le'et*).

CG CG CG

Take a Break!

אַךְ אֶת שַׁבְּתֹתַי תִּשְׁמֹרוּ כִּי אוֹת הִוא בֵּינִי וּבֵינֵיכֶם לְדֹרֹתֵיכֶם.

Only keep My Sabbaths! For it is a sign between Me and you for your generations.

(Ex. 31:13)

Ki Tissa continues with the instructions how to build the Ark, the Table, the Menora, and the other vessels. Right in the middle of the technical details, the Torah interrupts and introduces a completely different subject: "And the Lord spoke to Moses, saying: And you, speak to the Children of Israel and say, 'Only keep My Sabbaths! For it is a sign between Me and you for your generations, to know that I, the Lord, make you holy.'" Could there possibly be a connection between the two? Otherwise, how can we explain why the commandment to rest on the Sabbath day comes in the middle of the building project?

The two are indeed strongly connected and so, even in the midst of all the activity, we have to stop on Shabbat. However important and holy building the *Mishkan* is, all work must cease on the seventh day.

Moreover, the thirty-nine categories of labor that are forbidden on Shabbat are all derived from the work in the *Mishkan*. For thousands of years, halakhic decisions about what is permitted on Shabbat have been based on what was forbidden in the wilderness when all work on the *Mishkan* stopped for the day.

Some commentators maintain that everything is connected to the sin of the Golden Calf. In the aftermath of the sin, the Torah has to remind us once again what our attitude to holiness ought to be. The people sinned by using their jewelry to build the Golden Calf and worshiping it. This was a physical and material sin and therefore the way to correct the damage had to be refined and sophisticated, by contrast. The people were told to build the *Mishkan*, a physical edifice in which the Divine Presence would dwell, but even before the Torah tells us this commandment, we are told to cease all work on Shabbat. A new dimension is being introduced to our lives. We now have holiness in time, which is a more important dimension than holiness in space. From now on, our actions in the spatial dimensions will stop so that we can let the holiness of time enter our lives.

This pattern is as relevant to our lives as it was in the *Mishkan*. For six days a week man conquers nature and progresses through the dimensions of space, but on the seventh day, he stops conquering. I once heard a thought-provoking idea about this. For six days a week we rule over the world, and on the seventh, we try to rule over ourselves.

CB CB CB

The Origins of Repentance

וַיְחַל מֹשֶׁה אֶת פְּנֵי ה' אֱלֹהָיו וַיֹּאמֶר לָמָה ה' יֶחֱרֶה אַפְּךָ בְּעַמֶּךָ אֲשֶׁר
הוֹצֵאתָ מֵאֶרֶץ מִצְרַיִם בְּכֹחַ גָּדוֹל וּבְיָד חֲזָקָה.

Moses pleaded before the Lord, his God, and said, **"Why, O Lord, should Your anger be kindled against Your people whom You have brought up from the land of Egypt** with great power and with a strong hand?"

(Ex. 32:11)

It is really difficult to comprehend how the same people who stood at Mount Sinai and received the Ten Commandments amid the claps of thunder and flashes of lightning could forget everything so quickly and set up the Golden Calf.

One surprising explanation is given in the Talmud: "The Children of Israel created the Golden Calf only to give an opening for those who wish to repent and do *teshuva*."

This is an unbelievable statement which tells us that the Golden Calf occurred to open the potential for repentance in the future. Anyone who stumbles onto the path of sin will now have the prospect of repentance and be forgiven.

According to this optimistic explanation, we now have the option of making a fresh start, thanks to the sin of the Golden Calf. We all know that we received the Torah at Mount Sinai, but now we learned that we received the chance to do *teshuva* at the Golden Calf.

C３ C３ C３

What Was the Sin of the Golden Calf?

וַיְהִי כַּאֲשֶׁר קָרַב אֶל הַמַּחֲנֶה וַיַּרְא אֶת הָעֵגֶל וּמְחֹלֹת וַיִּחַר אַף מֹשֶׁה וַיַּשְׁלֵךְ מִיָּדָיו אֶת הַלֻּחֹת וַיְשַׁבֵּר אֹתָם תַּחַת הָהָר.

And when he drew closer to the camp and saw the calf and the dances, Moses' anger was kindled, **and he flung the tablets from his hands, shattering them at the foot of the mountain.**

(Ex. 32:19)

In the *Kuzari*, Rabbi Judah HaLevi explains the motives behind the sin of the Golden Calf. The Children of Israel were expectantly waiting to receive the tablets. The masses stood at the foot of Mount Sinai in anticipation. But what were they expecting to receive, the tablets of stone or what was written on them?

He explains that the people wanted to have a tangible object of holiness, which would become the iconic symbol of their religion.

However, some had forgotten that the purpose of the object was merely to be a physical representation of the spiritual message it conveyed. From their over-eagerness arose the Golden Calf; a medium instead of a message.

When Moses descended from the mountain and saw the people dancing around the Golden Calf, he understood their mistake and he responded in the only way he could. Moses shattered the tablets and thus taught them that the icon is nothing more than a tool and symbol. When the physical object no longer represents the spiritual message that it is meant to, it becomes meaningless, and even more dangerously, it becomes an object of idol worship.

CB CB CB

Some Things Are Hidden

וַיֹּאמֶר לֹא תוּכַל לִרְאֹת אֶת פָּנָי כִּי לֹא יִרְאַנִי הָאָדָם וָחָי.

And He said, "You will not be able to see My face, **for man shall not see Me and live.**"

(Ex. 33:20)

When I took a preparatory course for an aptitude test, we were advised to follow a process of elimination. If you have no idea what answer to choose in the multiple-choice question (as is often the case for me), first try to eliminate the answers which are definitely incorrect, and then circle the last remaining option.

A similar process takes place in this *parasha* when God and Moses hold a fascinating and complex dialogue. Moses wants to understand God's ways, and is given a partial answer. The conversation has been the basis of many philosophical discussions throughout the generations as commentators discuss whether a human being can even grasp the meaning of the concept of God.

The Kotzker Rebbe was fond of saying, "I would never want to worship a God whose ways are crystal clear to all humans." I think this is a powerful sentence that leaves space for humility and even mystery. This conversation between God and Moses is often explained by the same process of elimination, that we cannot understand who God is, but we do know what He is not. We should be careful to eliminate all kinds of shallow ideas about our Judaism and our Creator, ideas that are too physical or too cumbersome, and then we will slowly but surely get closer to understanding of His essence.

CR CR CR

Fragile: Handle with Care

וַיֹּאמֶר ה' אֶל מֹשֶׁה פְּסָל לְךָ שְׁנֵי לֻחֹת אֲבָנִים כָּרִאשֹׁנִים וְכָתַבְתִּי עַל הַלֻּחֹת אֶת הַדְּבָרִים אֲשֶׁר הָיוּ עַל הַלֻּחֹת הָרִאשֹׁנִים אֲשֶׁר שִׁבַּרְתָּ.

And the Lord said to Moses, "**Carve for yourself two stone tablets like the first ones.** And I will inscribe upon the tablets the words that were on the first tablets, which you broke."

(Ex. 34:1)

Moses was instructed to carve our two new tablets, to replace the first ones that he had shattered because of the sin of the Golden Calf. The second set of tablets, which had the same Ten Commandments engraved on them, signified the start of a new era of reconciliation.

The new era did not erase the past and from now on the Children of Israel would continue their journey through the wilderness carrying both the shattered and the whole tablets, which our sages say lay side by side in the Ark. This is not simply a technical description of their physical location, but a spiritual teaching. Wherever the Children of Israel wander, they will carry their sin and forgiveness, the shattered and the whole, with them. And the same applies to any individual who has sinned.

Cracks were formed in the idyllic existence, but from a certain perspective the new reality is even more whole. Those who have overcome crises or downturns will testify that they emerge stronger and more mature. Life's journey will continue, but one now possesses the knowledge that it is more complex, with ups and downs, and it is the memory of the failures which gives the strength to carry on. There is nothing more whole than a broken heart.

ଔ ଔ ଔ

One People, One Sin

וַיֹּאמֶר אִם נָא מָצָאתִי חֵן בְּעֵינֶיךָ אֲדֹנָי יֵלֶךְ נָא אֲדֹנָי בְּקִרְבֵּנוּ כִּי עַם
קְשֵׁה עֹרֶף הוּא וְסָלַחְתָּ לַעֲוֹנֵנוּ וּלְחַטָּאתֵנוּ וּנְחַלְתָּנוּ.

And he said, "If I have now found favor in Your eyes, O Lord, let the Lord go now in our midst for they are a stiff-necked people, and **You shall forgive our iniquity and our sin and take us as Your inheritance.**"

(Ex. 34:9)

When Moses prayed to God to forgive the Children of Israel after the sin of the Golden Calf, he used the first person plural, thus throwing his lot in with the sinners, "Forgive our iniquity and our sin," whereas one would have expected him to say, "Forgive their iniquity and their sin." Rabbi Yosef Hayim of Baghdad, better known as the *Ben Ish Hai*, explains why Moses begged for forgiveness for a crime he had not been part of:

In addition to being punished for sins he did commit, he is also punished for his fellows' sin because of collective respon- sibility. The Children of Israel are one body with many limbs. When the sages composed the *Viduy* confessional prayer, they wrote it in the plural, "We have transgressed, we have betrayed," etc. rather than in the singular. A person says the entire prayer in the plural even if he is certain that he is not guilty of any of these transgressions, and he need not fear that he is saying untruths because he is demonstrating his collective responsibility toward all other Jews. It is thus clear why Moses, the righteous person, begged for forgiveness for "our iniquity and our sin," because he was part of them.

Moses did not participate in the sin of the Golden Calf, but when he prayed on behalf of his people, he felt a sense of collective responsibility for them and used the plural form. We continue to do the same whenever we pray.

Vayak'hel

One for All

וַיַּקְהֵל מֹשֶׁה אֶת כָּל עֲדַת בְּנֵי יִשְׂרָאֵל וַיֹּאמֶר אֲלֵהֶם אֵלֶּה הַדְּבָרִים אֲשֶׁר צִוָּה ה' לַעֲשֹׂת אֹתָם.

And Moses assembled the whole congregation of the Children of Israel, and he said to them, "These are the things that the Lord commanded to do."

(Ex. 35:1)

The opening verse of this *parasha* tells us that Moses assembled the entire congregation and informed them about the commandment to keep the Shabbat. Why was it so important to have them all come together? What strength do we have in being one unit and what place does the individual have among the masses?

Abba Kovner was a member of the HaShomer HaTza'ir youth movement in pre-war Europe and a leader of the partisans during the Holocaust. He provided an answer to these questions during a speech about his experiences in Israel after the Holocaust and, in particular, one event that made him feel part of the congregation of Israel:

> Throughout the many calamities that befell me and threatened to break me, one thing remained firm and unbroken. I did not cease to be a believer...the first week after I arrived in Israel, I

went to the Western Wall. When I was just a few steps away from the stones, I felt that I did not belong, that I am part of another reality. I stood still, not wanting to get any closer. But then someone tugged at my sleeve and asked me to be the tenth man in a *minyan.* I put on a hat and joined in the Minha afternoon prayers. Now I felt I had arrived.

Being part of a *minyan* is a very Jewish thing, one of the more unique features of Judaism: to know that the nine need the tenth and that the tenth needs the other nine. Perhaps this is the core of Judaism, and nothing that I learned in my youth group is more special or Jewish than it. My prayer and hope is always to be one of a group, that my good words will join with the utterances of the other Jews. Even the person who leads the prayers only has the weight of one person and no more, just one member of the entire congregation.

03 03 03

Focus on Shabbat

שֵׁשֶׁת יָמִים תֵּעָשֶׂה מְלָאכָה וּבַיּוֹם הַשְּׁבִיעִי יִהְיֶה לָכֶם קֹדֶשׁ שַׁבַּת שַׁבָּתוֹן לַה'.

Six days work shall be done, and on the seventh day you shall have sanctity, a day of complete rest to the Lord.

(Ex. 35:2)

Did Rabbi Nahman of Breslov know anything about ADHD? Could he have written about the difficulty of focusing on just one task at a time? Did he provide a tool for dealing with this difficulty?

Rabbi Nahman offers the following explication of the verses about the idea of Shabbat in *Vayak'hel*:

> Each of our thoughts gets very mixed up with the others and so we go from one idea to the next, and one thought to the next ... the idea is that a person should suddenly pause and take a break from his

thoughts. This is the concept of Shabbat, that with all the thoughts and tasks and bothers during the week, one should rest on Shabbat.

Some two hundred years before we were bombarded with Facebook posts and Twitter feeds and push notifications, Rabbi Nahman described people as overloaded with thoughts and partial ideas such that they find it difficult to sit and have serious, uninterrupted thinking time. His solution was a Shabbat, a day in which we neutralize all these distractions.

Rabbi Nahman takes his idea one step further and writes about having a "Shabbat" in the middle of each weekday. He calls upon everyone to make time for quiet and seclusion during the day: "A person should always remember to bring some of the holiness of Shabbat into the six days of the week. In the middle of all the confusion, he should stop and rest, as if it were Shabbat, and if he does so he will be saved from all the bad thoughts."

CB CB CB

Wisdom of the Heart

וְכָל הַנָּשִׁים אֲשֶׁר נָשָׂא לִבָּן אֹתָנָה בְּחָכְמָה טָווּ אֶת הָעִזִּים.

And all the women **whose hearts lifted them up with wisdom,** spun the goat hair.

(Ex. 35:26)

The Lubavitcher Rebbe often spoke of the women's prominent role in building the *Mishkan* and, indeed, in building the world. The Torah talks about "every wise-hearted woman" and "all the women whose hearts lifted them up with wisdom," who took part in building the *Mishkan*. This combination of the brain and the heart is a special one which is emphasized by the Torah during this project. The Lubavitcher Rebbe emphasizes two points:

First, the men only brought the materials to the *Mishkan* but did not actually produce anything. We should not deduce from this that "sewing is a woman's job," but rather need to consider the spiritual suitability of men and women for this task. Most of the men worshiped idolatry with the Golden Calf and were considered less suited than the women, who did not sin. The women were considered to be on a higher spiritual level and did the task *leshem Shamayim*, with holy intent.

Second, some of the skilled jobs in the *Mishkan* were initiated by the women of their own accord. They were talented artists who used their skills to benefit the *Mishkan*. This lesson applies to men and women. If you have been blessed with special skills or senses, you should use them for a good purpose, and to plan and execute constructive projects. And in the Rebbe's words, "To make the whole world a *Mishkan* of goodness and faith."

 C3 C3 C3

Israel's Pleasant Face

וַיְצַו מֹשֶׁה וַיַּעֲבִירוּ קוֹל בַּמַּחֲנֶה לֵאמֹר אִישׁ וְאִשָּׁה אַל יַעֲשׂוּ עוֹד מְלָאכָה לִתְרוּמַת הַקֹּדֶשׁ וַיִּכָּלֵא הָעָם מֵהָבִיא.

And Moses commanded, and they announced in the camp, saying, **"Let no man or woman do any more work for the offering for the Holy."** And the people stopped bringing.

(Ex. 36:6)

During Operation Protective Edge in the summer of 2014, I interviewed the spokesman of the Soroka Medical Center in Beer Sheba. He came on air with an unusual request: "Please do not come to the hospital to bring food and drink, candy, and other goodies to the injured soldiers. We are being overrun with goodwill. Hundreds of people are coming to visit and the injured cannot eat all the marshmallows, even if the nurses help."

In the background, the television screen showed masses of people entering the hospital with pots full of home-cooked food, and teenagers with their guitars and darbuka drums. Everyone was so keen to help, but at some point they had to be asked not to come anymore. This was both heartwarming and amusing, and it reminded me of the scene described in our *parasha* when the people were so enthusiastic about bringing things to the *Mishkan* that they had to be stopped.

"And Moses commanded, and they announced in the camp, saying, 'Let no man or woman do any more work for the offering for the Holy.' And the people stopped bringing." Moses simply had to put an end to this outpouring of generosity. After seeing the ugly side of the Jewish people as revealed at the Golden Calf, we have here a full turnaround, as the pleasant face of the nation was revealed with an outpouring of goodwill.

Was this always so? No. With one sentence, the *parasha* describes how the same people so keen to contribute their jewelry to build the Golden Calf are now eager to build the *Mishkan*. The language used to describe the two "projects" is very similar, but one refers to idol worship and the other to holiness!

The Jerusalem Talmud explains the situation concisely: "It is impossible to understand this nation. When they are asked to donate to the Golden Calf, they do so. When they are asked to donate to the *Mishkan*, they do so."

The public can easily be swayed to either positive or negative action, depending on what goal they are aiming for. In both cases, the Children of Israel had the urge to give ceaselessly, understanding that some causes are more worthy than our possessions.

This may be the reason why Jews are often at the leadership of revolutions. Jews were at the forefront of communism and socialism and many other -isms, good or bad. Many commentators note that we learn from this *parasha* about the importance of channeling our spiritual energies into the right causes and distinguishing between "Golden Calf" and "*Mishkan*" projects.

Pekudei

How Much Does It Cost?

וַיְהִי זְהַב הַתְּנוּפָה תֵּשַׁע וְעֶשְׂרִים כִּכָּר וּשְׁבַע מֵאוֹת וּשְׁלֹשִׁים שֶׁקֶל בְּשֶׁקֶל הַקֹּדֶשׁ.

And the gold of the offering was **twenty-nine talents, and seven hundred and thirty shekels**, according to the holy shekel.

(Ex. 38:24)

Transparency, one of the latest buzzwords in Israeli public discourse, is also a key word in this *parasha*. Moses gives a detailed financial accounting, which takes up quite a few verses, about the cost of setting up the *Mishkan*, how much was collected and how it was used. There is a vital need for transparency about how the funds were used, even for a project involving a holy purpose (and maybe especially because of its holy purpose!). Moses is not exempt from the need to show financial transparency and he stands before the people to present his report.

Amos Hakham, the first winner of the Israel Bible Quiz and a Bible scholar, expanded on this theme:

> There is a moral lesson to be learned from Moses. Even though the *Mishkan* was steeped in holiness and there was no suspicion of any wrongdoing, nevertheless Moses himself gave a report of all the materials that were donated and how they were used. The details

of his report were published in the Torah. Precisely because of the holiness of the *Mishkan*, it was so important to publish the report.

A contemporary social initiative called "One Hundred Days of Transparency" demands that elected officials publish all their expenses and provide details of their meetings. In *Pekudei*, the Torah tells us about three thousand years of transparency.

ᘓ ᘓ ᘓ

The Art of Art

וַתֵּכֶל כָּל עֲבֹדַת מִשְׁכַּן אֹהֶל מוֹעֵד וַיַּעֲשׂוּ בְּנֵי יִשְׂרָאֵל כְּכֹל אֲשֶׁר צִוָּה
ה' אֶת מֹשֶׁה כֵּן עָשׂוּ.

**And all the work of the Tabernacle of the Tent of Meeting was
completed** and the Children of Israel had done according to all
that the Lord had commanded Moses, so they had done.

(Ex. 39:32)

Does Israeli culture exhibit a left-wing or right-wing bias? This question is discussed endlessly but first we need to ask what we mean by culture. What is the purpose of art? *Pekudei* is all about building the *Mishkan*, a major artistic undertaking. Rabbi Abraham Isaac HaKohen Kook had some fascinating views about art and its purpose:

Literature, painting, and sculpture give material expression to all
the spiritual concepts implanted in the depths of the human soul.
As long as even a single line hidden in the depth of the soul has
not been given outward expression, art, sculpture or literature
has a duty to bring it out.

Art is meant to express the ideas hidden in the depth of our souls and we must make every effort to bring forth our innermost thoughts. However, this must be qualified with the recognition that the soul contains both good and bad, high and low. Must absolutely everything contained in the soul be expressed? Does an artist have the right to exhibit every artistic creation? Rabbi Kook continues:

> But it is understood that it is good to uncover only those treasures that, in being opened up, add fragrance to the air of existence. However, the hidden things whose burial is their deserved disposal, we must close them up with a spade. Woe to the one who uses this spade for the opposite purpose, increasing a bad odor in the air.

There is great value to inspiring art that aims at improving reality, but other things are best hidden and buried. Woe to the artist who wastes his time on releasing all the filth hidden in his soul, only adding to the pollution in the world.

These quotes are from 1900, yet they are still relevant to discussions about art and culture today.

CB CB CB

Israel's Official Emblem

אֶת הַמְּנֹרָה הַטְּהֹרָה אֶת נֵרֹתֶיהָ נֵרֹת הַמַּעֲרָכָה וְאֶת כָּל כֵּלֶיהָ וְאֵת שֶׁמֶן הַמָּאוֹר.

The pure Menora, its lamps, the lamps to be set in order and all its implements, and the oil for the lighting.

(Ex. 39:37)

The official emblem of the State of Israel, the Menora, is first mentioned in *Pekudei*. The Torah described the Menora in the *Mishkan* with the seven branches, and instructed that it be made by hammering out the shape from one single unit rather than being made from separate units that were joined together. The Menora was first placed in the *Mishkan* in the wilderness and later in the Temple in Jerusalem, and has become one of Judaism's best-known symbols. Zechariah prophesied about the Menora and the olive branches, and the miracle about the rededication of the Menora and the jar of oil is celebrated annually on Hanukka. The Arch of Titus in Rome clearly shows the Menora as one of the vessels taken from the Second Temple. Shortly after the founding of the State of Israel, a call was issued for designing the official emblem of the state. The winning design was a seven-branched Menora flanked by two olive branches above the word "Israel."

Today we take this emblem for granted but after it was officially adopted, Gershom Schoken wrote an editorial in the *Haaretz* newspaper dated February 10, 1949, expressing his opposition:

> The State Council's decision this past Thursday ends the first session of our first parliamentary body in bad taste, if the following will not be swiftly corrected. If this emblem will be displayed at the council and soon at all official institutions of the State of Israel here and abroad, it will be a demonstration, on a worldwide scale, of the lack of taste and aesthetic culture by the government and its lawmakers. This small Menora is squeezed between two huge olive branches whose leaves resemble swords more than olive leaves, the symbol of peace. In addition, the empty space above the Menora is most ugly and bears witness to the designer's complete lack of sense. This emblem must be corrected before the good name and honor of the State of Israel in the world is damaged simply because the government ministers have no taste.

This "lack of taste, on a worldwide scale" continues to represent the State of Israel to this very day.

℘ ℘ ℘

This Is Also Worthy of a Headline

וַיַּרְא מֹשֶׁה אֶת כָּל הַמְּלָאכָה וְהִנֵּה עָשׂוּ אֹתָהּ כַּאֲשֶׁר צִוָּה ה' כֵּן עָשׂוּ וַיְבָרֶךְ אֹתָם מֹשֶׁה.

And Moses saw the entire work, **and behold they had done it as the Lord had commanded**, so had they done. And Moses blessed them.

(Ex. 39:43)

In *Teruma* and *Tetzaveh* the Torah gave detailed instructions about building the *Mishkan*, the vessels, and the priestly garments. Why is it necessary to repeat every single one of these instructions in *Pekudei*?

The Torah repeats these details because following all the instructions is no simple matter. A job done properly is worthy of a headline and the fact that the Children of Israel completed the task they had been given in the best possible way is worthy of praise. Keeping to a schedule, reaching set goals, and perfectly executing a task is not to be taken for granted. Anyone who has ever taken on a project knows this all too well.

The completion of the *Mishkan* project is described matter-of-factly: "In accordance with all that the Lord had commanded Moses, so the Children of Israel did do all the work. And Moses saw the entire work, and behold they had done it as the Lord had commanded, so had they done. And Moses blessed them."

Total execution of a project is certainly not self-evident, neither in the wilderness nor in the State of Israel. In the wilderness, there were no inquiry commissions, no Supreme Court, no scandals, and no strikes, no Golden Calf, and no complaints. Simply, "they did it as God had commanded."

೮೪ ೮೪ ೮೪

Filling the *Mishkan*

בְּיוֹם הַחֹדֶשׁ הָרִאשׁוֹן בְּאֶחָד לַחֹדֶשׁ תָּקִים אֶת מִשְׁכַּן אֹהֶל מוֹעֵד: וְשַׂמְתָּ שָׁם אֵת אֲרוֹן הָעֵדוּת וְסַכֹּתָ עַל הָאָרֹן אֶת הַפָּרֹכֶת.

On the day of the first month, on the first of the month, you shall set up the Tabernacle of the Tent of Meeting, **and you shall place the Ark of the Testimony there and hang the veil before the Ark.**

(Ex. 40:2–3)

Eliav Gelman was killed in a terror attack in Gush Etzion. When the *shiva*, the seven-day period of mourning, was over, his family began going through his notes and discovered new pearls of Torah wisdom he had written. While he was married with two children and an IDF officer, he still managed to devote many hours to learning Torah. One of the ideas found in his notebooks refers to building the *Mishkan*.

He quotes the Talmud, the *Kuzari*, Rabbi Kook, and the Maharal of Prague on the famous question of what comes first, the *Mishkan* or its vessels. Eliav writes that although the vessels, which symbolize the inner content, are more important, nevertheless we must first build a place to house them. The physical building comes first.

Eliav compares the *Mishkan* to the body and the vessels to the soul. The soul requires a body within which to operate. He then makes a comparison with the era in which we are living. The physical body, the State of Israel, is already standing, the National Home for the Jewish people exists. However, the soul, the culture, the spirit, and the content – these elements are not yet complete. We have the "*Mishkan*"; now we have to work on the "vessels" within.

CB CB CB

More to Come

כִּי עֲנַן ה' עַל הַמִּשְׁכָּן יוֹמָם וְאֵשׁ תִּהְיֶה לַיְלָה בּוֹ לְעֵינֵי כָל בֵּית יִשְׂרָאֵל בְּכָל מַסְעֵיהֶם.

For the cloud of the Lord was upon the Tabernacle by day, and there was fire within it at night, before the eyes of the entire house of Israel in all their journeys.

(Ex. 40:38)

We have made it. We have arrived at the end of the Book of Exodus. Now it is time to return to the beginning of the book and recall how it all started: "And these are the names of the sons of Israel who came to Egypt; with Jacob, each man and his household came." One family, not yet a nation, came down to Egypt because of a famine in the Land of Israel. Pharaoh died, slavery began, Moses was born, he saw the Burning Bush, the Ten Plagues, the Splitting of the Sea, the Revelation at Mount Sinai, and finally, the *Mishkan* was consecrated.

Now we jump to the final verse of Exodus: "For the cloud of the Lord was upon the Tabernacle by day, and there was fire within it at night, before the eyes of the entire house of Israel in all their journeys." The *Mishkan* has been consecrated, and this spiritual core will accompany the Children of Israel on their journey to the Land of Israel. We have come a long way in this book, but the journey of the Jewish people is far from over.

Leviticus is just around the corner, and it is a good idea to stop and take a break at the end of each stage of the journey, before commencing the next task. When the reading of one of the Five Books of the Torah is completed in synagogue, the entire congregation stands up and says, "*Hazak, hazak, venit'hazek* – Be strong, be strong, and may we be strengthened!"

Leviticus

We have finished Genesis, on the creation of the world, followed by Exodus, in which we went out from slavery to freedom. What next? Where do the readers, and the Jewish nation, continue from here?

The next stage is the Book of Leviticus, which is also called the "Book of Holiness." A high standard is expected of us: "You shall be holy, for I, the Lord, your God, am holy."

What does the Torah mean by this demand? The commentators explain that this relates to personal sanctity: we are meant to be holy people within our physical selves and the physical world. This holiness is expressed within the many small details listed in the Book of Leviticus dealing with the sacrifices, respectful dialogue, holidays, the *Shemitta* year, the laws of keeping kosher, etc. The entire book, and indeed the essence of the entire Torah, can be summed up by one famous phrase from the middle of Leviticus: "Love your neighbor as yourself."

Vayikra

The Constant Calling

וַיִּקְרָא אֶל מֹשֶׁה וַיְדַבֵּר ה׳ אֵלָיו מֵאֹהֶל מוֹעֵד לֵאמֹר.

And He called to Moses, and the Lord spoke to him from the Tent of Meeting, saying.

(Lev. 1:1)

The Lubavitcher Rebbe explains how we should understand "And He called," the first words of this *parasha* and of the entire Book of Leviticus:

> This is a calling for what a person must do in his life. Every single hour and day you are being called and told, "Get up. Be constantly on the move to improve yourself."
>
> This calling can be understood in two different ways. It is a challenge for a person already on a high level, who is told he or she must constantly strive to reach even greater heights. And for a person who has sunk to the depths, it is a call of encouragement telling him or her not to despair: "Despite your present situation you have the power within you to rise up and go out from darkness to light."

CB CB CB

Between the Lines

דַּבֵּר אֶל בְּנֵי יִשְׂרָאֵל וְאָמַרְתָּ אֲלֵהֶם אָדָם כִּי יַקְרִיב מִכֶּם קָרְבָּן לַה' מִן
הַבְּהֵמָה מִן הַבָּקָר וּמִן הַצֹּאן תַּקְרִיבוּ אֶת קָרְבַּנְכֶם.

Speak to the Children of Israel, and say to them, "When a man
from you brings a sacrifice to the Lord; **from animals, from cattle
or from the flock you shall bring your sacrifice.**"

(Lev. 1:2)

Before we read about the laws of the sacrifices, we are told that there
were pauses between each time God spoke to Moses to give him new
instructions. Rashi asks what the purpose of these gaps was and answers
that they were "to give Moses a break, to contemplate between one section and the next, and between one subject and another."

What a wonderful expression! It tells us that we can't bombard
ourselves constantly with non-stop information, even if it is important,
and maybe, precisely because it is so important and holy. We need a
break, to pause and ingest what we have been told and to contemplate
its content. The silences in the breaks are the main part of a lesson, and
of life itself.

I heard the following story from Rabbi Yehoshua Hartman, the
principal of Hasmonean School in London:

> Many years ago, I went to a lecture by Rabbi Moshe Shapira
> and brought along the latest technological invention, a voice-
> activated tape recorder. When the recorder detected a voice, it
> would spring into action; otherwise it would not record and
> thus save space on the tape. I was very excited to use this new-
> est piece of equipment and proudly placed it on the table in
> front of the rabbi in order to record the lecture. Rabbi Shapira
> noticed the machine and asked what was so special about it.
> When I told him about this invention that would only record
> his words and not his pauses, he looked at me and said, "If
> that is the case, then you will be missing out on the main part
> of my lecture!"

To really listen and take in what is being said, we need space to contemplate and absorb.

CB CB CB

The Point of Sacrifice

דַּבֵּר אֶל בְּנֵי יִשְׂרָאֵל וְאָמַרְתָּ אֲלֵהֶם אָדָם כִּי יַקְרִיב מִכֶּם קָרְבָּן לַה' מִן
הַבְּהֵמָה מִן הַבָּקָר וּמִן הַצֹּאן תַּקְרִיבוּ אֶת קָרְבַּנְכֶם.

Speak to the Children of Israel, and say to them, "When a man
from you brings a sacrifice to the Lord; from animals, from cattle,
or from the flock you shall bring your sacrifice."

(Lev. 1:2)

Let's be honest – the subject of sacrifice is difficult to understand in the
modern era. Why do we need to bring animals as sacrifices? Is there
any connection between the sacred values of Judaism that we know
and what seems to be a massive slaughterhouse operation? We will deal
with these questions again and again throughout the Book of Leviticus.
The following is a preliminary answer, taken from the *Sefer HaHinukh*,
which we will then put into contemporary language:

> Most thoughts of the heart are dependent on actions. Therefore,
> if a person sins, his heart will not be purified properly by words
> alone, if he just says to himself (or to the wall), "I have sinned,
> and I will not do it again." However, if he undertakes a major
> action because of his sin, to take sheep out of his personal prop-
> erty and take the trouble to come to the priest in the appointed
> place and perform all the actions that accompany a sin offering,
> then these major actions will imprint on his soul the severity of
> the sin, and he will avoid repeating the sin in the future.

In modern terms, sacrifice can be explained as follows: Most feelings
in the heart are dependent on actual deeds. If a person commits a sin,

he cannot simply clean his heart by mumbling a few words (or, as the *Sefer HaHinukh* puts it – to talk to the wall) admitting his sin and committing not to repeat it. He has to act, to take his own animals and set out on the long journey to Jerusalem. Only after he has gone through the entire procedure with the priest will his soul actually absorb how bad it is to sin; only then will he avoid doing so in the future.

This is an important educational principle, even in a world in which sacrifices no longer occur. It is not enough to think or talk about something, or even to decide to do something. You have to take action as well. A sacrifice.

CB CB CB

Messages from the Subconscious

נֶפֶשׁ כִּי תֶחֱטָא בִשְׁגָגָה מִכֹּל מִצְוֹת ה' אֲשֶׁר לֹא תֵעָשֶׂינָה וְעָשָׂה מֵאַחַת מֵהֵנָּה.

If a person sins unintentionally in any of the commandments of the Lord, which may not be done, and he shall do any one of them. (Lev. 4:2)

Moses continues to teach the Children of Israel the laws of sacrifice, including the one brought after committing an unintentional sin: "Speak to the Children of Israel, saying: 'If a person sins unintentionally.'"

If a person did not intentionally sin, why is it necessary for him to bring a sacrifice? According to hasidic thought, when we do something inadvertently, it is not coincidental, but rather a result of impulses and motives hidden deep down in our soul. These actions reveal what is going on in our subconscious mind and bring it to the fore. Thus, we are not asking for forgiveness for the actual sin, which was committed unintentionally, but for what occurred prior to the action. The true fault is in our bad habits, lack of self-control, negligence, and errant ways. All of them together cause the situation in which our misdeeds are committed, even though we certainly do not want to do them. Thus, we could go so far as to claim that accidental sins may even require a higher level of forgiveness than those committed on purpose. When we make a conscious choice to commit a sin, it is a bad decision but at least it is a known defect. However, an unintentional sin reflects what is going on in our subconscious. Precisely because this sort of sin reveals our hidden nature, we are required to pay more attention to what is going on deep down in our soul in order to prevent it.

ଓ ଓ ଓ

Shake It Off

אָדָם כִּי יַקְרִיב מִכֶּם קָרְבָּן לַה'.

When a person from you brings **a sacrifice to the Lord**.
(Lev. 1:2)

A few years ago, on a Friday night of the week when we read *Parashat Vayikra*, a terrorist entered the Fogel family home and murdered the parents, Udi and Ruti, and three of their children as they slept in their beds. During the painful funeral, all the eulogies spoke of these precious communal sacrifices. I had not known the Fogel family personally, but since the tragedy I have been privileged to get to know their families. Ruti's parents, Rabbi Yehuda and Tali Ben-Yishai, are raising the three remaining orphans, Tamar, Roie, and Yishai. During one of the memorial services, Tali gave a very personal speech. The following is an excerpt:

> I quickly felt the enormity of the loss, but I also see that what I still had was even greater. Yes, I allow myself to go to pieces, crying over how much I miss them, but one minute later I offer my heartfelt thanks, again and again, for what remains, for Udi and Ruti's wonderful children who live with us and will, please God, grow up with great strength. I understood that I am going to have to live in two worlds. I will live the day-to-day world to its fullest. I will cook, bake, tidy up, go shopping, plant flowers, enjoy the fresh fragrance of spring, plan for a family summer vacation, and organize my younger daughter's wedding. But I will also live in

the World to Come. How so? I will acknowledge that there are difficulties to be dealt with, but I will not give up on the great ideals of integrity and goodness. I live in the day-to-day world and will take advantage of every minute I am here, but I also know that the Resurrection of the Dead will occur. This is not some abstract term, or a far-off vision. It means that I will not allow the dead to be dead or forgotten. We resurrect them every moment of our lives. The very fact that we are here and go about our lives means that we keep our beloved ones alive.

We tend to refer to terror victims as "Sacrifices of Terror."

Yes, they are sacrifices (*korbanot*) but they are also close (*karov*) to us. And they are not the only sacrifices. We who are left behind in this world, who constantly bear a terrible burden, who feel different, who no longer can afford to care about trivial matters, we are also sacrifices. Yet our sacrifice does not turn us into pitiable people, nor does it cause us to give up on life. It brings us closer to our beloved ones who have passed on to the World of Eternity. We are close to those who have a difficult life, close to the true life.

Before the Jews were expelled from Gush Katif, Ruti and Udi lived in Netzarim, one of the Jewish communities in the Gaza Strip. During the protests prior to this move, Ruti took a large white sheet and, in large letters, wrote a line from the *Lekha Dodi* prayer, sung during the Friday night service, and hung the sheet outside her house:

"Arise now, shake off the dust,
Don your robes of glory – my people."

Through this action, Ruti was giving us a lesson about living. There are some unbearably difficult periods in life, but at a certain point we must rise up, shake off the dust and wear our robes of glory, befitting royalty.

Ruti's message echoes with me all the time, I hear her voice telling me, "Mom, wear your robes of glory." And I continue living.

For Now and for the Future

וַיְדַבֵּר ה' אֶל מֹשֶׁה לֵּאמֹר: **צַו אֶת אַהֲרֹן וְאֶת בָּנָיו לֵאמֹר.**

And the Lord spoke to Moses, saying: "**Command Aaron and his sons, saying.**"

(Lev. 6:1–2)

Before the Torah goes into the fine print of the *parasha*, Moses is commanded by God, "Command Aaron and his sons, saying." Rashi explains the imperative form of the verb *tzav* as being "an urging, for the present and also for future generations."

Aaron is commanded to hurry up, a charge which applies to all of us in every generation since. We are told to attend to all tasks, be they spiritual or material, at once.

Rabbi Moshe Hayim Luzzatto, the Ramhal, writes in *Mesillat Yesharim* (*The Path of the Just*), that the virtue of zeal is one of the first stages of how a person should work on refining his character. The following quote from his book indicates the importance of showing zeal for action:

A person's nature exercises a strong downward pull upon him. This is so because the heaviness which characterizes the substance of earthiness keeps a person from desiring exertion and labor. One who wishes, therefore, to attain to the service of the

Creator must strengthen himself against his nature and be zealous. If he leaves himself in the hands of his downward-pulling nature, there is no question that he will not succeed.

CB CB CB

The Eternal Flame

אֵשׁ תָּמִיד תּוּקַד עַל הַמִּזְבֵּחַ **לֹא תִכְבֶּה.**

A continuous fire shall burn upon the Altar; **it shall not go out.**
(Lev. 6:6)

This verse is far more than a technical instruction about maintaining a continuous fire on the Altar. This is a motto for life. An eternal flame burns continuously in every person's heart, an inner spark of enthusiasm, joy, and desire to be a good person and be close to goodness. Just as a fire must be continuously stoked with a fresh supply of wood, so a person must continually "light" his inner fire and constantly refuel it with new material so that it does not burn out. The materials that ensure the fire burns continuously are Torah, good deeds, and good people.

Hasidic thought has a lot to say about this inner "fire" within us which can be summarized in the following sentence: A hasidic rabbi was once asked about his mood. He replied: "I am always happy and I am never satisfied."

CB CB CB

Modeh Ani

אִם עַל **תּוֹדָה יַקְרִיבֶנּוּ** וְהִקְרִיב עַל זֶבַח הַתּוֹדָה חַלּוֹת מַצּוֹת בְּלוּלֹת בַּשֶּׁמֶן.

If he is bringing it as a thanksgiving offering, he shall offer, along with the thanksgiving offering, unleavened loaves mixed with oil.
(Lev. 7:12)

One of the sacrifices mentioned in the *parasha* is the thanksgiving offering. The halakha lists four situations for which a person is obliged to bring a special offering of thanks after safely emerging from them: one who traveled on the high seas and arrived safely on dry land, one who traveled through the desert and safely reached his destination, one who was thrown in jail and then released, and one who was sick and recovered. In these cases, people were in danger, despairing that their end had come, only to emerge safely. These four instances are connected to the blessing of *HaGomel* that is recited nowadays after recovering from difficult situations, and which women recite after childbirth.

Many commentators explain that the thanksgiving offering is meant to teach us to pay constant attention to changing situations in our lives, and to know when to express gratitude. The first words we utter when waking up each morning are an expression of thanks, the *Modeh Ani* prayer: "I thank You, living and eternal King, for You have returned my soul within me with compassion – great is Your faithfulness."

It is written in our sources that in the time of Redemption, in the perfect world, many other sacrifices will be abolished but the thanksgiving offering will remain in effect. This is because the feeling of thankfulness is eternal and must be continuously nurtured. We must constantly be aware of all that is good in our life and we take note when we have to give thanks, when our lot has improved and when we are the recipients of kindness.

Rabbi Nathan of Nemirov writes about gratitude:

Nowadays, when we cannot bring a sacrifice, we have to utter heartfelt thanks, which is an expression of joy, because the main aspect of joy is to thank God. This is the main aspect of correcting ourselves when we come out of a dire situation, that we should correct that which was wrong and which caused the trouble, and that is sadness. We must give thanks, to talk of the kindness God bestowed upon us, that everything turned out for the best.

Shemini

Have You No Shame?

וַיֹּאמֶר מֹשֶׁה אֶל אַהֲרֹן קְרַב אֶל הַמִּזְבֵּחַ וַעֲשֵׂה אֶת חַטָּאתְךָ וְאֶת עֹלָתֶךָ
וְכַפֵּר בַּעַדְךָ וּבְעַד הָעָם וַעֲשֵׂה אֶת קָרְבַּן הָעָם וְכַפֵּר בַּעֲדָם כַּאֲשֶׁר צִוָּה ה'.

And Moses said to Aaron, "Come near the Altar and perform
your sin offering and your burnt offering, atoning for yourself
and for the people, and perform the people's sacrifice, atoning
for them, as the Lord has commanded."

(Lev. 9:7)

During the festive ceremony of dedicating the new *Mishkan*, Moses
summons Aaron to come near and begin the services: "And Moses said
to Aaron, 'Come near the Altar.'" In his commentary, Rashi notes that
Moses had to specially call Aaron to the *Mishkan* "because Aaron was
ashamed and frightened to come near. So Moses said to him, 'Why are
you ashamed? You have been chosen for this!'"

After the sin of the Golden Calf, Aaron did not want to
approach the Altar. Moses had to convince him to overcome his
natural shame, hesitation, and reticence since, after all, he had been
chosen for the task

Rashi's comment can be read in an alternative manner: Why are
you ashamed? Precisely for this reason you were chosen! The shame that

you feel is the very reason why you were selected. The fact that you are not vocal and decisive, that you do not see issues as clear-cut, that you are hesitant and think before you act, that you feel you are not worthy of the position, that you are not full of self-confidence, these are the very qualities that make you a leader.

On this reading, a little bit of shame goes a long way.

C３ C３ C３

Murky Feelings

וַיִּקְחוּ בְנֵי אַהֲרֹן נָדָב וַאֲבִיהוּא אִישׁ מַחְתָּתוֹ וַיִּתְּנוּ בָהֵן אֵשׁ וַיָּשִׂימוּ עָלֶיהָ
קְטֹרֶת וַיַּקְרִבוּ לִפְנֵי ה' אֵשׁ זָרָה אֲשֶׁר לֹא צִוָּה אֹתָם.

And Aaron's sons, Nadav and Avihu, each took his pan, put fire in them, and placed incense upon it, and **they brought before the Lord a foreign fire, which He had not commanded them.**
(Lev. 10:1)

The festivities are in full swing, the historic *Mishkan* is being dedicated, and then tragedy strikes. The Children of Israel had worked hard and anticipated this moment and Aaron's two sons die suddenly. We are told that they "brought before the Lord a foreign fire which He had not commanded them." For thousands of years, generations of commentators have been asking what was so terrible about the sin that Nadav and Avihu committed that they deserved to die during the dedication ceremony.

Rabbi Samson Raphael Hirsch explains that they were governed by their feelings rather than by logic. We are familiar with expressions such as "It feels right to me," "This speaks to me," or "I do not feel any connection to it," and "What does it have to do with me?" Rabbi Hirsch calls for a diametrically opposed approach to life which involves obedience, precision, commitment, and devotion in observance of commandments. It comes as no surprise that he lived in Germany, land of the "*yekke.*" The following is his explanation of the "foreign fire":

To fulfill God's commandments we are not required to invoke the murky area of our soul with the feelings of excitement and imagination, but to use a clear, logical, and realistic mind. The sons of Aaron died because they were trapped by their excitement. This is the lesson that all future priests and, indeed, all future teachers must learn. Do not teach only what your heart tells you, and do not let your imagination cause you to err or lead you astray.

ଔ ଔ ଔ

Next to Best

וַיֹּאמֶר מֹשֶׁה אֶל אַהֲרֹן הוּא אֲשֶׁר דִּבֶּר ה' לֵאמֹר **בִּקְרֹבַי אֶקָּדֵשׁ** וְעַל פְּנֵי כָל הָעָם אֶכָּבֵד וַיִּדֹּם אַהֲרֹן.

And Moses said to Aaron, "This is what the Lord said: '**I will be sanctified through those near to Me**, and before all the people I will be glorified.'" And Aaron was silent.

(Lev. 10:3)

After the death of Aaron's two sons, we read an expression that causes me to shudder, "I will be sanctified through those near to Me," which is meant to explain the deaths. As if God takes those nearest to Him, the holiest ones, the best ones, back to Him. Unfortunately, many times during my professional work reporting on funerals I have heard the expression "God takes the best."

Rabbi Shmuel ben Meir, the Rashbam, offers an alternative reading. He explains that the near ones are not the ones who have passed away, but those who remain alive and have to deal with the tragedy. A person who has lost a dear one is the one who becomes close and holy; he is the one who must continue building and living. According to the Rashbam, Aaron is being given a lesson after the death of his two sons. He is told not to mourn and cry, not to cease doing his work. He is advised to continue with his priestly work and not let death prevent the continuation of life.

This is a very powerful message for people who have lost their dearest ones. A holy person is not only the deceased, but also the one who remains alive and manages, despite his loss, to deal with the tragedy, gather his strength, and continue with his work.

ॐ ॐ ॐ

Sorry, I Forgot

וַיִּשְׁמַע מֹשֶׁה וַיִּיטַב בְּעֵינָיו.

And Moses heard this, **and it pleased him.**
(Lev. 10:20)

An embarrassing incident occurs in this *parasha*. Moses is angry with Elazar and Itamar due to a misunderstanding about how the sacrifices were offered. Their father Aaron explains to Moses why they had acted as they did. Moses' reaction is described in this short, profound verse: "And Moses heard this, and it pleased him." He is convinced by Aaron's explanation, which pleases him. Our sages have a deeper insight on what pleased him: "He admitted [Aaron was correct] and was not embarrassed [for he could have covered himself] by saying, 'I never heard this'; rather he said, 'I heard and then forgot.'" Moses was not embarrassed by the incident. He simply admitted that he had once known a certain law, and had now forgotten it.

The capacity to listen to the opposing side when you are angry, to be convinced by what they say, to own up to your mistakes and admit you once knew something but forgot it and now you have been reminded: this shows the true character of a leader.

For this reason, among others, he is known as Moses our Teacher.

Tazria

Ugliness Begets Ugliness

אָדָם כִּי יִהְיֶה בְעוֹר בְּשָׂרוֹ שְׂאֵת אוֹ סַפַּחַת אוֹ בַהֶרֶת וְהָיָה בְעוֹר בְּשָׂרוֹ
לְנֶגַע צָרָעַת וְהוּבָא אֶל אַהֲרֹן הַכֹּהֵן אוֹ אֶל אַחַד מִבָּנָיו הַכֹּהֲנִים.

If a man shall have on the skin of his flesh a rising, or a scab,
or a bright spot, and it becomes the plague of leprosy in the
skin of his flesh, then he shall be brought unto Aaron the priest,
or unto one of his sons the priests.

(Lev. 13:2)

Tzaraat, commonly but incorrectly translated as leprosy, is a spiritual
disease with physical manifestations of blemishes on a person's skin.
It is seen as a punishment for improper speech, especially negative
talk about other people. You say something and suddenly you see a
blemish appear on your skin, as if there is a cosmic law determining
these matters.

The not very aesthetic details of the symptoms form the main
part of the *parasha*. We do not understand the physiological definition
of *tzaraat* – it was treated by the priest, the spiritual leader, and not
by a physician. *Tzaraat* goes beyond the realm of the physical, and
the spiritual aspect of the skin blemishes teaches us about cause and
effect, crime and punishment. If you speak negatively, you skin will

look negative. These are difficult ideas for us to conceptualize now, but there is an inner logic. Is it science fiction? Or is it a lot more rational than we care to think?

CR CR CR

What Exactly Is *Lashon HaRa*?

נֶגַע צָרַעַת כִּי תִהְיֶה בְּאָדָם וְהוּבָא אֶל הַכֹּהֵן.

When the plague of leprosy is in a man, **he shall be brought to the priest**.

(Lev. 13:9)

What do we mean when we say *lashon hara* (lit. evil tongue)? Israeli civil law defines it as defamation but permits publication of information which is true and not defamatory under the Defamation Law. However, the Torah's definition of slander is different. This is because speech has power and every word we utter is significant.

In his classic work *The Gates of Repentance* (*Shaarei Teshuva*), Rabbi Yona Gerondi defines six categories of *lashon hara*:

1. "When you place a blemish on someone, and the blemish will not be on him," meaning that we invent a flaw about someone. For example, Yossi is intelligent but we say that he is dumb.
2. "Someone who says *lashon hara* which is not telling a lie." For example, Yossi really is unintelligent, and we state this fact.
3. "A slanderer who spreads hate in the world and causes animosity among family and friends." This is a gossiper who goes from one person to the next, causing discord between them.
4. "Dust of *lashon hara*" is a difficult term to define. It is the prevailing atmosphere which causes someone to speak *lashon hara* by offering exaggerated praise about someone else or by

hinting at something negative. (For example, "I do not want to tell you what happened with Yossi.")

5. "Profanity" is speech which pollutes the atmosphere. We don't need to look hard for examples, just look on the internet for some online comments!

6. "Complaining" is when a person grumbles and sees the bad in everything.

At least we now know what is meant by *lashon hara*.

෮ ෮ ෮

If You Don't Have Anything Nice to Say…

צָרַעַת נוֹשֶׁנֶת הִוא בְּעוֹר בְּשָׂרוֹ.

It is an old leprosy **on the skin of his flesh**.
(Lev. 13:11)

A new style seems to have taken over the world. Whether in reality shows, the media, or in politics, we are all expected to be authentic and show our true selves, whatever the results. We admire those who are totally blunt, and praise people who say things as they are and do not beat about the bush.

Who decided that whatever we think or feel needs to be said? Since when is telling your "inner truth" the most important value? Are we supposed to "let it all hang out" or should we aim for discretion? Are we simply ruled by our impulsiveness or should personal growth be our guiding principles?

Speech-related issues, and especially *lashon hara*, dominate this *parasha*. For thousands of years, the Jewish people have discussed the merits of measured, level-headed speech. Life would become unbearable if we would say the first thing that came into our head. The Torah demands that we strike a fine balance between truth and peace. Of course it is important to tell the truth and not to lie, but we also need to strive for peace among people. Sometimes peace takes priority over truth.

When we speak politely and respect others, when we think once, twice, or even three times before we speak so as not to insult someone, we may end up with fewer "likes" on our Facebook page, but we are building the foundations of a more likeable, healthy society.

ભ ભ ભ

Don't Reward Slander with Attention!

כָּל יְמֵי אֲשֶׁר הַנֶּגַע בּוֹ יִטְמָא טָמֵא הוּא בָּדָד יֵשֵׁב מִחוּץ לַמַּחֲנֶה מוֹשָׁבוֹ.

All the days the plague is upon him, he shall remain unclean. He is unclean; **he shall dwell isolated; his dwelling shall be outside the camp.**

(Lev. 13:46)

How do we punish someone who speaks *lashon hara*? Or for that matter, how does the public react to someone who makes a violent, extreme, vitriolic, or biting statement. We tend to give them free publicity by constantly mentioning the comment and by analyzing it from every possible angle. The speaker is interviewed on every news outlet and repeatedly asked to retract his comments. The headlines proclaim that "the musician/politician/actor refused to apologize."

If headline news is not enough, other protesters organize online petitions, go to the courts to get an injunction, or call for a ban on the offender. Before we know it, the weekend papers are running feature articles about the terrible new trend afflicting society. It works very simply. A famous person says a few words which are blown out of all proportion into a scandal, which controls the news cycle (until the next scandal erupts).

The Torah has a completely different approach to those who speak *lashon hara*. They are not given a stage to air their negative opinions about someone, but are sent into isolation: "He shall dwell isolated; his dwelling shall be outside the camp." Rashi elaborates that "since the slanderer caused a separation between husband and wife or between two friends because of his gossip, so he also must be separated." The rationale is that if you try to cause a rift between different sectors of society, and speak badly about everyone, you are sent away from society for a few days to reflect on your actions and see how you can make amends, and only then may you return.

If you don't use the power of speech correctly, you are isolated for a few days, far from the glare of the spotlight.

Metzora

Speak More, but Speak Morally

זֹאת תִּהְיֶה תּוֹרַת הַמְּצֹרָע בְּיוֹם טָהֳרָתוֹ וְהוּבָא אֶל הַכֹּהֵן.

This shall be the **law of the leper in the day of his cleansing**, he
shall be brought to the priest.

(Lev. 14:2)

The main theme of *Parashat Metzora* is the laws of purity and impurity,
but the first part is a continuation of the previous chapters about the
laws of *tzaraat*. One might get the feeling from these *parashot* that we
would be better off taking a vow of silence and living in a monastery.
But we would be mistaken if we thought that the intense preoccupation
with the prohibition about speaking *lashon hara* sends us the message
that it is better to keep silent.

Rabbi David Cohen, known as "the Nazir," was one of Rabbi
Abraham Isaac HaKohen Kook's leading disciples. Born in Lithuania,
he studied in the yeshiva in Radin headed by the Hafetz Hayim, Rabbi
Yisrael Meir HaKohen, who penned an eponymous book on guarding
one's tongue and taking great care in one's speech. Rabbi Cohen related
the following story about the Hafetz Hayim:

> When a fire broke out in Radin, all the students at the yeshiva in
> the town were sent away to neighboring villages. I was sent to a

village with a group of ten students and, from time to time, we would return to Radin. On one of these journeys, I accompanied the Hafetz Hayim and I was surprised that he talked non-stop. It is no big deal to talk less and avoid speaking *lashon hara*, but I noticed that he was very careful when speaking about someone else. The Hafetz Hayim did not talk less, he simply ensured that he spoke correctly, without insulting anyone else. That is the right way to speak.

The Hafetz Hayim taught us to be careful when speaking, but not to keep silent. We are not called upon to take a vow of silence, but precisely to observe the laws of not speaking *lashon hara* while engaging in regular speech.

CB CB CB

Speech in the Land of Israel

כִּי תָבֹאוּ אֶל אֶרֶץ כְּנַעַן אֲשֶׁר אֲנִי נֹתֵן לָכֶם לַאֲחֻזָּה וְנָתַתִּי נֶגַע צָרַעַת בְּבֵית אֶרֶץ אֲחֻזַּתְכֶם.

When you come into the land of Canaan, which I am giving you as a possession, and I put the plague of leprosy in a house of the land of your possession.

(Lev. 14:34)

Take a look at the history of the Jewish people and you will see that speech and exile are intertwined. The connection traces back to the dawn of history, in the Garden of Eden. The serpent speaks *lashon hara* about God Himself and tells Eve untruths about Him. ("And the serpent said to the woman, 'You will surely not die for God knows that on the day that you eat thereof, your eyes will be opened, and you will be like angels, knowing good and evil.'") Adam and Eve believed the serpent, sinned, and were punished with exile from the Garden of Eden.

Later in Genesis, Joseph tells his father Jacob *lashon hara* about his brothers: "And Joseph brought evil tales about them to their father." The outcome was exile to Egypt. In the wilderness, the spies spoke badly about the Land of Israel, saying that it is a difficult and bad land, "a land that consumes its inhabitants." The punishment was forty years of wandering in the wilderness en route to the Land of Israel. Our sages teach that the Davidic kingdom was broken up because of strife and *lashon hara* among King David's soldiers and once again we were sent into exile. From all these examples, we have to realize that a society's resilience is vital to its survival. If members of a society curse, shame, and gossip about co-members, then there is no future for this society and it will eventually disintegrate.

The correct use of speech is our entry code into the Land of Israel. Rabbi Tzvi Yehuda Kook said that after the long two-thousand-year exile, we needed to return to the Land of Israel and correct our way of speaking. Therefore, in the generation prior to our return and the Ingathering of Exiles, God sent us the Hafetz Hayim to instill in us the awareness of not speaking *lashon hara* and the importance of correct speech. Perfect historical timing! Just before we returned to the Land of Israel, we were given the tools to speak correctly and be worthy of returning.

CB CB CB

You're on Candid Camera!

וּבָא אֲשֶׁר לוֹ הַבַּיִת וְהִגִּיד לַכֹּהֵן לֵאמֹר כְּנֶגַע נִרְאָה לִי בַּבָּיִת.

And the one to whom the house belongs comes and tells the priest, saying, "It seems to me as if a **plague is in the house.**"
(Lev. 14:35)

The *parasha* describes an unbelievable, even apocalyptic situation in which houses get struck by *tzaraat*. If a person does not behave correctly within his home, then the signs of *tzaraat* appear on the walls, visible for all to see. Our sages say that extreme stinginess or not lending belongings to others are examples of improper behavior that cause *tzaraat*.

To explain the connection between the physical walls and ethical behavior within the home, our sages say that "the walls of a person's house bear witness to him." While we might behave very differently inside and outside the home, *tzaraat* of the house does not allow for such hypocrisy or two-faced behavior.

We are being given a warning that if we turn our homes into our castles and are not welcoming enough to strangers, if we distance ourselves from society's needs, or if we behave or speak improperly within our home, we will not be able to keep it a secret forever. The walls of our house will tell the truth. A home which sees violent or selfish behavior will be stained by *tzaraat*.

How interesting that, thousands of years after the Torah was written, a popular television show format involves installing cameras in a home to continuously monitor every detail of the inhabitants' lives. In contrast, the Torah warns us, through the threat of *tzaraat* on our houses, to behave "as if we are live, on-air."

Aharei Mot

The Original Scapegoat

וְנָתַן אַהֲרֹן עַל שְׁנֵי הַשְּׂעִירִם גּוֹרָלוֹת גּוֹרָל אֶחָד לַה' וְגוֹרָל אֶחָד לַעֲזָאזֵל.

And Aaron shall place lots upon the two goats: **one lot for the Lord, and the other lot for Azazel.**

(Lev. 16:8)

The source of the word scapegoat (*sa'ir laAzazel* in Hebrew) is found in this *parasha*, which describes the priestly order of service on Yom Kippur. The priest would place lots on the two goats, one for God which would be sacrificed in the Temple, and the other for *Azazel* which would be sent to its death by being thrown over the rocks in the wilderness.

Rabbi Samson Raphael Hirsch explains that this is not just some ancient rite, but a choice that everyone must make at any given moment in time:

> In the world of powers without freedom, man is the sole being possessing freedom. This freedom implies also having the ability to set oneself against the Divine will. A person can be "for God" or "for *Azazel*" and he has to make the choice. He decides which direction to turn, to the Temple or to the wilderness. To be respected or disregarded, great or small, rich or poor, today or yesterday – at any given moment every person may choose. And

the decision to choose "for God" only has meaning and value because at that moment the possibility of choosing "for *Azazel*" is available. And the decision "for *Azazel*" is only a disgrace to man, because at the same moment he could have chosen to remain faithful to God.

If the message is not explicit enough, Hirsch continues: "The entire dignity and worth of man lies just in the ability to sin, the possibility afforded him to disobey the will of God. This is his ethical advantage. Choice."

ଓ ଓ ଓ

One Day a Year

כִּי בַיּוֹם הַזֶּה יְכַפֵּר עֲלֵיכֶם לְטַהֵר אֶתְכֶם מִכֹּל חַטֹּאתֵיכֶם לִפְנֵי ה׳ תִּטְהָרוּ.

For on this day He shall make atonement for you **to cleanse you. Before the Lord, you shall be cleansed from all your sins.** (Lev. 16:30)

This *parasha* talks about Yom Kippur, the most powerful and meaningful day of the entire year. This is a day of prayer and fasting, forgiveness and reconciliation, which has a special atmosphere felt by nearly all sectors of Jewry. In Israel, a majority of Jewish citizens choose to commemorate Yom Kippur, despite no laws encouraging such behavior.

The *Sefer HaHinukh*, written some seven hundred years ago, explains each one of the 613 commandments in the Torah. In beautiful language, the book describes the special quality of Yom Kippur as an opportunity to reboot, to go back to the starting point and erase all the sins of the entire world:

> In God's kindness toward the Jewish people He established one day a year when they can atone for their sins through repentance (*teshuva*). If their sins would accumulate each year, their limit would be reached within a few years and the world would have to be destroyed. Therefore, in order for the world to persist, God,

in His wisdom, established one day a year to enable those who repent to receive atonement for their sins. From the beginning of Creation, He set aside this day and made it holy for this purpose, such that it acquired from God the power to assist in atonement.

The Torah tells us about the festivals, but we do not read this *parasha* in Tishrei when Yom Kippur is actually observed. So, take the opportunity when reading this *parasha* in the middle of the year to remind yourself that on the tenth day of Tishrei a wonderful gift awaits us.

C8 C8 C8

The Jewish Tweet

וּשְׁמַרְתֶּם אֶת חֻקֹּתַי וְאֶת מִשְׁפָּטַי אֲשֶׁר יַעֲשֶׂה אֹתָם הָאָדָם וָחַי בָּהֶם אֲנִי ה'.

You shall observe My statutes and My ordinances, which if a man shall **do he shall live by them. I am the Lord.**

(Lev. 18:5)

I met Rabbi Jonathan Sacks to interview him and he opened our conversation with a quote from the *parasha*, "And he shall live by them," adding, "He should not die by them." Rabbi Sacks is the former chief rabbi of the United Kingdom, a knighted peer in the British House of Lords, and one of the most prominent Jewish speakers and philosophers in the world. In recent years, he has taken upon himself the task of rebranding religion. During the interview, Rabbi Sacks repeated the phrase, "And he shall live by them," and offered his thoughts on religion:

> Religious terror is rife, especially in the name of Islam. I want to prove that we are all the children of Abraham and we are betraying his legacy. When we murder in His name, God weeps. We have to challenge the regnant narrative. I do not claim to be tolerant; I am a zealot too. God is also a zealot, a zealot for peace. The Jewish people have always been zealots – for life and

for love. It is precisely because we know what it means to "walk in the valley of the shadow of death" that we treasure the holiness of life. The Jewish people have always been outsiders, so they know how to be sensitive to others. This is our zealousness. The idea that zeal equals terror is a pagan one. It is a forbidden concept and my goal is to prove that religion is not the problem, it is the solution, the cure for all conflicts in the world. The Jews and Israel are supposed to inspire and bring blessing to the whole world. How on earth can we be considered the villains in this movie?

Rabbi Sacks wants to spread his message through his writings, but also on social media.

Moses prayed for forty days and nights on behalf of the Children of Israel, but when the situation called for it, he knew how to be very brief and needed just sixteen characters to pray on behalf of his sister Miriam, "Please God, Heal Her," a prayer short enough to be tweeted on Twitter. Brief does not necessarily mean superficial. We must make the Torah and its message accessible and attractive to all. The world is starving for serious content and we must get it out, using the latest technology to make a *Kiddush Hashem*.

03 03 03

The Sanctity of Marriage

אִישׁ אִישׁ אֶל כָּל שְׁאֵר בְּשָׂרוֹ לֹא תִקְרְבוּ לְגַלּוֹת עֶרְוָה אֲנִי ה'.

No man shall **come near to any of his close relatives, to uncover their nakedness.** I am the Lord.

(Lev. 18:6)

In modern, liberal society people expect to live their private lives exactly as they wish and, as long as they do not harm others, no authority may tell them what to do. Almost anything goes, as long as it is consensual. In *Parashat Aharei Mot*, the Torah introduces the concepts of holiness and impurity, which are totally alien concepts in modern-day society. We are told that certain acts cause an impure spirit, while others bring a holy spirit. Transgressing and fulfilling commandments influence a person's soul as well as the entire community. Every act leaves its mark on ourselves and on the world at large.

Many prohibitions are listed in *Aharei Mot*, particularly in the area of the personal relationship between husband and wife. The Jewish home is governed by a set of laws which sets out what is permitted and forbidden and throughout history, despite the prevalent culture, Jews kept to these laws.

The Torah is full of universally accepted ethics and concepts that appeal to the general public, but the Jewish people are required to live by completely different standards in their intimate lives. The Torah uses words such as abomination, incest, and promiscuity which are not socially acceptable in modern-day society and also repeatedly invokes holiness, an equally rare word.

Standing under the canopy during the Jewish wedding ceremony, the groom addresses the bride and says, "Behold you are consecrated to me with this ring." Of course a marriage involves going on dates, taking out a mortgage, having fun, and arguing over who takes the garbage out, but let us not forget that this relationship is holy.

ೞ ೞ ೞ

Earning the Land

וַתִּטְמָא הָאָרֶץ וָאֶפְקֹד עֲוֹנָהּ עָלֶיהָ וַתָּקִא הָאָרֶץ אֶת יֹשְׁבֶיהָ.

And the land became defiled, and I visited its sin upon it, **and the land vomited out its inhabitants.**

(Lev. 18:25)

Aharoni Bernstein, who learns at the hesder yeshiva in Ramat Gan, told me the following. A mother's love for her child differs from the love between a husband and wife. Motherly love is unconditional and ever-lasting. A child's very being is what makes him loved and, regardless of whether he disappoints her with his actions, he will always be her child. By contrast, the relationship between husband and wife is one of conditional love, less maternal, more demanding, and it causes people to change and improve themselves.

The relationship between the Jewish people and the Land of Israel is akin to that of husband and wife. The land has a sensitive stomach and, if our lifestyle is not fitting, it will vomit us out. What a strange and offensive comment! The Torah apparently does not think so, as it describes a situation in which the land expels its inhabitants. Unfortunately, this has already happened twice in Jewish history with the destruction of the two Temples. We did not return to the Land of Israel just to have a safe shelter. More is demanded of us if we are to be worthy of living here. In a certain sense, the Land of Israel is a gift to us, calling on us to become better people, to be a beacon of light.

Kedoshim

Living a Holy Life

דַּבֵּר אֶל כָּל עֲדַת בְּנֵי יִשְׂרָאֵל וְאָמַרְתָּ אֲלֵהֶם קְדֹשִׁים תִּהְיוּ כִּי קָדוֹשׁ אֲנִי ה׳ אֱלֹהֵיכֶם.

Speak to the entire congregation of the Children of Israel, and say to them, "**You shall be holy, for I, the Lord, your God, am holy.**" (Lev. 19:2)

At the start of this *parasha*, we are commanded to be holy, but what does this entail? Let us look at the list of subjects covered in *Kedoshim* and see if there is one predominant theme telling us how to be holy: honor your parents, keep Shabbat, do not worship idols, leave a corner of the produce of your field for the poor, do not steal, do not tell lies, do not delay paying salaries. The list continues with more commandments: "Do not put a stumbling block before a blind person," "Judge your fellow man with righteousness," "Do not go gossiping among your people," and "Love your neighbor as yourself." The Torah discusses laws of clothing, intimate relationships between husband and wife, the prohibition against tattoos, agriculture, standing up for the elderly and treating them with respect, treating a convert fairly, and keeping kosher.

An entire range of subjects, encompassing almost every aspect of life, comes under the heading of "holiness." This is not a holiness that requires us to aspire to reach mystical heights. It is found in our relationships with our spouse, family, friends, community, business partners, and the court. So the predominant theme in this *parasha* is actually the same as the central one of the entire Torah – how to live our lives.

C3 C3 CJ

Friendship

לֹא תִקֹּם וְלֹא תִטֹּר אֶת בְּנֵי עַמֶּךָ וְאָהַבְתָּ לְרֵעֲךָ כָּמוֹךָ אֲנִי ה׳.

You shall neither take revenge from nor bear a grudge against the members of your people; **you shall love your neighbor as yourself, I am the Lord.**

(Lev. 19:18)

This verse is one of the most well-known in the entire Tanakh. Innumerable explanations have been written about "Love your neighbor as yourself," one of the core principles of the Torah. First and foremost, a person is expected to love himself. After all, how can he love another person as himself, if he does not love himself? Unfortunately, this is not always so obvious to all of us. This demand seems to be impossible to fulfill. Is it really possible to love one's friend as much as one loves himself?

Among the many answers given to the question, the following one asks us to continue reading until the less familiar end of the verse, "love your neighbor as yourself, I am the Lord." When you understand that you were both created by God who gave you both a soul, then you will love your neighbor because you are both part of humanity, and the bonds of solidarity and commitment connect you. The prophet Malachi expressed this idea, which may be considered a continuation of the verse in *Kedoshim*: "Have we not all one Father? Has not one God created us? Why should we deal treacherously every man against his brother, profaning the covenant of our forefathers?" (Mal. 2:10).

In short, I love you because I love myself, because we are both part of the same whole.

૪૪ ૪૪ ૪૪

He Can't Even Hear

לֹא תְקַלֵּל חֵרֵשׁ וְלִפְנֵי עִוֵּר לֹא תִתֵּן מִכְשֹׁל וְיָרֵאתָ מֵאֱלֹהֶיךָ אֲנִי ה׳.

You shall not curse a deaf person. You shall not place a stumbling block before a blind person, and you shall fear your God. I am the Lord.

(Lev. 19:14)

Parashat Kedoshim continues with the standards expected of a holy person in all aspects of life. One of the interesting demands is that we are forbidden to curse a deaf person. Since we are told elsewhere in the Torah that it is forbidden to curse anyone, men, women, and children, and, in any case, the deaf person cannot even hear the curse, what is the Torah telling us by making a special point in this verse?

Maimonides explains that "the Torah was not only concerned about the cursed person, but is also strict with the one cursing, that he should not train his soul to aim at revenge or accustom it to getting angry." The Torah knows that the deaf person cannot hear the curse, but it is concerned with the perpetrator's soul.

Who is a greater cause of concern? The driver who is shouted at, or the abusive driver who shouts at him? The basketball referee who is cursed by fans, or the hecklers themselves? *Kedoshim* raises the bar and tells us that it does not matter at all whether the person can hear the insult and get offended by it. We should be far more concerned about the curser.

૪૪ ૪૪ ૪૪

Breaking the Cycle

וְכִי יָגוּר אִתְּךָ גֵּר בְּאַרְצְכֶם לֹא תוֹנוּ אֹתוֹ. כְּאֶזְרָח מִכֶּם יִהְיֶה לָכֶם הַגֵּר אִתְּכֶם וְאָהַבְתָּ לוֹ כָּמוֹךָ כִּי גֵרִים הֱיִיתֶם בְּאֶרֶץ מִצְרָיִם.

And if a stranger sojourns with you in your land, you shall not taunt him. The stranger who sojourns with you shall be as a native from among you, and you shall love him as yourself; **for you were strangers in the land of Egypt.**

(Lev. 19:33–34)

Unfortunately, an abused child often becomes an abusive parent, and a child who is bullied will often bully others. The Exodus from Egypt tried to stop this vicious cycle by taking the Jewish people out of slavery into freedom. The sequence of being abused and then becoming abusive must be stopped.

The Torah tells us how to treat the outsiders and weaker members of society, and remind us that "you were strangers in the land of Egypt." This verse is just one of many instances in which we are reminded of our past and warned not to continue the cycle of violence in which only the fittest survive.

If you suffered at the hands of a Pharaoh and were lucky enough to survive, it doesn't mean that you can be excused for becoming a Pharaoh yourself. Just because you suffered does not grant you the legitimacy to do whatever you want. In fact, the opposite is true. You are obliged to break the cycle and change the direction of your life.

03 03 03

Why Jews Don't Eat Pork

וְהִבְדַּלְתֶּם בֵּין הַבְּהֵמָה הַטְּהֹרָה לַטְּמֵאָה וּבֵין הָעוֹף הַטָּמֵא לַטָּהֹר וְלֹא
תְשַׁקְּצוּ אֶת נַפְשֹׁתֵיכֶם בַּבְּהֵמָה וּבָעוֹף וּבְכֹל אֲשֶׁר תִּרְמֹשׂ הָאֲדָמָה אֲשֶׁר
הִבְדַּלְתִּי לָכֶם לְטַמֵּא.

And you shall distinguish between clean animals and unclean ones, and between unclean birds and clean ones; thus you shall not make yourselves disgusting through animals and birds and anything which crawls on the earth, **that I have distinguished for you to render unclean.**

(Lev. 20:25)

The *parasha* stresses the importance of distinguishing between pure and impure animals. Rashi explains that keeping kosher is the basis of holiness and adds that a person should not say "pork disgusts me," as Rashi's puts it or, in contemporary language, "I'm not interested in eating a cheeseburger." We are told that we should not be ashamed to say "I really want to eat it, but what can I do – God forbids it!"

Parashat Kedoshim is full of laws that we can identify with and feel good about observing them. "Love your neighbor as yourself," "Get up for the elderly," and "Honor an older person" seem logical and moral. Rashi feels that in the middle of all these intuitive commandments, it is important to emphasize that there are other laws that are based on commandedness, where we must simply accept God's rulings. The Torah tells us that we may not eat pork. It is not a question of taste, it is because God forbade it.

ശ ശ ശ

Life and Death

וַיֹּאמֶר ה' אֶל מֹשֶׁה אֱמֹר אֶל הַכֹּהֲנִים בְּנֵי אַהֲרֹן וְאָמַרְתָּ אֲלֵהֶם לְנֶפֶשׁ לֹא
יִטַּמָּא בְּעַמָּיו.

And the Lord said to Moses, "Speak to the priests, the sons of
Aaron, and say to them: '**Let none of you defile himself for a
dead person among his people.**'"

(Lev. 21:1)

The first of many laws in *Parashat Emor* intended only for priests, the
spiritual leaders of the nations, is an unequivocal demand to keep away
from the dead. This prohibition still applies today and priests do not
enter cemeteries.

This prohibition was given to the priests shortly after the Children of Israel had left Egypt, the land of the pyramids. In these mag-
nificent edifices, the Egyptian priests led elaborate rituals to glorify
the dead. These included ceremonial grave processions replete with
magic chants, burying personal effects with the deceased, and, of
course, embalming.

In contrast, the Jewish priests are meant to be exemplary models
for the living and not to serve the "industry of death." In Egyptian law,
the embalming process lasted ten days, whereas we are commanded to
bury our dead as soon as possible, of course with much reverence and
according to Jewish law, but without pompous rites. The Torah's message to the priests is very clear: Jewish spiritual leaders and priests are
meant to focus on the living and not on the dead.

Emor

Enlighten Your Students!

וַיֹּאמֶר ה' אֶל מֹשֶׁה אֱמֹר אֶל הַכֹּהֲנִים ... וְאָמַרְתָּ אֲלֵהֶם.

And the Lord said to Moses, "**Speak to the priests**...and say to them."

(Lev. 21:1)

The *parasha* opens with God giving instructions and commandments to the priests. Rashi asks why two verbs are used in this verse, "Speak to the priests...and say to them," and answers that it is "to warn the adults about the children." The adult priests (and educators) are meant to warn their junior charges.

A famous hasidic reading of Rashi's use of the word "to warn – *lehazhir*" understands it to mean "to light up – *zohar*." Teachers and parents have two ways to influence their students and children. They can warn, informing their charges what is forbidden to do, but they must also show the light and give love and warmth.

This two-pronged approach to education is common in the ethical beliefs of the *Musar* movement. One way of teaching is likened to pouring wine from a goblet into a glass, a technical process of transferring a message from place to place, from teacher to student. The other method is to cause the goblet to overflow and influence everything nearby. No force is used to convey the message, but the teacher is so full of the subject matter that it simply flows out and is transferred to all who hear it.

CR CR CR

Total Devotion

וְהַכֹּהֵן הַגָּדוֹל מֵאֶחָיו אֲשֶׁר יוּצַק עַל רֹאשׁוֹ שֶׁמֶן הַמִּשְׁחָה וּמִלֵּא אֶת יָדוֹ לִלְבֹּשׁ אֶת הַבְּגָדִים אֶת רֹאשׁוֹ לֹא יִפְרָע וּבְגָדָיו לֹא יִפְרֹם.

And the priest who is elevated above his brothers, upon whose head the anointment oil has been poured or who has been inaugurated to wear the garments, he shall not leave his hair unshorn or tear his garments.

(Lev. 21:10)

Chabad emissaries are found in all four corners of the globe and are known for their total devotion to all Jews. When asked what motivates them to live such a lifestyle, often under difficult physical conditions, they answer with an idea their leader, the Lubavitcher Rebbe, taught about this verse.

Priests are forbidden to enter a graveyard and must keep away from any contact with a dead body. The one exception in which they are allowed, and even commanded, to be involved is when the deceased has no one else to bury him. Even if the High Priest is in the middle of services in the Temple on Yom Kippur, he is required to drop everything and deal with the burial of this abandoned person. The Lubavitcher Rebbe says that total devotion to a fellow Jew is more important than any spiritual experience, however lofty.

He explains that there are many situations in our life which are compared to the abandoned dead body, because no one else is available to deal with them. The most important task for the Jewish people is to provide spiritual and material assistance to all Jews and to spread belief in God. So we are commanded to leave aside all our other affairs and make the needs of our fellow Jews our top priority. We may find this idea difficult to implement, but if the High Priest was commanded to leave the Holy of Holies on Yom Kippur and go and deal with a deceased person, just imagine the importance of doing everything to revive a living Jew.

ଔ ଔ ଔ

One Day at a Time

וּסְפַרְתֶּם לָכֶם מִמָּחֳרַת הַשַּׁבָּת מִיּוֹם הֲבִיאֲכֶם אֶת עֹמֶר הַתְּנוּפָה שֶׁבַע שַׁבָּתוֹת תְּמִימֹת תִּהְיֶינָה.

And you shall count for yourselves, from the day after the rest day from the day you bring the Omer offering for seven complete weeks.

(Lev. 23:16)

The first time I saw this at a synagogue I found it rather odd. At the conclusion of the evening prayers, a man announces what day of the Omer it is, and all those present repeat this counting. From Passover which commemorates the Exodus from Egypt until Shavuot which commemorates the giving of the Torah, we are commanded to count each one of the forty-nine days.

There are deep kabalistic meanings to the numbers counted in this period, but on the simplest level counting the Omer is all about a process. We are taught to believe in the journey, not what happens at this precise moment, but in the gradual, step-by-step development. A nation is freed from slavery and proceeds, one day at a time, on a journey which culminates in receiving the Torah. Since that seminal event thousands of years ago, Jews have been commemorating the seven-week journey one day at a time. In our culture, this seems particularly difficult. We may have the technology to download an app to remind us to count the Omer every evening, but who today is prepared to wait seven whole weeks, making slow progress, until something actually happens?

The fridge in our home tells a story of the process. Among the wedding invitations and bills that need to be paid which are stuck on our fridge, we hung an Omer counting chart one of our children brought home from her nursery school. It was one of those scratch cards, and every evening we were supposed to scratch off a little bit of the silvery cover to see what number of the Omer we had reached. Just like a lottery card, except that we had to scratch a little bit at a time and not all at once. I recalled that we received the same chart a year ago but then our daughter could not hold herself back and scratched the entire card at once, reaching from one to forty-nine in one shot, moving hastily from Passover to Receiving the Torah in a few minutes. A year later, she was older and more patient, and was able to scratch one day at a time until she reached her goal.

I feel that the Omer chart on our fridge symbolizes the journey we make from Passover to Shavuot. We learn the value of patience and restraint, that we do not need instant gratification, and that slow progress leads to great things.

Behar

Take a Break from Everyday Life

דַּבֵּר אֶל בְּנֵי יִשְׂרָאֵל וְאָמַרְתָּ אֲלֵהֶם כִּי תָבֹאוּ אֶל הָאָרֶץ אֲשֶׁר אֲנִי נֹתֵן
לָכֶם וְשָׁבְתָה הָאָרֶץ שַׁבָּת לַהי.

Speak to the Children of Israel and you shall say to them: "When you come to the land that I am giving you, **the land shall rest a Sabbath to the Lord.**"

(Lev. 25:2)

The first thing we are supposed to do when we enter the Land of Israel is to rest. We are not meant to feel an immediate sense of ownership over the land. Quite the contrary, at the beginning of *Behar* we are told to loosen our hold on it: "When you come to the land that I am giving you, the land shall rest a Sabbath to the Lord."

While we were still in the wilderness, the Torah told us that when we eventually enter the Land of Israel, we will be required to keep the laws of *Shemitta*, the Sabbath of the Land, in addition to the weekly Sabbath. Once every seven years we have to reset all our systems, stop working hard to earn a living and for an entire year let go of our continual control over our affairs. At a time when agriculture was the dominant occupation, this meant that trade and employment slowed down significantly.

In a more ideal world, the *Shemitta* year would be observed in the State of Israel. We would "rest" more, we would keep all the laws in the fields, and would feel that the entire year was one long Shabbat in which we would choose to busy ourselves with spiritual matters rather than with physical ones and feel free from the shackles of six years of hard work.

Even though now is not the *Shemitta* year and most of us are not farmers, we can still learn a lot from this important principle of life. Rabbi Kook wrote that "for growth and progress in life to be promoted, there must be a pause and break to shake off the tumult of everyday life."

C3 C3 C3

Fraud Goes Beyond Money

וְלֹא תוֹנוּ אִישׁ אֶת עֲמִיתוֹ וְיָרֵאתָ מֵאֱלֹהֶיךָ כִּי אֲנִי ה' אֱלֹהֵיכֶם.

And you shall not wrong one another, and you shall fear your God, for I am the Lord, your God.

(Lev. 25:17)

In *Behar*, we are told not to wrong our fellow Jew. Rashi explains that this is not a question of monetary fraud but about verbally wronging someone by insulting them or giving a bad piece of advice.

We might think about fraud as a criminal offense, related to Israel's National Fraud Investigations Unit, or the IRS. But *Parashat Behar* tells us that there is also a religious injunction against using words to harm others.

Throughout the ages, our sages have given many examples of such verbal wrongdoings, such as deliberately reminding a convert or a person who has become more religious about their past; or insisting on publicly asking someone a question, even though we know full well that he does not know the answer; or asking a store assistant to show us more and more merchandise when we have no intention of actually buying anything; or harassing a waiter when we go out to eat in a restaurant. The common theme in all these examples is that the perpetrator has sense of power, cheats, is arrogant and patronizing, and thus verbally humiliates another person. In all these cases, the Torah warns us not to "wrong one another."

CB CB CB

Free Humanity from the Shackles of Freedom

וְהָאָרֶץ לֹא תִמָּכֵר לִצְמִתֻת כִּי לִי הָאָרֶץ.

The land shall not be sold permanently, for the land belongs to Me.

(Lev. 25:23)

Once every fifty years is the Jubilee year, when all land returns to its original owner. It is difficult to imagine the mechanism described by the Torah that everyone works hard and acquires money, possessions, and land and then once every fifty years everything resets to zero and we begin again. Tal Lesser is a social worker who wrote about the idea of the Jubilee year:

> Freedom is a wonderful thing, but when it has no limitations problems begin and then it becomes the biggest form of slavery. For example, an adolescent who has total freedom to do whatever he wants without any parental supervision is very likely to turn to drugs and crime.
>
> Similarly, in the economic sphere, the free market which promotes competition is a wonderful thing but at some point the forces become unequal. Anyone who has ever played Monopoly knows that at a certain point in the game, one of the players gains an advantage and from then on, he will only get richer and the other players will only get poorer until they are forced to declare bankruptcy.
>
> That is why the Torah creates a balance between competition in a free market economy, with reallocation every fifty years in the Jubilee year, as the "cards are reshuffled," and the land (or means of production) is returned to the original owners. However, freedom cannot be limited by simply hitting someone over the

head; they have to feel emotionally connected to the idea of the Jubilee. The adolescent who does not have any limits does not only need rules and regulations, he needs a connection with his parents and to understand why it is important that they supervise him. Also, in the economic sphere, it is not possible to limit the natural human instinct to earn more money at the expense of the weaker competitors. Communism tried to curb economic freedom and millions were killed in the eventually failed experiment.

There is a need to gain an inner recognition that the land does not belong to us: "The land shall not be sold permanently, for the land belongs to Me, for you are strangers and temporary residents with Me." Only by internalizing this sense, and educating around these themes, will it be possible to create the correct balance and release humanity from the shackles of freedom.

03 03 03

The Entry Code to the Land

כִּי גֵרִים וְתוֹשָׁבִים אַתֶּם עִמָּדִי.

For you are strangers and temporary residents with Me.
(Lev. 25:23)

The speeches Israeli politicians give on Yom HaShoah, Yom HaZikaron, Yom HaAtzma'ut, and Yom Yerushalayim all have one recurring theme, that the land is ours. The Torah tells us a different message: "The land shall not be sold permanently, for the land belongs to Me, for you are strangers and temporary residents with Me."

Abraham uses the same expression, "a stranger and temporary resident," when he introduces himself to the children of Heth after Sarah's death. Many years later, when we already have sovereignty and a kingdom, King David gathers all the people to pray together in Jerusalem and declares, "For we are strangers before You, and temporary residents like all our forefathers." Why did he not say that we are the owners of the land? Why do we always need to feel a little bit like strangers? Why did Abraham and David not speak with the same self-confidence so common among our politicians today?

Many commentators have explained that the rules of the game are completely different in the Land of Israel. It belongs to us precisely in accordance with our behavior. Just as a safe has an entry code, so does the Land of Israel. If we want to access that code, we are expected to live up to a certain standard of behavior. Of course, it goes without saying that this is where the Jewish people belong, and we must speak up and fight against those who wish to erase our rights to the land. But the land is not automatically ours. We need to show some humility, hoping that our conduct makes us worthy of having it.

It might be a better idea to speak not of our rights to the land, but of our obligations to it.

ের ের ের

Early Detection

וְכִי יָמוּךְ אָחִיךָ וּמָטָה יָדוֹ עִמָּךְ וְהֶחֱזַקְתָּ בּוֹ גֵּר וְתוֹשָׁב וָחַי עִמָּךְ.

If your brother becomes destitute and his hand falters beside you, **you shall support him as a convert or a resident so that he shall live with you.**

(Lev. 25:35)

It can be difficult to see the first cracks. It is easy to miss those moments when it is still possible to mend the situation easily. This verse is about when a person's financial situation begins to worsen, and the Torah demands that "you shall support him." Rashi writes that we must not allow him to fall and collapse completely, but must support him while he is still faltering, before he has completely fallen. Rashi compares this to a donkey carrying a heavy load. If the burden becomes unsteady when it is still on the donkey, one person can stabilize it. However, once the burden has fallen to the ground and its contents are strewn all over, even five people cannot return the burden to its previous state. Early detection is needed.

It is also worth noting that when someone can still be helped in the early stages of a crisis it is less newsworthy. When everything has collapsed and a person has fallen into the gutters of society and lives on the street, then we have a news item.

The same principle applies to other crises in life. Do we start marital therapy when small problems begin or do we wait until, God forbid, the marriage has come to a dead end? Do we begin worrying about at-risk youngsters only once the situation has already blown up, or do we try to help them at an early stage? Do we go for treatment when we are already sick or do we undertake tests that enable detection of the disease in its early stages? At what point do we begin therapy for emotional problems?

The Torah's commandment should make us aware about ourselves and others and try and detect problems when they first emerge.

CS CS CS

Slaves

כִּי לִי בְנֵי יִשְׂרָאֵל עֲבָדִים עֲבָדַי הֵם אֲשֶׁר הוֹצֵאתִי אוֹתָם מֵאֶרֶץ מִצְרַיִם אֲנִי ה' אֱלֹהֵיכֶם.

For the Children of Israel are servants to Me; they are My servants, **whom I took out of the land of Egypt.** I am the Lord, your God. (Lev. 25:55)

I came across the following idea in Rabbi Nahman of Breslov's writings. I am not sure if I understand it fully and I certainly have not successfully implemented it, but it caught my attention and I wanted to understand it further. The Torah talks about slavery and declares a release from all physical labor. Rabbi Nahman applies this verse to the body and soul. We must always be conscious of which is the master and which is the slave, because most of us have it backwards.

For most people eating, drinking, and other bodily desires are not considered work at all, whereas doing good deeds and fulfilling God's commandments are considered difficult and wearisome. So a substitution has taken place, with the king and slave changing roles. The desire of the soul, which is the true king, is considered to be work, and the desire of the body, which is nothing but a slave, is not considered by them to be slavery. Instead the body is considered, God forbid, to be the king over the soul. The truth is completely the opposite: the soul is the true king and the body is the slave. Just as a slave must serve his master, so the body must fulfill the will of the soul and put the soul's desires before the body's desires.

Behukkotai

Engraving the Law

אִם בְּחֻקֹּתַי תֵּלֵכוּ וְאֶת מִצְוֹתַי תִּשְׁמְרוּ וַעֲשִׂיתֶם אֹתָם: וְנָתַתִּי גִשְׁמֵיכֶם בְּעִתָּם וְנָתְנָה הָאָרֶץ יְבוּלָהּ וְעֵץ הַשָּׂדֶה יִתֵּן פִּרְיוֹ.

If you follow My statutes and observe My commandments and perform them I will give your rains in their time, the land will yield its produce, and the tree of the field will give forth its fruit. (Lev. 26:3–4)

The opening words of this *parasha* echo a recurrent theme throughout Leviticus: "If you follow My statutes…I will grant peace in the land." The Land of Israel demands that we live according to the rules and values set out in our contract with this special place.

The use of the word "*Behukkotai*" indicates that we are not talking about the technical aspects or the dry letter of the law (even though we do have a contract with the One who rented this place to us) but about something more fundamental. The root of the word "*Behukkotai*" is the same as "to engrave – *hakak*." If you use a pen to write instructions on a piece of paper, two separate items are needed and they never really become one entity. However, if you engrave words in stone, the letters and the stone merge to become one inseparable unit.

The Torah is meant to be engraved on our heart, so that we identify totally with what it says and internalize the laws until we and the

Torah become one entity. This is what the Torah means by "If you follow My statutes." The statutes are engraved in us and are part of our essence. We keep them willingly because they come from within.

෨ ෨ ෨

Synergy

וְרָדְפוּ מִכֶּם חֲמִשָּׁה מֵאָה וּמֵאָה מִכֶּם רְבָבָה יִרְדֹּפוּ וְנָפְלוּ אֹיְבֵיכֶם לִפְנֵיכֶם לֶחָרֶב.

Five of you will pursue a hundred, **and a hundred of you will pursue ten thousand**, and your enemies will fall by the sword before you.

(Lev. 26:8)

According to one commentator on this verse, everyone should think that they are the best, that they have a really important and influential role to play in this world. Even if you normally keep clear of math problems (I certainly do), read the equation in this verse. It is a simple math exercise, but it has deep significance for every one of us.

The above blessing tells us that only five people are needed to pursue one hundred enemies and overcome them, with a ratio of 1:20. The verse continues with another mathematical formula, "and a hundred of you will pursue ten thousand." If we use the original formula of five people defeating one hundred, then two thousand people would be needed to pursue ten thousand enemies using the same ratio of 1:20. So how come the Torah says that only one hundred people are needed? How does the math work out?

Rashi explains that "there is no comparison between a few who fulfill the Torah and many who fulfill the Torah." When people come together as a group they have tremendous power and, as more and more people join, their power grows disproportionally and leads to far better results than the actual size of the group would suggest.

In her commentary on this verse, Professor Nehama Leibowitz writes:

This disproportion teachers us how much responsibility is placed on the shoulders of each and every one of us. The individual person should not think, "How can I possibly have an influence if I join the small group of people who 'fulfill the Torah'? How much can I, an insignificant number, add to the power of the group?" We are told that the opposite is true and every single person who joins the group of the good people increases its power in a disproportional manner.

We learn from this mathematical formula that the power of each individual is far greater than they think when they are part of a group.

CB CB CB

How to Learn?

וַאֲכַלְתֶּם יָשָׁן נוֹשָׁן וְיָשָׁן מִפְּנֵי חָדָשׁ תּוֹצִיאוּ.

And you will eat old produce that has been stored for a long time, **and you will clear out the old from before the new.**

(Lev. 26:10)

Do you find yourself having difficulties learning? Do you feel your brain is stuffed with old information? The Torah has some advice for you: "Clear out the old from before the new." We are promised that the Children of Israel will have so much produce from the harvest that there will be no space left in the silos and storehouses. They will have to make room for all the new produce that needs to be stored.

According to hasidic thought, this verse is not only talking about material produce but also about spiritual treasures. If you wish to renew yourself with new knowledge and achievements or if you wish to develop in new directions, make sure that there is room in the storehouse of your mind and clear out old thoughts and teachings.

How are we supposed to make room in our soul? By taking what we have already learned, which is stored in our brain, and teaching it to someone else. If you keep all your knowledge safely locked up in you

like in a vault, then you will have no room to spare. But if you share all
the wisdom, knowledge, beliefs, and life experiences that you have accumulated with your friends and surroundings, you will have spare room.
By teaching others, they benefit, but so do you, and you now have space
to learn new things. "You will clear out the old from before the new."

03 03 03

The Real Peace Process

וְנָתַתִּי שָׁלוֹם בָּאָרֶץ וּשְׁכַבְתֶּם וְאֵין מַחֲרִיד וְהִשְׁבַּתִּי חַיָּה רָעָה מִן הָאָרֶץ
וְחֶרֶב לֹא תַעֲבֹר בְּאַרְצְכֶם.

And I will grant peace in the land, and you will lie down with
no one to frighten you; I will remove wild beasts from the land,
and no army will pass through your land.

(Lev. 26:6)

We are all so familiar with speeches about internal peace and unity
within the Jewish people that they can sound like clichés. This *parasha*
makes it abundantly clear that internal peace and unity are not overrated
words but are critically important. Solidarity among us is vital and is a
cornerstone of our existence as a people.

The Torah promises us that if we follow the correct path, then
"I will grant peace in the land," and only then are we promised that "no
army will pass through your land." This second promise refers to a time
when we will be at peace with our enemies, when there will be no wars
with them and no swords will be seen in our land. So what peace is
being referred to in the first promise, "I will grant peace in the land"?

Nahmanides gives a definite answer: "I will grant peace in the
land – that there will be peace between you and you will not fight one
another." Before we have peace with our enemies, we need to make peace
at home. Rabbi Hanan Porat wrote about peace within the Jewish people.

Peace in the land refers to peace at home, within the Jewish people,
without civil war. It refers to peace between husband and wife,

a person and his friends, between different sectors and ethnic groups, between different political parties and camps, so that we do not eat each other alive, much to the delight of our enemies. Peace at home is not the "backup plan" when we have no option to make peace with our enemies abroad. To the contrary: only when we have true peace among everyone at home can we muster the strength needed to make peace with our enemies. We must work internally to foster a spirit of goodness and peace, among family and friends, among Israel and the Jewish people, and even with our non-Jewish neighbors in the country. We must learn to see the good in everyone. As this spirit grows in strength within us, it will eventually overcome and subdue the spirit of hate and divisiveness in a person's soul.

Amen!

છ છ છ

When Ehud Banai Travels Back in Time

וְזָכַרְתִּי אֶת בְּרִיתִי יַעֲקוֹב וְאַף אֶת בְּרִיתִי יִצְחָק וְאַף אֶת בְּרִיתִי אַבְרָהָם
אֶזְכֹּר וְהָאָרֶץ אֶזְכֹּר.

And I will remember My covenant with Jacob, and also My covenant with Isaac, and also My covenant with Abraham I will **remember; and I will remember the land**.

(Lev. 26:42)

I was once the moderator for a panel discussion with two singer-songwriters, Ariel Horowitz and Ehud Banai. They both talked about our connection to the Land of Israel and how we treat it, which is one of the central motifs of this *parasha*. Ariel is the son of famed singer song-writer Naomi Shemer, who composed *Jerusalem of Gold*. He recalled that he is often asked if he shares the same right-wing political views as his late mother and that he has a standard answer to this question: "We are too obsessed with the width of the land, busy arguing about its borders, and split among ourselves between right- and left-wing. This is a terrible shame because we are so concerned about the width that we have little energy left to discuss its depth, questions of culture, spirit, and substance."

Ehud Banai spoke about the Land of Israel in a similar vein:

> I am very fond of American Blues and of songs that tell the story of a journey. I was always jealous of American musicians who go on never-ending musical tours and write about their experiences on the road from New Orleans to Memphis and on to New York. Here in Israel if you want to write about the long and winding road, your choice would be about the road from Acre to Safed, which is only an hour's drive.
>
> In one of my songs I wrote, "I am taking time again, between Peki'in and Bet Jan," but the whole journey takes six minutes, in traffic, at least according to Waze. Another song talks about "Pardes Hanna and Karkur," which are less than five minutes apart. All I want is space and freedom. I want to get behind the wheel and just travel as far as I can. I always hoped that the day would come when I could drive to the border, cross it and continue on my journey.
>
> My friend Oded Peled lives in Kibbutz Bet HaNassi and translates American poetry into Hebrew. When I shared my frustrations about the lack of distance in this country, he told me that we have something here that the Americans do not. We have a time span going back three or even four thousand years, whereas American history goes back at most two or three hundred years.
>
> His idea gave me a new perspective on our country and I look at it with new meaning. Now I understood why I was attracted to writing songs that talk about our Jewish heritage: "The Golden Calf," "David and Saul," and "City of Refuge." These are topics that send me back to earlier eras and this is my compensation for not having geographical space here. So instead I sing about the time span of this wonderful country.

Numbers

The Hebrew name for the Book of Numbers is *Bemidbar* (In the Wilderness) and the sages ask what the significance is of giving the Torah there and not in Egypt or the Land of Israel. Why was it so important that it be given in an empty and desolate spot? I have gathered a few of our sages' answers. There is no one "correct" answer and they are all interrelated.

- "If a person makes himself like a desert, which is available to all, the Torah is given to him as a gift."
- "The Torah was given in the wilderness, in a place open to all, so that whoever wants to receive it can come and take it."
- "If the Torah had been given to them in the Land of Israel, the tribe in whose territory it had been given would say, 'I am the most important.' Therefore the Torah was given in the wilderness where all are equal."

When a person acts with modesty and humility and gives of himself to others then he can receive the Torah. And not just people. The Torah itself is given in an open space that does not belong to anyone, without power struggles over ownership and borders, so that everyone will feel an equal connection to it.

Let us set out to the wilderness.

Bemidbar

Camping Round

אִישׁ עַל דִּגְלוֹ בְאֹתֹת לְבֵית אֲבֹתָם יַחֲנוּ בְּנֵי יִשְׂרָאֵל מִנֶּגֶד **סָבִיב לְאֹהֶל מוֹעֵד יַחֲנוּ.**

Each man of the Children of Israel by his division with the flag staffs of their fathers' house; **a good way off shall they pitch round the tent of meeting**.

(Num. 2:2)

What did life look like for the Children of Israel in the wilderness? How did this huge population manage their affairs? The *Mishkan*, or Tent of Meeting, stood at the heart of the camp, with three tribes encamped on each of its four sides, totaling twelve tribes. Each tribe had its own banner as a symbol of its particular identity. This is commonly used to demonstrate the pluralism and variety in Judaism, with each group having its own distinct character. This is of course true, but we should be aware that they were all surrounding the same object. Although each tribe is different, they all focus on the same thing.

Rabbi Samson Raphael Hirsch describes the camping of the Children of Israel as follows:

> The tribes camped around the *Mishkan*, which is the mission. Each individual returns to his family, each tribe returns to its

camp, and all these camps encamp and travel precisely around the *Mishkan*, which is an important educational lesson. This is the way to educate individuals, families, and tribes to live with the Torah in the center, uniting the entire nation into one unit. This is the life and soul of the entire people. All of them, from the prince of the camp to the newborn, are all the same distance from the *Mishkan*, which is the center of the joint mission that goes with them, within their sight, wherever they go.

CR CR CR

What's Our Banner?

וַיַּעֲשׂוּ בְּנֵי יִשְׂרָאֵל כְּכֹל אֲשֶׁר צִוָּה ה' אֶת מֹשֶׁה כֵּן חָנוּ לְדִגְלֵיהֶם וְכֵן נָסָעוּ אִישׁ לְמִשְׁפְּחֹתָיו עַל בֵּית אֲבֹתָיו.

And the Children of Israel did all that the Lord had commanded Moses; they encamped by their banners, **and so they journeyed each man with his family, according to his father's house.**

(Num. 2:34)

In *Bemidbar* each tribe is given its own banner and position in the camp, and each one is counted within the crowd. The *Netivot Shalom* expands on this historic event:

Just as each nation and each military corps has a unique banner which denotes its special task, so too each and every individual has his own banner and special task. The worst possible thing is when a person exists in the world without purpose or mission and has no idea what he is living for, for what purpose he was born into the world. The purpose of the banners in the wilderness was to clarify the mission of each person. One tribe bears the banner of Torah, another of labor, another of good deeds, and they come together to form a whole unit. This is a hint to future generations. Each person has his own task and way of life, and there is no one who does not have a banner he belongs to. A person must look after his own banner and not exchange it for issues that are not his task. When a person finds out what his mission in the world is, he has found out the secret of his life.

How are we supposed to discover this secret? How can we find out what our mission and banner are? The *Netivot Shalom* suggests that Shabbat, the day in which we focus more on our inner selves, can help us:

> One of the *zemirot* we sing around the Shabbat table is "Who-ever protects the Shabbat properly from desecration, each in his own camp, each under his own banner." A person is distracted and confused during the six days of the week and does not have the clarity to know what his camp and banner is. Only on the holy Shabbat does he have the peace of mind to be a person of his own camp, under his own banner.

C３ C３ C３

Mom, Dad, Teacher

וְאֵלֶּה תּוֹלְדֹת אַהֲרֹן וּמֹשֶׁה בְּיוֹם דִּבֶּר ה' אֶת מֹשֶׁה בְּהַר סִינָי.

These are the generations of Aaron and Moses on the day that the Lord spoke to Moses at Mount Sinai.

(Num. 3:1)

Rashi asks why the Torah says that these are the generations of Aaron and Moses, when only Aaron's descendants are listed. To answer, he cites the talmudic saying, "Whoever teaches Torah to his friend's son is considered as having given birth to him." Thus, Aaron's sons who were taught Torah by Moses are considered to be like his own sons.

This statement has far-reaching consequences. When you edu-cate a person, you give him life. Of course, no one is suggesting that a teacher can substitute for a parent, and that is why Rashi says "consid-ered as if." Yet, when you add Torah to someone's life, you add vitality, energy, and novelty.

From Rashi's statement we can draw three conclusions: the rabbi, teacher, or even nursery school teacher has the power to help someone be reborn; the student has the capacity to be reborn; and the Torah has the power to make it all happen.

CʒCʒCʒ

Peer Pressure

וְהַחֹנִים לִפְנֵי הַמִּשְׁכָּן קֵדְמָה לִפְנֵי אֹהֶל מוֹעֵד מִזְרָחָה מֹשֶׁה וְאַהֲרֹן וּבָנָיו שֹׁמְרִים מִשְׁמֶרֶת הַמִּקְדָּשׁ לְמִשְׁמֶרֶת בְּנֵי יִשְׂרָאֵל.

Moses, Aaron and his sons, the keepers of the charge of the Sanctuary, camping in front of the Tabernacle, in front of the Tent of Meeting to the east, were as a trust for the Children of Israel.

(Num. 3:38)

Who does not remember their parents telling them to stay away from bad friends? Who has not heard about peer pressure and been told that "he is really a good kid at heart, but his friends…"

The Torah tells us how the tribes were encamped around the *Mishkan* and (as is usually the case) this is no mere technical description. The location of each tribe had a profound influence on its character. Our sages say that the tribes of Judah, Zebulun, and Issachar, who camped near to Moses and Aaron, produced leading Torah scholars, whereas the tribe of Reuben, who camped near the family of Kehat, was negatively influenced to join the rebellion led by Korah, a member of the Kehat family. The sages draw two conclusions from the location of each tribe in the camp: "Woe to an evil person, and woe to his neighbor" and "It is good for the righteous person, and good for his neighbor."

We learn the importance of social and environmental influences from this *parasha*. The people you choose to be your neighbors and friends are the ones you will end up identifying with. They will influence not only you but also your descendants. By choosing your friends, you have the power to decide whether that influence will be positive or negative.

"So if your friends tell you to jump off the Empire State Building, would you do it?" We have all been asked this rhetorical question by our parents during our teenage years when the most important thing for us is to be like all our friends and adopt their values. Psychological studies have shown how peer pressure causes individuals to change their behavior and values, without even realizing it.

Naso

Order!

וְזֹאת מִשְׁמֶרֶת מַשָּׂאָם לְכָל עֲבֹדָתָם בְּאֹהֶל מוֹעֵד קַרְשֵׁי הַמִּשְׁכָּן וּבְרִיחָיו
וְעַמּוּדָיו וַאֲדָנָיו.

This is the charge of their burden for all their service in the Tent
of Meeting: **the planks of the Tabernacle, its bars, its pillars,
and its sockets.**

(Num. 4:31)

Naso tells us of the logistics of journeying in the wilderness. The Torah
relates which tribe was responsible for carrying what, and how the
Mishkan was taken apart when the Children of Israel moved from one
place to the next.

None of this could be achieved without discipline, organization,
and order. If the physical moves are not done in the correct order, and
in collaboration, the content on the inside will be flawed.

Some people think that feeling "spiritual" means going with the
flow, and freeing yourself from any obligations so that you can do what
you want when you feel like it. Others believe that the opposite leads to
spirituality and only when you are live within an orderly framework can
you reach spiritual heights. Rabbi Yeruham Levovitz, one of the great
spiritual leaders in pre-war Europe, who headed the Mir yeshiva, wrote:

Order, which on its own is not important, helps preserve all the good in the world. Order is an important virtue, and is possibly the most important one. When we use order to regulate our spiritual life and help us keep the Torah and its laws then it certainly influences a person to be better. Someone who lives without order is missing the chance for perfection and wholeness.

03 03 03

Every Single Person Counts

עַל פִּי ה' פָּקַד אוֹתָם בְּיַד מֹשֶׁה אִישׁ אִישׁ עַל עֲבֹדָתוֹ וְעַל מַשָּׂאוֹ.

According to the commandment of God they were appointed by Moses, **each man to his service, and to his burden.**

(Num. 4:49)

Rami Levi is a self-made businessman who heads a discount supermarket chain with branches throughout Israel. We met when he spoke at a panel discussion that I moderated at Bar-Ilan University about the importance (or unimportance) of formal education.

"No one had time for me. I dropped out of school at the end of eighth grade because I was dyslexic and I was not accepted to my preferred high school. By the time I was fourteen I was already working full time," he said.

He related that he once went to a wholesale store with his mom. The salesman had no patience for this woman who wanted to buy just a small quantity of goods but to pay wholesale prices and he rudely told her to go to a regular store and not to bother him anymore. At that moment, Rami spotted a great business opportunity. He decided to open a store which would sell to the general public at wholesale, discounted prices. This one store eventually grew to be one of Israel's largest supermarket chains. "I had to work hard because from an early age, I was a nobody. I was never considered to be worth much and was always looked down upon."

It is interesting to note that the Israeli slang for considering someone worthless is *lo sofer oto* (lit. "he does not count him"). *Naso* teaches
us the opposite. We are told to count every single individual in the census
because everyone is valuable. We do not count in bulk, but one by one.
Maimonides writes: "God instructed to give each person the honor of
counting him individually. Do not ask the head of each family how large
his family is, how many children he has. No, each person comes before
you with fear and respect and you count them one by one."

This is one of the most important lessons to be learnt from the
Book of Numbers – from the census long ago to today's dyslexic kid
whose business acumen is waiting to be discovered and counted.

ೞ ೞ ೞ

This Blessing

וְשָׂמוּ אֶת שְׁמִי עַל בְּנֵי יִשְׂרָאֵל וַאֲנִי אֲבָרֲכֵם.

They will bestow My Name upon the Children of Israel, **and I
will bless them.**

(Num. 6:27)

The Priestly Blessings have accompanied the Children of Israel from
the time they were given in the wilderness to the Temple in Jerusalem,
through every synagogue, and to every Jewish home when parents bless
their children on Friday night. The blessings bestow on us God's blessing, protection, radiance, grace, and peace.

In synagogue, when the priests ascend to the ark to say the blessings, they raise their hands up high, as if pointing to and praying for a
faraway place, an ideal world. They raise their hands above their heads
to express yearning and prayer for a complete and perfect future world.

In addition to the messages of hope in the blessings, let us not
forget how the verse continues: "They shall bestow My Name upon
the Children of Israel, and I will bless them." The priests are a conduit,
messengers who convey blessings from God. We must not confuse the

agent with the source. God gives the blessings, "And I will bless them," through the priests.

People tend to look for good luck charms and blessings from various sources to help them. We need to look no further than the words of the Torah, fifteen words in Hebrew that contain wonderful blessings from God via His priests.

CR CR CR

My Unique Fingerprint

וַיַּקְרִיבוּ הַנְּשִׂאִים אֵת חֲנֻכַּת הַמִּזְבֵּחַ בְּיוֹם הִמָּשַׁח אֹתוֹ **וַיַּקְרִיבוּ הַנְּשִׂיאִם אֶת קָרְבָּנָם לִפְנֵי הַמִּזְבֵּחַ.**

And the princes brought the dedication offering on the day that it was anointed, **and the princes brought their offering before the altar.**

(Num. 7:10)

In case we had any doubt that the Torah is not a storybook, *Naso* proves the point. The Torah could have related the dramatic moments when the *Mishkan* was consecrated and given us a sense of the excitement and joy at this momentous event. Yet instead we are given a detailed description of the sacrifices brought by each one of the twelve princes of the tribes of Israel.

When the same verses are repeated twelve times in what seems to be a boring list, the Torah must be sending us a message. People are not robots. The list of sacrifices cannot be compared to a shopping list that is repeated twelve times. Each one of the princes has his own feelings, thoughts, and personal touch which he brings with him when he offers the sacrifices. The list may be the same, but each person's offering is important in its own right.

We all have unique fingerprints. Each one of us is a singular creation, a one-hit wonder. Each one of us also forges his or her own connection to the Torah, a connection that can also be compared to a fingerprint. When you study the Torah, you are bonding with it in your unique way, which no one else can reproduce. You can copy homework from someone else or ask someone else to study on your behalf, but when it comes to your bond with the Torah, no one but you can create your unique connection.

In this *parasha* as well, each prince is a separate individual, each has his own thoughts and feelings about his sacrifices and thus each of the twelve sets is different. It would be pointless for one prince to bring the sacrifices on behalf of all the others. Each has his own role to play, and each adds his unique, individual imprint.

Behaalotekha

The Happy Match

דַּבֵּר אֶל אַהֲרֹן וְאָמַרְתָּ אֵלָיו בְּהַעֲלֹתְךָ אֶת הַנֵּרֹת אֶל מוּל פְּנֵי הַמְּנוֹרָה יָאִירוּ שִׁבְעַת הַנֵּרוֹת.

Speak to Aaron and say to him, "**When you light the lamps**, the seven lamps shall cast their light **toward the face of the Menora**."

(Num. 8:2)

Aaron is commanded to light the lamps in the *Mishkan* and Rashi comments that he was told to light them "until the flame rises by itself." As the commentators explain, he brought the fire near to the wick until the flame burned on its own. There is no need to use force, just let go and allow the flame to burn on its own.

We learn from Aaron an important principle in educating our children and teaching our students. There is no need to stifle your children and/or students if you want to educate them well. It is sufficient to inspire them, and to light the flame in their hearts to excite them. Stay close but know that sometimes you need to step back and let the flame rise by itself.

ೞ ೞ ೞ

213

Think Inside the Box

וַיַּעַשׂ כֵּן אַהֲרֹן אֶל מוּל פְּנֵי הַמְּנוֹרָה הֶעֱלָה נֵרֹתֶיהָ כַּאֲשֶׁר צִוָּה ה' אֶת מֹשֶׁה.

And Aaron did so; he lit the lamps toward the face of the Menora, as the Lord had commanded Moses.

(Num. 8:3)

Many of the events I attend are "out of the ordinary," or have an "alternative" format, or so the producers tell me. At the end of a lecture I gave to a group of IDF soldiers, one of them told me, "All our lecturers tell us to think outside the box. This dogma has almost become a compulsory statement."

While the wish to renew ideas is indeed a positive one, the Torah gives us a timely reminder of the other side of the equation. After the command to light the Menora, the Torah emphasizes that Aaron did indeed fulfill the task given to him, "And Aaron did so," and Rashi elaborates that the Torah tells us that, "in order to praise Aaron that he did not deviate." He did not do more or less than what he was commanded, he did not look for new or different ways to fulfill the commandment, and he did not suggest an alternative meaning or a new format for lighting the Menora. It is not as simple as it sounds to do something exactly as you are told to.

"The King of Israeli Rock," as Shalom Hanoch is known, sings, "It is not easy to be simple, you always want more." Two hundred years earlier, Rabbi Nahman of Breslov wrote a sentence that I find absolutely amazing: "The time will come when being an upright and simple person will be as revolutionary as being the Baal Shem Tov."

Have we already come to the point when everything is so confusing and challenging that the person who is not constantly reinventing things and thinking out of the box is in fact the biggest novelty of them all?

෮ ෮ ෮

Hope

וַיְהִי אֲנָשִׁים אֲשֶׁר הָיוּ טְמֵאִים לְנֶפֶשׁ אָדָם וְלֹא יָכְלוּ לַעֲשֹׂת הַפֶּסַח בַּיּוֹם
הַהוּא וַיִּקְרְבוּ לִפְנֵי מֹשֶׁה וְלִפְנֵי אַהֲרֹן בַּיּוֹם הַהוּא.

**But there were certain men, who were ritually unclean from
the dead body of a man,** so that they could not keep the Passover
on that day; and they approached Moses and Aaron on that day.
(Num. 9:6)

A group of people come to Moses with a strange request. They had
become impure and so were unable to take part in the Passover festivities with the Pascal lamb. They ask him, "Why should we be excluded"
and not be allowed to celebrate? Moses asks God and is given a surprising answer: Whoever is impure during Passover, or whoever lives far
away and did not get to the Temple in Jerusalem on time, will be given
a second chance on the "Second Passover" on the fourteenth day of Iyar,
exactly one month after the day of the Exodus from Egypt.

Our rabbis learn from this that there is always a second chance,
that we are always able to repair previous actions. Everyone has hope, no
matter what happened in the past, no matter how many missed opportunities they had. One of Rabbi Nahman's most famous sayings is "There
is no despair in the world at all." It is worth reading his entire statement:

> He taught us the way of repentance, because there is no despair
> in the world at all. Even if the appropriate time of restoration has
> passed and we have become impure because of our actions, there
> is still hope. Even if not at its proper time, wonderful and hidden
> ways of restoration exist, which can help us even now, and every
> day. The most important thing is not to give up on crying out to
> God and praying to Him.

In the words of *HaTikva*, Israel's national anthem, "Our hope is not yet lost."

CB CB CB

What Can the Wandering Teach Us?

עַל פִּי ה' יַחֲנוּ וְעַל פִּי ה' יִסָּעוּ אֶת מִשְׁמֶרֶת ה' שָׁמָרוּ עַל פִּי ה' בְּיַד
מֹשֶׁה.

At the Lord's bidding they would encamp, and at the Lord's bidding they would travel; they kept the charge of the Lord by the word of the Lord through Moses.

(Num. 9:23)

Each time the Children of Israel travel from one place to the next in the wilderness, the move is described by the words, "At God's bidding they would encamp, and at God's bidding they would travel." Their journey echoes that of IDF soldiers in basic training, who are given orders without advance notice, and who never know what is coming next. The Children of Israel did not know in advance how long they would stay at each camp, yet whenever they stopped, the first thing they would do is to set up the *Mishkan* so that the order of services and sacrifices would continue on as normal. They did not know that some stops would be for a short time only, while others would last many years, but at all times they ensured that the most important aspect of their lives, the *Mishkan*, ran smoothly. We can learn several lessons from this and apply them to our own lives.

First, we are not really the ones who plan and control our lives, and things happen that we did not plan or ask for. We have to face this fact of life and internalize that we must expect the unexpected.

Second, we do not need to put our lives on hold whenever we find ourselves temporarily moving from place to place. We should not wait until we reach our destination, until we enter the Land of Israel. We have to learn to live every moment to the fullest, even when we are still on the journey. There is no point in waiting until we reach our final destination, because we really have no idea how long each stage of the journey will last.

Life does not begin when we finish our studies, or our army service, or when we find a new job or begin a family. Life is right now, this very moment.

ೞ ೞ ೞ

The Power of Music

עֲשֵׂה לְךָ שְׁתֵּי חֲצוֹצְרֹת כֶּסֶף מִקְשָׁה תַּעֲשֶׂה אֹתָם וְהָיוּ לְךָ לְמִקְרָא הָעֵדָה וּלְמַסַּע אֶת הַמַּחֲנוֹת.

Make for yourself two silver trumpets; you shall make them from a beaten form; they shall be used by you to summon the congregation and to announce the departure of the camps.

(Num. 10:2)

When the words cease and the music begins, everything changes. The world of music is higher than the world of speech, and the Torah tells us to go up a notch every so often and let the music take over. Moses is instructed to prepare two silver trumpets and blow them on certain occasions, such as when he wants to assemble the entire nation, when they are forced to go to war, or for happier events and offering sacrifices during the festivals.

The *Sefer HaHinukh* explains the reasons for this special commandment of blowing the trumpets. Although the explanation was written seven hundred years ago, its message is still relevant today.

> Given a person's physical nature, one needs great awakening to do things, and there is nothing that will awaken more than the sound of music, especially the sound of the trumpets, the greatest sound of any musical instrument. There is another advantage of the sound of the trumpet, in addition to the fact that it awakens a person to act. The sound of the music also brings a person to remove thoughts of all other matters from his heart, so that he can focus only on the sacrifice. Why should I speak at length about this sound? Anyone who has listened to the sound of the shofar with concentration will understand my point.

The author of *Sefer HaHinukh* explains that we are awakened when we hear a musical tune and our thoughts and concerns are washed away. He added that he has no need for lengthy explanations; anyone who has ever listened to the shofar blowing will understand what he means.

Shelah

Intellectual Independence

וַיַּעֲלוּ בַנֶּגֶב וַיָּבֹא עַד חֶבְרוֹן.

And they went up in the south, **and came to Hebron.**

(Num. 13:22)

The Torah describes twelve spies entering the Land of Israel, and only one of them, Caleb the son of Yefuneh, went to Hebron to visit the Cave of Machpela. Rashi adds that "he was the only one who went to prostrate himself at the graves of the Patriarchs to pray that he would not be enticed by his colleagues to be part of their incitement." Caleb went to pray at the graves of the Patriarchs and Matriarchs to ask for clarity of vision, that he would have the strength to withstand the influence of his fellow spies and not be influenced by their negative peer pressure, and that he would retain his faith and optimism. And so only Joshua and Caleb, out of all twelve spies, avoided being swept up in the tide. They returned from their mission with a positive message.

The Torah is giving us a revolutionary message in this *parasha*. Going to the graves of the righteous is meant to stimulate within us intellectual and spiritual independence, so that we can gain imagination and inspiration. We should not be drawn after popular fads, but

maintain a clean (and inspired!) conscience by "prostrating yourself at
the graves of holy people."

⊂ઝ ⊂ઝ ⊂ઝ

Fake News

וַיּוֹצִיאוּ דִּבַּת הָאָרֶץ אֲשֶׁר תָּרוּ אֹתָהּ אֶל בְּנֵי יִשְׂרָאֵל לֵאמֹר הָאָרֶץ אֲשֶׁר
עָבַרְנוּ בָהּ לָתוּר אֹתָהּ אֶרֶץ אֹכֶלֶת יוֹשְׁבֶיהָ הִוא וְכָל הָעָם אֲשֶׁר רָאִינוּ
בְתוֹכָהּ אַנְשֵׁי מִדּוֹת.

**And they spread an evil report about the land which they
had scouted**, telling the Children of Israel, "The land we passed
through to explore is a land that consumes its inhabitants, and
all the people we saw in it are men of great height."

(Num. 13:32)

What is the media's job? To provide facts or opinions? Does the media
only tell us what actually happened or does it also decide for us who is
an extremist and who is a moderate? Who represents the mainstream
and who is sectorial? Who is "one of us" and who is an outsider?

Twelve spies are sent to the Land of Israel from the wilderness in
order to scout out the land. Ten of them return with a harsh and negative report, sowing despair in the hearts of the people by telling them
that it is not a good idea to continue their journey to the Land of Israel
as it is a country that "consumes its inhabitants." As a punishment for
the historical sin of the spies, the Children of Israel were told that they
would wander in the wilderness for forty years, one year for each day
that the spies were in the Land of Israel.

Why was their sin considered so devastating? After all, they simply shared their feelings with the people. But that's just the point. They
did not distinguish between the facts and their personal feelings. They
presented their opinions as fact, and thus took on the role of advisors
instead of simply being reporters. Their charge had been to bring back
information but they returned to tell not only the dry facts but also their
personal interpretation of what they saw. The people heard the spies

and reacted with bitterness and frustration, losing their motivation to continue on the journey to the Land of Israel.

What a relevant lesson for us today! When we watch a news program or read an article, we must use our critical thinking skills. Are we simply being given information or is the program or article trying to educate us? We must ask ourselves if we are interested in this educational influence.

The spies did not succeed in brainwashing the Children of Israel with their opinions. Thousands of years later, we read *Shelah*, in the land which they had recommended avoiding because there was no chance we would reach it and be able to live there.

೫ ೫ ೫

Extremism Is Not the Solution

וַיַּשְׁכִּמוּ בַבֹּקֶר וַיַּעֲלוּ אֶל רֹאשׁ הָהָר לֵאמֹר הִנֶּנּוּ וְעָלִינוּ אֶל הַמָּקוֹם אֲשֶׁר אָמַר ה' כִּי חָטָאנוּ.

They arose early in the morning and ascended to the mountain top, saying, "We will go up to the place of which the Lord spoke, for we have sinned."

(Num. 14:40)

Shelah is more than just the sin of the spies, which takes up the lion's share of the *parasha*. There is also the little-mentioned incident of the *maapilim*. In modern-day Israel, this word has a very positive connotation and is used to describe the illegal immigrants who resisted the British Mandate that had severely curtailed Jewish immigration and managed to reach Palestine. However, in its original form in the Torah, the word *maapilim* has a very negative connotation.

Immediately after the long and detailed description about the spies and their lack of belief or desire to go to the Land of Israel, the Torah relates, in seven verses, what followed after the sin and punishment. A group of people feel that they want to right the wrong and go to the Land of Israel. Immediately. They want to run ahead, as if to prove that the sin is a thing of the past. They are going to the Land of Israel to demonstrate that they are prepared for the challenge. Moses warns them that this is not the right way to rectify the sin and, indeed, they are killed in the battle against Amalek.

What can we learn from this incident for our lives? If we have made a mistake, the right way to correct it is not necessarily by going to the opposite extreme. Most of the spies were paralyzed by fear, but showing exaggerated self-confidence in knowing what is the right thing to do will not correct the wrong. Life is more complicated than that.

ೞ ೞ ೞ

Do Not Wander

וְהָיָה לָכֶם לְצִיצִת וּרְאִיתֶם אֹתוֹ וּזְכַרְתֶּם אֶת כָּל מִצְוֹת ה' וַעֲשִׂיתֶם אֹתָם
וְלֹא תָתוּרוּ אַחֲרֵי לְבַבְכֶם וְאַחֲרֵי עֵינֵיכֶם.

This shall be fringes for you, and when you see it, you will remember all the commandments of the Lord to perform them, and **you shall not wander after your hearts and after your eyes.**

(Num. 15:39)

The most common verb used in the story of Moses sending the spies to the Land of Israel is "*latur* – to spy": "And Moses sent them to spy out the land of Canaan," "And they went up, and spied out the land," "And they returned from spying out the land." The spies returned with a negative interpretation of what they had seen, so their mission failed and ended tragically. The Children of Israel were doomed to wander in the wilderness for forty years and entry into the Land of Israel was deferred while they underwent a process of education to ensure that they were worthy of entering the Promised Land.

The *parasha* continues with the commandment to wear tzitzit, the ritual fringes, and the verb *latur* appears again, in the sense of "to wander": "And it shall be to you for fringes, and when you see it, you will remember all the commandments of the Lord to perform them, and you shall not wander after your hearts and after your eyes." By using the same verb, the Torah is telling us that tzitzit is the corrective to the failure of the spies. Man is commanded to place the tzitzit on his clothes as a concrete reminder not to wander. The spies went to the Land of Israel as tourists (*tayar*), and even today tourists look upon sites with a critical eye. We are meant to come to the Land of Israel to live there with a sense of purpose and belonging, not as tourists.

The tzitzit are meant to be a sign that will help us recall all the other commandments, and to be a constant reminder not to get confused or carried away by all that our eyes see. The tzitzit enable us to focus on the idea that something bigger is above us, "and when you see it…you will remember…and you will not wander."

Korah

The Dangers of Boredom

וַיִּקַּח קֹרַח בֶּן יִצְהָר בֶּן קְהָת בֶּן לֵוִי וְדָתָן וַאֲבִירָם בְּנֵי אֱלִיאָב וְאוֹן בֶּן פֶּלֶת בְּנֵי רְאוּבֵן.

And Korah, the son of Yitzhar, the son of Kehat, the son of Levi, with Datan and Aviram, the sons of Eliab, and On, the son of Pelet, sons of Reuben, took men.

(Num. 16:1)

What happens during the long summer vacation, when the end seems so far away? Some fifty years ago, Rabbi Benzion Firer wrote an essay entitled "The Danger of Doing Nothing" ("*HaSakana SheBeHoser Maas*"), in which he analyzed Korah's character and said that when a person has no goal or task or direction in life, he begins to be concerned about himself, his honor, his status, and his ego.

When did Korah start his rebellion against Moses? After the sin of the spies, when the Children of Israel were punished with having to wait forty years in the wilderness. They now had plenty of spare time on their hands, and Korah seized the opportunity to stir them up into a frenzy of dangerous arguments. Rabbi Firer elaborates:

> When a nation is busy planning the capture of its homeland, it has no time for arguments and divisions. The overriding goal unites

all sectors of the population and prevents them from becoming involved with trifling matters or abandoning the main idea. Even if one person becomes obsessed by insignificant details of misplaced honor or other personal issues, he will find that he has no followers. However, after the sin of the spies, the Children of Israel are not busy with anything and they have time to waste. A person with too much spare time must find something to do with himself. When you have nothing to look forward to, you begin to make trouble.

CB CB CB

Holiness Isn't Automatic

וַיִּקָּהֲלוּ עַל מֹשֶׁה וְעַל אַהֲרֹן וַיֹּאמְרוּ אֲלֵהֶם רַב לָכֶם כִּי כָל הָעֵדָה כֻּלָּם **קְדֹשִׁים** וּבְתוֹכָם ה' וּמַדּוּעַ תִּתְנַשְּׂאוּ עַל קְהַל ה'.

And they assembled against Moses and Aaron, and said to them, "You take too much upon yourselves, **for the entire congregation are all holy**, and the Lord is in their midst. So why do you raise yourselves above the Lord's assembly?"

(Num. 16:3)

The argument between Korah and Moses is the clash between two opposing outlooks on life. The Children of Israel have barely recovered from the spies and now a new argument threatens to tear them apart. This new attack on Moses' leadership comes from a different angle.

The two different outlooks can be summarized in their address to the people. Korah questions why only Moses and Aaron have been singled out as leaders and he attacks them by saying, "The entire congregation are all holy." Contrast this with a similar sounding, but fundamentally different, command. Moses tells them: "You shall be holy."

Korah's claim sounds logical. He says that we are all equal, all holy, all the same, and we all deserve to have the same. As Korah demands justice in the realm of holiness, his assertion is reminiscent of the 2011 social protests in Israel, which demanded equality and social justice.

He says that holiness already exists among all the people, and therefore speaks in the present tense. This claim sounds great but is, in fact, a populist shallow claim without any factual basis.

Moses has a different approach. He does not flatter the people with empty slogans. He makes demands of them and sets a goal for them to aspire to: "You shall be holy." He speaks in the imperative, not promising everyone sanctity but charging them to pursue it. We must work hard in order to make progress. Are we all holy? We all have the potential to achieve that status, but we have to work at it.

These two opposing approaches are at the heart of the *parasha*, and extend far beyond. Moses confronts the people who say that they are already perfect and do not need to work on improving themselves. He reminds them, and us, that when we received the Torah at Mount Sinai, we did not automatically become holy; instead, we received the option of introducing holiness into our lives.

ᏯᏯᏯ

Truth in Advertising

הַמְעַט כִּי הֶעֱלִיתָנוּ מֵאֶרֶץ זָבַת חָלָב וּדְבַשׁ לַהֲמִיתֵנוּ בַּמִּדְבָּר כִּי תִשְׂתָּרֵר
עָלֵינוּ גַּם הִשְׂתָּרֵר.

Is it not enough that you have brought us **out of a land flowing with milk and honey** to kill us in the desert, that you should also exercise authority over us?

(Num. 16:13)

Anything goes. If you tell a lie, but package it nicely, it will sell. For example, a manufacturer takes water, corn syrup, caramel food coloring, caffeine, artificial flavoring, and phosphoric acid and sells this unhealthy black beverage throughout the world with the slogan "Life Tastes Good." Taste? Life? The very opposite is true!

We are constantly bombarded with ads and reports that simply turn bad into good, wrong into right. In the Talmud, this confusing reality is called "an upside-down world."

Datan and Aviram, Korah's partners, use these same tricks and hurl an unbelievable accusation at Moses: "Is it not enough that you have brought us out of a land flowing with milk and honey to kill us in the desert, that you should also exercise authority over us?" The expression "a land flowing with milk and honey" is generally synonymous with the Land of Israel. In their crafty and cunning manner, Datan and Aviram dared to take this slogan and use it to describe Egypt. Yes, Egypt, the very same country in which infants were thrown into the Nile River, which enslaved Israel and embittered their lives, is suddenly seen in a positive light, and fondly recalled as "a land flowing with milk and honey"! And some people even buy the argument.

CR CR CR

Humility and the Apple

וַיֹּאמֶר מֹשֶׁה בְּזֹאת תֵּדְעוּן כִּי ה׳ שְׁלָחַנִי לַעֲשׂוֹת אֵת כָּל הַמַּעֲשִׂים הָאֵלֶּה כִּי לֹא מִלִּבִּי.

And Moses said, "With this you shall know that **the Lord sent me to do all these deeds,** for I did not do them of my own mind." (Num. 16:28)

In the summer of 2010, during the week in which *Parashat Korah* is read, Rabbi Mordechai Eliyahu, the former Sephardi chief rabbi, spiritual leader, and halakhic authority passed away. I heard the following story from a teenager who witnessed Rabbi Eliyahu's special nature firsthand:

One morning I went with my high-school class to join Rabbi Eliyahu during the Shaharit prayers and when he finished we accompanied him back to his home. We were told to move along so as not to hold up the rabbi, who had another engagement to go to. From afar, a strange looking man called to get Rabbi Eliyahu's attention. The bodyguards tried to keep him away but Rabbi Eliyahu stopped and faced the man. In an earnest voice, the man said, "Honored Rabbi, what is the blessing for an apple?" We were all so embarrassed: How can you ask one of the leading rabbis of the generation such a simple question? It was an insult to his greatness!

However, Rabbi Eliyahu did not laugh at him. He stopped, pretended to think deeply about the question, and replied: "You asked a really important question and in order to give you a full answer, I would have to know whether you are talking about a solid, raw apple, in which case you would say the regular blessing for fruit. But if it was apple juice then a different blessing would be in order. If the apple was cooked and puréed then you would have to say another blessing. I suggest that you come to my yeshiva someday so that we can discuss this difficult matter at length."...

The man was very moved by the time and attention Rabbi Eliyahu gave to him, demonstrating that he was worth something. All those who saw this spectacle, who just a few minutes earlier were laughing at the neighborhood weirdo, had received an important lesson in life.

Since his passing, I have heard many stories about Rabbi Eliyahu's greatness and the wondrous deeds he did to help people in need. I find it particularly apt that the rabbi passed away in the week we learn that leadership and holiness are the antithesis of pride and arrogance. This particular story sticks in my mind because it shows how he cared for every single Jew, every question, and every apple.

೮೮ ೮೮ ೮೮

Mixing Business with Pleasure

וְאַתָּה וּבָנֶיךָ אִתְּךָ תִּשְׁמְרוּ אֶת כְּהֻנַּתְכֶם לְכָל דְּבַר הַמִּזְבֵּחַ וּלְמִבֵּית לַפָּרֹכֶת **וַעֲבַדְתֶּם עֲבֹדַת מַתָּנָה אֶתֵּן אֶת כְּהֻנַּתְכֶם.**

And you and your sons shall keep your priesthood in all matters concerning the Altar, and concerning what is within the Veil, and you shall serve; I give you the priesthood as **a service of gift**. (Num. 18:7)

This verse contains a strange expression, "a work of gift," which in this context applies to the work performed by the priests in the *Mishkan*. However, our sages view each person as a potential leader and public figure, as if one is a high priest in one's place of work. Therefore "a work of gift" is applicable to any one of us.

The combination of the two words seems to be an oxymoron. After all, work is an obligation and a hassle, whereas we receive a gift without making any effort. Our aim in life should be to reach a state of "a work of gift" in which obligations are also a privilege. We should work hard and strive to achieve something, but at the same time, we should feel that we have received a worthy gift, that we have been privileged to be a part of it.

I once heard an interesting explanation about how Judaism views "a work of gift." On the one hand, we are definitely expected to work hard to fulfill our obligations, but at the same time we have the merit to be in contact with The Boss of the world on a daily basis.

Hukkat

Philosophy and the Red Heifer

זֹאת חֻקַּת הַתּוֹרָה אֲשֶׁר צִוָּה ה' לֵאמֹר דַּבֵּר אֶל בְּנֵי יִשְׂרָאֵל וְיִקְחוּ אֵלֶיךָ
פָרָה אֲדֻמָּה תְּמִימָה אֲשֶׁר אֵין בָּהּ מוּם אֲשֶׁר לֹא עָלָה עָלֶיהָ עֹל.

This is the statute of the Torah which the Lord commanded, saying, "Speak to the Children of Israel and **they shall bring to You a
perfectly red unblemished heifer**, upon which no yoke was laid."
(Num. 19:2)

The opening commandment of this *parasha* to bring an unblemished red
heifer in order to purify an impure person is a mystery. The introduction
to this commandment tells us that this is a "statute" or *hok*, one that has
no reason. Unlike other logical and understandable ones, we are told that
this commandment is beyond reason and we should not search for any.

For generations, our sages and philosophers have discussed
the reasons for the commandments, both the obvious and the hidden
meanings, in a determined effort to understand them. Some questioned
whether human beings should even try to understand everything.

Maimonides writes: "It is appropriate for a person to meditate
on the judgments of the holy Torah and know their ultimate purpose
according to his capacity. If he cannot find a reason or a motivating rationale for a practice, he should not regard it lightly. Nor should he break
through to ascend to God, lest God burst forth against him."

Yes, we are given a challenge to learn as much as we possibly can, to search deeply for reasons, and to try and fathom the difficult-to-understand statutes, but we have to know when to stop. We are specifically warned not to belittle the value of those commandments that we cannot explain to ourselves: "He should not regard it lightly."

Some things will always remain hidden, and we will never understand them.

CB CB CB

What Is a Babysitter's Payment?

וַיָּבֹאוּ בְנֵי יִשְׂרָאֵל כָּל הָעֵדָה מִדְבַּר צִן בַּחֹדֶשׁ הָרִאשׁוֹן וַיֵּשֶׁב הָעָם בְּקָדֵשׁ וַתָּמָת שָׁם מִרְיָם וַתִּקָּבֵר שָׁם.

And the entire congregation of the Children of Israel arrived at the desert of Zin in the first month, and the people settled in Kadesh. **And Miriam died there and was buried there.**

(Num. 20:1)

You may at times ask an older child to look after a younger sibling for just a few minutes, and you certainly remember your parents asking you to do the same when you were young. Rabbi Avigdor Nebenzahl discusses this issue in an article he wrote entitled "The Reward for Looking After a Younger Brother" (*"Sekhar HaHashgaha al Ah Katan"*).

In this *parasha* we learn of the death of Moses and Aaron's sister, Miriam the Prophetess, who was one of the leaders of the Exodus from Egypt. She features prominently in two incidents in the Torah: first when she watches over the infant Moses in his crib on the Nile River, and second when she suffers from *tzaraat* after she speaks *lashon hara*. The Children of Israel then wait seven days for her until she returns to the camp, "And the people did not travel until Miriam was brought in again." In trying to discern why Miriam merited this great honor of the entire nation waiting for her, our sages make the connection between these two events and say that "Miriam waited one hour for Moses; therefore the people waited seven days for her in the wilderness."

As a young six-year-old girl, Miriam looked after her infant brother at a time when it was dangerous to be a Jewish child in Egypt. According to some commentators, she had only looked after him for fifteen minutes (!) before Pharaoh's daughter found Moses and drew him out of the water. Her reward for those fifteen minutes was that an entire nation, including her brother Moses and the *Mishkan* with its vessels, waited an entire week for her. Is it conceivable that because a young girl listened to her mother and agreed to look after her baby brother for fifteen minutes she would merit such a wonderful reward many years later?

Rabbi Nebenzahl answers with an emphatic "Yes":

> Every minute of helping others and doing good deeds is counted. The reward for a young girl's good deed to her brother is beyond any proportion to the time involved. This teaches us the tremendous influence of our deeds. A small action that we do has the potential to change the world. We do not know how it is recorded in heaven, but we should be aware that even seemingly insignificant acts such as smiling at a passerby, or welcoming a new resident to the neighborhood, are all recorded and are important. When we learn to realize that every single good deed we do becomes headline news above, we will acquire the power to take control over our own lives and not be swept along with the tide.

CB CB CB

Leading with Love

וַיָּרֶם מֹשֶׁה אֶת יָדוֹ וַיַּךְ אֶת הַסֶּלַע בְּמַטֵּהוּ פַּעֲמָיִם וַיֵּצְאוּ מַיִם רַבִּים וַתֵּשְׁתְּ הָעֵדָה וּבְעִירָם.

And Moses raised his hand **and struck the rock with his staff twice, and an abundance of water gushed forth**, and the congregation drank as did their livestock.

(Num. 20:11)

For thousands of years our commentators have been trying to understand what the big deal was here. Does it really matter how the water came out of the rock? So what if he hit the rock instead of talking to it, the main thing was that water gushed forth! For hitting instead of talking he was punished and told he would not enter the Land of Israel? Why was this mistake so fundamental that it caused such a harsh reaction? It seems that this incident is meant to teach us something important about leadership, the people, and the entry into the Land of Israel. Also, it seems that the water is a metaphor for the Torah.

Rabbi Eliyahu Blumenzweig, the head of the hesder yeshiva in Yeruham, explains the allegory. In life a person often comes up against a "rock," a wall that blocks your way and does not let you by. What do you do? You can hit it, but if you really want to get through to the inner strengths, to allow the water stored in the rock to flow out, then you have to speak. Your task is to speak, to explain, to convince, and to forge a connection. This is a more mature style of leadership. The Jewish people are about to enter the Land of Israel. The way to lead them is about to change and hitting is no longer of any avail. We can apply the same principle in our lives. The best way to lead is through education and explanation. We may see a stumbling block ahead of us, but living water stands right behind it. The way to access it is by using the correct language, not by hitting.

೮೮ ೮೮ ೮೮

Staying on Track

נַעְבְּרָה נָּא בְאַרְצֶךָ לֹא נַעֲבֹר בְּשָׂדֶה וּבְכֶרֶם וְלֹא נִשְׁתֶּה מֵי בְאֵר דֶּרֶךְ הַמֶּלֶךְ נֵלֵךְ לֹא נִטֶּה יָמִין וּשְׂמֹאול עַד אֲשֶׁר נַעֲבֹר גְּבוּלֶךָ.

Please let us pass through your land; we will not pass through fields or vineyards, nor will we drink well water. We will walk along **the king's highway, and we will turn neither to the right nor to the left** until we have passed your border.

(Num. 20:17)

The Jewish nation requests international backing and assistance and is rebuffed. Moses asks the king of Edom for permission to pass through his land on the way to the Land of Israel. He addresses him in a colloquial manner – "So says your brother Israel" – and promises that his people will not cause any damage to Edomite property. But it is to no avail. The king refuses to give permission and so the Children of Israel have to take a lengthy detour.

The hasidic masters understand this verse on a completely different level: "Please let us pass through your land; we will not pass through fields or vineyards, nor will we drink well water. We will walk along the king's highway, and we will turn neither to the right nor to the left until we have passed your border."

When the soul descends from heaven and enters the physical world in a person's body, it is given the following message: We are now descending into the physical world, but we do not want to settle down and allow it to become our master. We know that it is necessary to eat, drink, and work hard, but we will try not to get distracted by the temptations on the side of the road. We will try to stay on "the straight and narrow," on the king's highway, and remain faithful to the original task we have been given in the body, until we reach our final goal.

08 08 08

Elie Wiesel's *Havruta*

אָז יָשִׁיר יִשְׂרָאֵל אֶת הַשִּׁירָה הַזֹּאת.

Then Israel sang **this song**.
(Num. 21:17)

Elie Wiesel died in July 2016 during the week that we read *Hukkat*. In their eulogies, Barak Obama called him "the conscience of the world," and Bill Clinton said he was "a monument to memory." I was never privileged to meet him in person, but a few years ago, I saw him from afar at the

Western Wall, along with the thousands of people who throng the plaza and surrounding areas on Shavuot night. He was wrapped in his tallit, standing in prayer next to Rabbi Aharon Bina, the head of the Yeshivat Netiv Aryeh in the Old City. I admit I was surprised to see Elie Wiesel there; I had always imagined him in formal attire, wearing tux and tails, and hobnobbing with world leaders, addressing the United Nations or some other exclusive event. I did not expect to see him huddled together with the masses at the Kotel. On the day that Wiesel was buried in New York, I contacted Rabbi Bina in Jerusalem who gave me insight into an unknown part of the life of the famous Holocaust survivor, author, and Nobel Peace Prize laureate:

> Every Shavuot night, for eighteen consecutive years, Elie Wiesel learned Torah in my house. Ira Rennert, a New York businessman, introduced us, and the three of us would learn together throughout the night and in the morning we would go to the Kotel. Elie really knew how to learn, to ask difficult questions and give good answers. We would spend half the night arguing; when he criticized people's behavior, I would tell him "to stay off the Jews and concentrate on Judaism." We learned the *Minhat Hinukh*, a book that deals with all 613 commandments in the Torah. Each year we would focus on several commandments and I believe we got to study about thirty-five in total.
>
> Two years ago he was already a sick person, but he would not give up his annual custom. During the meal, the *zemirot* he sang were those he remembered from his father, a Vizhnitz Hasid. We were able to learn together for "only" an hour and a half before he felt weak and had to rest. However, a few hours later he was strong enough to go to the Kotel to pray. As usual, he requested to read the *haftara* after the Torah reading.
>
> Elie Wiesel often asked difficult questions about faith in God. I felt that here of all the places in the world, as he stood at the Kotel, in Jerusalem, the capital of the State of Israel, his memories from Auschwitz would return to haunt him. Yet he considered it vital to continue his Jewish heritage, so that the

chain should not be broken and that Judaism would continue. He wanted to continue the song of life, the song of the Torah. I always told him, "Reb Elie, if we should ever think that we understand exactly what God does, either we are crazy or we think that we are God Himself."

Balak

Love, Hate, and Donkeys

וַיָּקָם בִּלְעָם בַּבֹּקֶר וַיַּחֲבֹשׁ אֶת אֲתֹנוֹ וַיֵּלֶךְ עִם שָׂרֵי מוֹאָב.

And Balaam rose up in the morning, and **saddled his donkey**, and went with the princes of Moab.

(Num. 22:21)

As Balaam sets off to curse the Jewish nation, the Torah adds a small detail: "And Balaam rose up in the morning, and saddled his donkey." He got up early to do the job himself. Rashi comments that this teaches us that "hate distorts the normal order of things as he saddled it himself." Balaam was an important person and he surely had servants to help him, but he chose to saddle the donkey himself so that he could set off as early as possible to curse the Jews. When a person is driven by hate, the rules of the game change.

Our sages note the difference and similarity with another instance involving a donkey: "And Abraham arose early in the morning, and he saddled his donkey." Abraham also got up early and ran to prepare his donkey. In this case, Rashi comments that "love distorts the normal order of things."

Hate and love. They both goad us into action, motivate us to act quickly and personally undertake the job to ensure it gets done properly and quickly. Our task is to investigate what causes us to spring into action.

CR CR CR

A Curse, a Blessing, or a Challenge?

כִּי מֵרֹאשׁ צֻרִים אֶרְאֶנּוּ וּמִגְּבָעוֹת אֲשׁוּרֶנּוּ הֶן עָם לְבָדָד יִשְׁכֹּן וּבַגּוֹיִם לֹא יִתְחַשָּׁב.

For from the top of the rocks I see it, and from the hills I behold it, **it is a nation that will dwell alone, and will not be reckoned among the nations.**

(Num. 23:9)

Balaam stands opposite the Children of Israel and utters a proclamation that has echoed throughout the world ever since: "It is a nation that will dwell alone, and will not be reckoned among the nations." Did Balaam bless or curse the Jewish people? Have we been doomed ever since to be isolated among the nations and subject to constant anti-Semitism? Or have we been blessed with an eternal uniqueness setting us apart from all the other nations of the world?

The greatest Jewish minds have grappled with the question of the boundaries between the Jewish nation and all the other nations of the world. Do we choose insularity or openness? Racism? Spiritual independence? Survival or assimilation? It is neither blessing nor curse, nor an eternal promise. It is a challenge. This is the view of Rabbi Naphtali Zvi Yehuda Berlin of Volozhin, known by the acronym of his name, the Netziv. He explains the challenge as follows:

> "It is a people alone" – If the people preserve their own culture and heritage,
> "It will dwell" – it will survive.

"Among the nations" – If it tries to imitate the nations and assimi-
late among them, thus forgetting its task in the world,
"It will not be reckoned" – the nations will not take the Jews into
account, they will simply ignore them.

 War War War

Everyday Heroism

הֶן עָם כְּלָבִיא יָקוּם וְכַאֲרִי יִתְנַשָּׂא לֹא יִשְׁכַּב עַד יֹאכַל טֶרֶף וְדַם חֲלָלִים
יִשְׁתֶּה.

**Behold, a people that rises like a lioness and lifts itself up like
a lion.** He does not lie down until he eats its prey and drinks the
blood of the slain.

(Num. 23:24)

Balaam testifies that we are "a people that rises like a lioness and lifts
itself up like a lion." The imagery of military heroism is clear: we are a
nation that rises up and fights its enemies until victory.

This well-known verse gained a special significance after the Holocaust. *Balak* is the bar mitzva *parasha* of the late Naphtali Lau-Lavie, which
he read in his home town of Piotrkow, Poland, before the War. He took
the words "a people that rises like a lioness" as his motto in life. With this
phrase he survived the Holocaust, saved the life of his younger brother
(former Chief Rabbi Yisrael Meir Lau), made *aliya* to Israel, and was part
of the generation that established the State of Israel. He also titled his
Hebrew autobiography "A Nation as Strong as a Lioness" (published as
Balaam's Prophecy in English) which became a best-seller.

How are we to apply this verse in our lives, in a generation that is not
living through life-altering historical events? Drinking a cup of coffee is not
exactly a heroic way to start the day. So how do we "rise up like a lioness"?
Rashi provides an answer: "When they wake up in the morning, they demonstrate the vigor of a lion in grabbing mitzvot. They put on tzitzit, recite
the *Shema*, and don their tefillin." These small actions by the individual

also have value. It is important to get up in the morning with vigor. Our day-to-day schedule is sometimes like a battlefield and at times we require the heroism of a lion to get through it and do what we are supposed to.

CR CR CR

Repeating the Good Words

וַיַּרְא בִּלְעָם כִּי טוֹב בְּעֵינֵי ה' לְבָרֵךְ אֶת יִשְׂרָאֵל וְלֹא הָלַךְ כְּפַעַם בְּפַעַם לִקְרַאת נְחָשִׁים וַיָּשֶׁת אֶל הַמִּדְבָּר פָּנָיו.

And Balaam saw that it pleased the Lord to bless Israel; so he did not go in search of divination as he had done time and time again, but turned his face toward the desert.

(Num. 24:1)

Balaam ends up blessing the Children of Israel, but what value do blessings have when they come from a wicked person? Rabbi Yosef Hayim of Baghdad, the *Ben Ish Hai*, answers this question.

> His blessings have a great purpose, because they were recorded in the Torah, so when the righteous people study them every year while learning the *parasha*, all of Israel will be blessed through the merit of this study. In addition, when Balaam's blessings are recorded in the Torah, and God then reads them to Moses, and Moses repeats them aloud, the Children of Israel are blessed by God and by Moses His prophet.

When a person, even if he is evil, says good things ("A nation that rises like a lioness" and "How goodly are your tents, Jacob") his words have a value. Each time they are repeated, we are blessed again. There is good reason to repeat positive sayings. In every generation, and every year, we return to these good words and are blessed again.

CR CR CR

The Right to Privacy

מַה טֹּבוּ אֹהָלֶיךָ יַעֲקֹב מִשְׁכְּנֹתֶיךָ יִשְׂרָאֵל.

How goodly are your tents, O Jacob, your dwelling places, O
Israel!

(Num. 24:5)

There is an age-old philosophical question: "If a tree falls in the forest
and no one is around to hear it, does it still make a sound?" We could
paraphrase it in contemporary terms and ask: "If two friends go to the
mall and do not take a selfie, did they really go?" If something is not
posted, tagged, or publicized on Facebook, did it really take place?

We live in a time when everything is recorded and we have
no privacy. This is exactly the point that Balaam focused on when he
observed the tents of the Children of Israel. He could not help but
be impressed by what he saw, as he blesses them, "How goodly are
your tents, O Jacob, your dwelling places, O Israel," a verse which has
become famous from the prayer book. Rashi explains what impressed
Balaam so much: "He saw that their openings were not facing each
other." Each tent's opening faced a different direction so no one could
peep into his neighbor's tent.

Balaam came from a culture that knew no limits and now he
meets the modesty that provides each family with a personal private
space. He is so moved that he blesses them, "How goodly are your
tents, O Jacob."

We have been faced with this challenge ever since. To what extent
should we be open to the wider world? Should we be looking over our
shoulder, or to the other side of the fence to see if the neighbor's grass
is greener? How can we preserve our privacy in a society in which walls
have become transparent, in which Google and Facebook know everything about us and share it with the world? On a personal level, we need
to be aware of which feelings, experiences, and news have no place in
the public domain and should remain in our own private "tent."

൬ ൬ ൬

Balak

Beyond Victory

אֶרְאֶנּוּ וְלֹא עַתָּה אֲשׁוּרֶנּוּ וְלֹא קָרוֹב דָּרַךְ כּוֹכָב מִיַּעֲקֹב וְקָם שֵׁבֶט
מִיִּשְׂרָאֵל וּמָחַץ פַּאֲתֵי מוֹאָב וְקַרְקַר כָּל בְּנֵי שֵׁת.

I see it, but not now; I behold it, but not soon. **A star has gone
forth from Jacob, and a staff will arise from Israel** which will
crush the princes of Moab and uproot all the sons of Seth.

(Num. 24:17)

Balaam was an oddity, a prophet but not a Jew, a person who wanted
to curse the Jewish people but ended up blessing them. There are many
midrashim in which our sages discuss the personality of this mysterious character and his role in history. They usually contrast him with the
Jewish prophets, noting differences in moral fiber and behavior, such as
Moses' humility versus Balaam's haughtiness.

Another, less noted, difference is in the content. Even when
Balaam does say good things about the Children of Israel, he can only
describe a military victory: "A star has gone forth from Jacob, and a staff
will arise from Israel…and Israel shall triumph." He does not envision
world peace or redemption for humanity. The furthest that history can
reach, as far as he can prophesy, is victory on the battlefield.

The prophets of the Jewish nation have a different vision for the
world. Victory in war is but one part of this vision, but they also speak
about victory over human failings and envision the world as a better
place at the End of Days: "Nation shall not lift the sword against nation,
neither shall they learn war anymore" (Is. 2:4); "But they shall sit every
man under his vine and under his fig-tree, and none shall make them
afraid" (Mic. 4:4); "And a wolf shall live with a lamb, and a leopard shall
lie with a kid" (Is. 11:6); "For the land shall be full of knowledge of the
Lord as water covers the sea" (Is. 11:9).

As we see from these quotations, military victory is not our final
goal. It is barely the starting point.

Pinhas

A False Sense of Security

פִּינְחָס בֶּן אֶלְעָזָר בֶּן אַהֲרֹן הַכֹּהֵן הֵשִׁיב אֶת חֲמָתִי מֵעַל בְּנֵי יִשְׂרָאֵל
בְּקַנְאוֹ אֶת קִנְאָתִי בְּתוֹכָם וְלֹא כִלִּיתִי אֶת בְּנֵי יִשְׂרָאֵל בְּקִנְאָתִי.

Pinhas the son of Elazar the son of Aaron the priest has turned
My anger away from the Children of Israel in that he was zeal-
ous in avenging Me among them, so that I did not destroy the
Children of Israel because of My jealousy.

(Num. 25:11)

The beginning of this *parasha* is connected to the end of the previous one,
Balak. In the midst of idol worship and the worst kind of promiscuity,
Pinhas got up and acted. He was pained that people who had recently
stood at Mount Sinai and received the Torah had suddenly thrown off
all their morals and openly embraced idolatry.

Some commentators see a connection between the two *parashot*.
Balaam lulled the Children of Israel into a false sense of security with his
profusion of positive blessings, flattery, and praise. They were thrown off
guard and didn't notice the spiritual danger that was about to ensnare
them, which it certainly did.

Balaam's blessings entered the Jewish pantheon and have
become part of our prayers and our lexicon: "How goodly are your
tents, O Jacob, your dwelling places, O Israel!" and "Behold, a people

that rises like a lioness and lifts itself up like a lion." Contrast these wonderful blessings with the messages of the prophets who came from within the Jewish people. They did not hesitate to rebuke the people and warn that they are going in the wrong direction. Balaam, on the other hand, had no educational motive. He did not care if they became better people as a result of his prophecies. The Jewish prophets considered themselves as spiritual shepherds who guided their flock toward a particular goal. So their message had a purpose, even if it was delivered harshly, as they preferred to criticize rather than heap praise on the people. The outpouring of blessings and praises that Balaam showered upon the Children of Israel made them so excessively sure of themselves that their protective mechanisms failed and the warning bells did not ring. Rabbi Sholom Dovber Schneerson, the fifth Lubavitcher Rebbe, used to tell his followers: "Love criticism, because it lets you know your proper stature."

The lesson we can learn from Balaam and Pinhas is that excessive praise goes to people's heads, knocking them off balance and causing them to miss the Evil Inclination, which is lurking in the background waiting to pounce.

ଓ ଓ ଓ

Exclusive: Korah's Sons Did Not Die

וּבְנֵי קֹרַח לֹא מֵתוּ.

Korah's sons, however, **did not die.**
(Num. 26:11)

This short verse is one of the most optimistic ones in the Torah, surprising us with the news that Korah's sons are alive and well. Korah had led an aggressive uprising against Moses, attracting many followers, which was quashed when the earth opened up and swallowed them up alive. Korah, his family, and followers all died in this tragic end to the rebellion. Or so we thought. Rashi tells us that at the last minute, as they were about to die, Korah's sons had a change of heart and "during the dispute they contemplated repentance." At the eleventh hour, they realized what a terrible mistake their father had made and decided to abandon the rebellion, saving their lives.

What a message of hope for us! Even when all seems lost, we can still change course. Even if we have erred, it is never too late to rethink our path in life. It takes a lot of courage to announce our mistakes and our intention to mend our ways, but it can be done. We can go against our surroundings, and our family, we can stand up to a charismatic father, even when the battle has already begun. Just look at Korah's sons. They did it and did not die.

ଔ ଔ ଔ

Men Are from Sinai, Women Are from the Land of Israel

וַתִּקְרַבְנָה בְּנוֹת צְלָפְחָד בֶּן חֵפֶר בֶּן גִּלְעָד בֶּן מָכִיר בֶּן מְנַשֶּׁה לְמִשְׁפְּחֹת מְנַשֶּׁה בֶן יוֹסֵף וְאֵלֶּה שְׁמוֹת בְּנֹתָיו מַחְלָה נֹעָה וְחָגְלָה וּמִלְכָּה וְתִרְצָה.

And the daughters of Tzlofhad the son of Hepher, the son of Gilead, the son of Machir, the son of Manasseh, of the families of Manasseh the son of Joseph, came forward, and his daughters' names were **Mahlah, Noah, Hoglah, Milcah, and Tirzah**.

(Num. 27:1)

In his hugely popular book, *Men Are from Mars, Women Are from Venus*, John Gray claimed that men and women come from completely different planets. I am not so sure that the differences are so extreme, but in this *parasha* we come across one issue in which men and women showed totally contrasting attitudes.

Tzlofhad's five daughters come to Moses and ask to receive their portion of land as an inheritance in the Land of Israel: "Give us a portion along with our father's brothers." Moses is unsure how to answer them and asks God, who tells him that their request is justified and they should be given a portion of land.

Rashi makes an interesting comment about the difference between men and women in the wilderness: "The women were not

247

included in the decree enacted after the sin of the spies, for they cherished the land. The men said, 'Let us appoint a leader and return to Egypt,' but the women said, 'Give us a portion.'" The men wanted to reverse course, whereas the women pushed ahead because they loved the Land of Israel. As a result, for the forty years following the sin of the spies, all the men of that generation died in the wilderness, while the women, the elderly and widowed women who loved the land, merited to enter it.

Rabbi Shlomo Ephraim of Luntschitz, known as the *Kli Yakar*, writes an even more radical commentary. He claims that the reason the spies failed in their mission is because they were men, and that if women had been sent they would have come back and given an optimistic report about the Land of Israel. Four hundred years ago, the *Kli Yakar* wrote that "the men hated the land and the women cherished it, so God said, 'In My opinion it would have been better to send women who cherish the land and would not speak badly about it.'"

The sin of the spies might have been averted if female spies had been sent.

C3 C3 C3

Moses & Sons?

וַיֹּאמֶר ה' אֶל מֹשֶׁה קַח לְךָ אֶת יְהוֹשֻׁעַ בֶּן נוּן אִישׁ אֲשֶׁר **רוּחַ בּוֹ** וְסָמַכְתָּ אֶת יָדְךָ עָלָיו.

And the Lord said to Moses, "Take for yourself Joshua the son of Nun, **a man of spirit**, and you shall lay your hand upon him." (Num. 27:18)

Shortly before his death, Moses requested that his sons be appointed as his heirs. This is not uncommon in the business world, so we might have expected to have Moses & Sons in the spiritual world.

The Midrash says that God refused his request and informed him that Joshua was the most suitable person to serve as his successor. Rabbi Yaakov Edelstein notes that "the only way to become a Torah scholar is to study hard and diligently over a long period of time." And all along, Joshua was simply more diligent than Moses' sons. Rabbi Edelstein continues his idea and adds that one should never think that the Torah is passed down from father to son as an inheritance. The danger in such thinking is twofold. First, if your father is not a rabbi, then you will feel that you have no chance of progressing in your Torah studies and becoming a rabbi in your own right. Second, if your father is a rabbi, you may think that you do not need to concentrate on your Torah studies because you will inherit the job. He adds, "So if you see a dynasty of great rabbis and leading Torah scholars then you have proof that each one studied hard and achieved what he did in his own right and not through nepotism." Rabbi Edelstein's idea can be applied to the father-son relationship. It is not at all simple to be the "son of…" and to follow in your father's footsteps without losing your own original imprint.

He tells the story of Rabbi Aharon Rokach who was appointed to head the Belz Hasidim in place of his father. The elder Hasidim asked him if he would follow in the ways of his father's leadership. He replied, "Of course I will! Just like he did not imitate his father and chose to act independently, I plan to do the same."

ଔ ଔ ଔ

Wait, Don't Go!

בַּיּוֹם הַשְּׁמִינִי עֲצֶרֶת תִּהְיֶה לָכֶם כָּל מְלֶאכֶת עֲבֹדָה לֹא תַעֲשׂוּ.

On the eighth day you shall have a solemn assembly: you shall not do any mundane work.

(Num. 29:35)

The latter part of the *parasha* deals with the festivals: Passover, Yom Kippur, Sukkot, and Shemini Atzeret. This festival is celebrated immediately after the last day of Sukkot and Rashi comments that it is a short festival coming at the end of a long one. During Sukkot we bring a total of seventy cows as sacrifices to represent the seventy nations of the world on whose behalf we pray and sacrifice. Rashi adds: "When they were about to depart from the Temple, God said to them, 'Please make a small festive meal for Me so that I can enjoy your company alone.'"

"It is as if God is having an intimate conversation with the Children of Israel. In Rashi's words, God says to them: "'Stay with Me a little longer,' expressing His affection for Israel. It is like children taking leave of their father, who says to them, 'It is difficult for me to part from you, please stay one more day.'"

Shemini Atzeret comes after Elul, Rosh HaShana, Yom Kippur, and Sukkot, a long sequence of festivals, and we may feel a bit of "overload." Rashi's parable puts a nice touch on this mini-festival. He compares it to children about to leave the table after all the guests have left, but their father asks them to stay for a bit longer so that they can enjoy each other's company more intimately.

Matot

A Word About Words

אִישׁ כִּי יִדֹּר נֶדֶר לַה' אוֹ הִשָּׁבַע שְׁבֻעָה לֶאְסֹר אִסָּר עַל נַפְשׁוֹ לֹא יַחֵל דְּבָרוֹ כְּכָל הַיֹּצֵא מִפִּיו יַעֲשֶׂה.

If a man makes a vow to the Lord or makes an oath to prohibit himself, he shall not violate his word; whatever came out of his mouth, he shall do.

(Num. 30:3)

The world was created with words: "And God said, 'Let there be light,' and there was light." Humans are the only living creature with the almost godly ability to speak. We tend to take speech for granted, not thinking of the immense power our words have. *Matot* begins with a discussion of the significance of the vows, oaths, and promises that we utter: "If a man makes a vow to the Lord or makes an oath to prohibit himself, he shall not violate his word; whatever came out of his mouth, he shall do."

This is not the place for a halakhic discussion on the different types of vows and what happens when they are broken. However, the message emanating from these words is that words create and change reality. Indeed, they have the power to build or destroy worlds. There is no such thing as empty words. During the wedding ceremony, the groom places a ring on his bride's finger and declares, "Behold you are betrothed to me," creating a new reality that did not exist a moment earlier. In a similar vein, "You are ugly and stupid" creates a new relationship between two people which cannot easily be erased.

Some of us are familiar with the verse "Death and life are in the power of the tongue" (Prov. 18:21). In another verse, Isaiah tells us that the Messiah will use words and not swords to shape the new reality: "And he shall smite the earth with the rod of his mouth and with the breath of his lips he shall put the wicked to death" (Is. 11:4).

In his final days, Rabbi Shlomo Wolbe told his students: "If only we could understand that just as there is a physical reality in which we can see tangible objects, so there is another reality, a spiritual one, in which we create with our words and prayers."

C8 C8 C8

Bye-Bye Balaam

וְאֶת מַלְכֵי מִדְיָן הָרְגוּ עַל חַלְלֵיהֶם אֶת אֱוִי וְאֶת רֶקֶם וְאֶת צוּר וְאֶת חוּר
וְאֶת רֶבַע חֲמֵשֶׁת מַלְכֵי מִדְיָן **וְאֶת בִּלְעָם בֶּן בְּעוֹר הָרְגוּ בֶּחָרֶב.**

And they killed the Midianite kings upon their slain: Evi, Rekem, Zur, Hur, and Reba, the five kings of Midian, and **Balaam the son of Beor they killed by sword.**

(Num. 31:8)

While describing the war against Midian, the Torah devotes a few words to "settling accounts" with Balaam and tells us that he was killed by the sword. Rashi asks why it is important for us to know the method of his killing. He answers:

He came to fight Israel and exchanged his craft for theirs. For they [Israel] are only victorious with their mouths through prayer and supplication, and he [Balaam] came and adopted their craft to curse them with his mouth. So they too arose against him and exchanged their craft for that of the nations who come with the sword.

The Jews have always been a people of words. We use speech for prayer, supplication, study, begging, explaining, and persuading. We are not a people of the sword. Balaam tried to attack the Jewish people through spiritual means, using "our craft" to pray against them. He failed in his mission and the Children of Israel were forced to fight him on the battle-field, using "his craft," the sword.

Ever since, the Jewish people have resorted to the use of the sword only when we have no other choice. So, it is no coincidence that the IDF is called the Israel Defense Forces. When we are forced to, we kill Balaam and all our enemies by sword. Yet we must remember that our preferred choice is to avoid war whenever possible.

CB CB CB

The Side-Effects of Anger

וַיֹּאמֶר אֶלְעָזָר הַכֹּהֵן אֶל אַנְשֵׁי הַצָּבָא הַבָּאִים לַמִּלְחָמָה זֹאת חֻקַּת הַתּוֹרָה אֲשֶׁר צִוָּה ה' אֶת מֹשֶׁה.

And Elazar the priest said to the men of war who went to the battle, "This is the statute of the law which God commanded Moses."

(Num. 31:21)

The Torah relates that it was Elazar the priest, and not Moses, who taught the people a certain point in Halakha: "And Elazar the priest said to the men of war who went to the battle, 'This is the statute of the law which God commanded Moses.'" This seems strange because Moses, who knew all the laws, was still alive! What happened to him? Our sages direct us back seven verses earlier for the answer. At the end of the battle against Midian, the Torah says that "Moses was angry with the officers of the army" and our sages add, "Since he was angry, he forgot the halakha."

The Talmud is full of statements that anger is more than a bad characteristic. It causes you to lose the spiritual assets you have already gained: "Anger causes a sage to lose his wisdom, a prophet to lose his prophecy, and a person destined for greatness to forfeit it." Maimonides adds that "One who becomes angry is as though he has worshiped idols."

Rabbi Chaim Friedlander expands on these statements and explains that losing one's wisdom is not a punishment for anger but its natural outcome. The Torah cannot dwell in a "vessel" that also contains bad characteristics:

> The proper vessel for the wisdom of the Torah is a body pure of any negative traits. When such a characteristic is formed, his wisdom disappears immediately, not as a punishment but because of a natural result. A bad characteristic drives wisdom away.
>
> Therefore we should avoid any hint of anger at all costs... we should try not to become confused or lose our peace of mind, and most certainly not become angry because we then lose our spiritual qualities and endanger our material lives, and most importantly we lose our peace of mind.

Masei

Children and Property: A Proper Sense of Priorities

וּמִקְנֶה רַב הָיָה לִבְנֵי רְאוּבֵן וְלִבְנֵי גָד עָצוּם מְאֹד וַיִּרְאוּ אֶת אֶרֶץ יַעְזֵר
וְאֶת אֶרֶץ גִּלְעָד וְהִנֵּה הַמָּקוֹם מְקוֹם מִקְנֶה.

The descendants of Reuben and Gad had a very great abundance
of livestock and they saw the land of Yazer and the land of Gilead,
and **behold, the place was fitting for livestock.**

(Num. 32:1)

This verse is an example of when the text is so blatantly clear that very
little commentary is needed to drive home the point the Torah wishes to
make. Before they even go out to fight, the tribes of Reuben and Gad ask
Moses for permission not to cross the Jordan River into the Land of Israel.
They ask to leave their property and children behind and then conquer
the land, together with the other tribes. They propose to Moses that "we
will build sheepfolds for our livestock here and cities for our children."

In his reply, Moses reverses the order and tells them, "Build
yourselves cities for your children and enclosures for your sheep." Your
children come first, and only then your flock. Obviously, this is not simply a matter of chronological order but a question of priorities. Rashi
makes the point simply but forcefully: "They were more concerned
about their possessions than about their sons and daughters, as they
mentioned their livestock before their children. Moses told them: 'This

255

is not correct. Treat the matter of primary importance first, and the matter of secondary importance second. First build cities for your children and then enclosures for your sheep.'"

The purpose of having a career is to help the family and not the other way round. For some reason, this point reminds me of a contemporary situation. As a result of a few tragic deaths when infants were left behind in the car during the hot Israeli summer, campaigns have been launched to avoid the recurrence of such tragedies. One piece of advice for parents is to leave their mobile phones next to the car seat. No parent will ever forget to take their phone with them.

CS CS CS

Keep on Going

אֵלֶּה מַסְעֵי בְנֵי יִשְׂרָאֵל אֲשֶׁר יָצְאוּ מֵאֶרֶץ מִצְרַיִם לְצִבְאֹתָם בְּיַד מֹשֶׁה וְאַהֲרֹן.

These are the journeys of the Children of Israel who left the land of Egypt in their legions, under the charge of Moses and Aaron. (Num. 33:1)

The *parasha* tells of the journeys of the Children of Israel in the wilderness and mentions the forty-two geographical names they passed on their journey – Ramses, Refidim, Sukkot, Hatzerot, etc. Jeremiah alludes to this journey: "I remember to you the loving-kindness of your youth, the love of your nuptials, your following Me in the desert, in a land not sown."

The details of the journey may be explained in various ways. Nahmanides writes that "The journey is a commandment from God, but the secret of the journey has not been revealed to us." So we have this mystery, which we must try to resolve. Perhaps the history of the Jewish people is, in actual fact, the solution to the mystery. After all, the journey of our nation is not yet over; the Torah may have listed the spots we visited on our way, but we have not yet reached the end of the journey. The Children of Israel are about to enter the Land of Israel but will be exiled from it in the future, only to return, be exiled a second time, and then merit to return to the land again in our times.

The phrase "these are the journeys" is not merely a summary of a past journey but also a prophecy for the future. We are going to make many more than forty-two stops during our journey. Just think how many cities and villages, shtetls and ghettoes, mellahs and camps, we have endured, lived in, and departed from in our journey in the wilderness until this very day.

According to hasidic thought, this journey can be also be explained not only on a national level but on a personal one. We are told that a person should constantly look back and review his life's journey, to be aware that there is a reason for everything that happens to him, and to always try to proceed to the next stop, remembering that life's journey never ceases.

Rebbetzin Esther Jungreis was a Holocaust survivor who wrote that the Jewish people must always retain the spark of godliness throughout its journeys:

> Amidst all the atrocities that the Nazis did, I always told myself that, despite everything, I am grateful that I am on the side of the murdered ones and not the murderers. I saw how the most cultured nation on Earth could stoop to such a low level and commit such terrible crimes. When I look at our journeys, I think that the name survivors is inappropriate. We should be called victors. The Jewish people did not survive the Holocaust. We beat it, and we must continue to win.

CB CB CB

Destruction and Rebuilding

וַיַּעַל אַהֲרֹן הַכֹּהֵן אֶל הֹר הָהָר עַל פִּי ה' וַיָּמָת שָׁם בִּשְׁנַת הָאַרְבָּעִים לְצֵאת בְּנֵי יִשְׂרָאֵל מֵאֶרֶץ מִצְרַיִם בַּחֹדֶשׁ הַחֲמִישִׁי בְּאֶחָד לַחֹדֶשׁ.

And Aaron the priest ascended Mount Hor at the Lord's bidding and died there, on the first day of the fifth month in the fortieth year of the Children of Israel's Exodus from Egypt.

(Num. 33:38)

The Jews are about to enter the Land of Israel, forty years after the Exodus, and the Torah relates that Aaron died: "And Aaron the priest ascended Mount Hor at the Lord's bidding and died there, on the first day of the fifth month in the fortieth year." The actual date of his death is recorded, the first day of the month of Av. (The Torah counts the months of the year starting in Nisan and not Tishrei.)

The month of Av later became a time of mourning because of the destruction of the Temple: "When the month of Av begins, we reduce our happiness." Is there a possible connection between Aaron's death and the destruction of the Temple? Our sages felt that the two events are indeed connected and said that "the death of a *tzaddik*, a righteous person, is comparable to the burning of God's home."

The death of a holy person is a time of weeping and mourning, but also the best time to learn from their good deeds and continue in their ways, thus serving as a living memorial to his heritage.

The days of mourning for the Temple have a similar potential. Of course we are commanded to mourn for the destruction and for the fact that we have not yet merited the rebuilding, but these are also days in which we are commanded to increase our *ahavat hinam*, baseless non-judgmental love. This is our way of repenting for *sinat hinam*, baseless hatred, which was the cause of the destruction of the Temple and end of Jewish sovereignty. Given that the theme of the month of Av is baseless love, the connection with Aaron becomes obvious. Aaron is considered the epitome of someone who shows love to everyone, as described by the sages in Ethics of the Fathers: "He loves peace and pursues it, loves people and brings them closer to the Torah."

೮೮ ೮೮ ೮೮

How to Influence Others

וַיֹּאמְרוּ אֶת אֲדֹנִי צִוָּה ה' לָתֵת אֶת הָאָרֶץ בְּנַחֲלָה בְּגוֹרָל לִבְנֵי יִשְׂרָאֵל וַאדֹנִי צֻוָּה בַה' לָתֵת אֶת נַחֲלַת צְלָפְחָד אָחִינוּ לִבְנֹתָיו.

And they said, "The Lord commanded my master to give the land as an inheritance through lot to the Children of Israel, and our master was commanded by the Lord **to give the inheritance of Tzlofhad our brother to his daughters**."

(Num. 36:2)

At the end of the *Masei*, right at the end of the Book of Numbers, the Torah once again relates the request of Tzlofhad's five daughters for a portion in the Land of Israel. These women became the symbol of the feminine optimism of that generation. The gender lines were also split along the issue of belief. The men were pessimistic about entering the land and so they died in the wilderness, whereas the women who did not sin at the Golden Calf or the spies, but instead waited expectantly to enter, merited to cross the Jordan and enter the Land of Israel.

Rabbi Moshe Tzvi Neriah, who founded the network of Bnei Akiva Yeshiva High Schools and was a very influential figure in the national-religious sector, discussed why the women succeeded where the men had failed. He said that Moses and Aaron were responsible for educating the men, whereas Miriam was responsible for the women, and explains the difference between their distinct educational styles:

Miriam was more successful than her two brothers. They did not merit to bring the masses to the required spiritual level, whereas Miriam succeeded. How can we explain this? The secret to success in education is the personal connection between teacher and student. Miriam sang and danced with the women. The Torah only relates that she did this once, after the Splitting of the Red Sea, and we assume that she would dance and sing on every joyous occasion with the celebrating family or tribe. The Torah does not give details of day-to-day life in the wilderness, but the one example given of Miriam's dancing implies that she did so regularly and thus was able to form a close connection with the women. This connection had a decisive influence on the women and Miriam was successful where Moses and Aaron came up short.

Rabbi Neriah was known for his prayers and singing and the influence he had on his students. His comments tell us that if you want to teach a message, it is not enough to give a lecture. You have to dance and sing, spend time with your students, and form a personal connection.

Deuteronomy

The opening verse of Deuteronomy, the fifth and final book of the Pentateuch, is: "These are the words which Moses spoke to all Israel on the other side of the Jordan." The Jewish people were camped at the border; they could have easily entered the Land of Israel at this point. However, the Torah adds a fifth book, which primarily consists of one long and fascinating speech given by Moses, interspersed with poetry, rebuke, reminiscences, and lessons to be learned for the future. Some people consider the opening phrase, "These are the words," to be an expression of excitement. It is as if the Torah is telling us: Listen carefully. After all we have learned in the previous four books, now is the time to pay close attention to Moses' final, valedictory address, which gives us the preparatory spiritual food as we prepare to enter the land.

These are the words!

Devarim

The Double Lament

אֵיכָה אֶשָּׂא לְבַדִּי טָרְחֲכֶם וּמַשַּׂאֲכֶם וְרִיבְכֶם.

How can I bear your trouble, your burden, and your strife **all by myself?**

(Deut. 1:12)

Parashat Devarim is always read in the week preceding Tisha B'Av, the day of mourning which commemorates the destruction of the two Temples. The word *eikha* is found both in this *parasha* and in the opening of the Book of Lamentations (*Eikha*) which is read on Tisha B'Av. Moses uses the word *eikha* to express to the people his pain and sadness, as he alone has to bear their troubles, burdens, and strife. When it is read from the Torah, this verse is customarily read in the same mournful tune used to read the Book of Lamentations.

Rashi uses strong language to explain Moses' complaint:

> It teaches that they were heretics. If Moses was early leaving his tent they would say, "Why does the son of Amram leave so early? Perhaps he is not at ease inside his house?" If he left late, they would say, "Why does the son of Amram not leave? What do you think? He is sitting and devising evil schemes against you and formulating plots against you!"

What a preposterous and dismal state of affairs. Why would anyone want to keep tabs on when Moses leaves his home? Why would anyone give a negative interpretation to everything Moses does on their behalf?

The sages see a connection between the two occurrences of *eikha*. Before we read the monumental lamentation about the destruction of the Temple and the ensuing war, we first read a small lamentation in this *parasha* which is the source of all the trouble. Moses is lamenting the people's suspicion and lack of faith. A direct line connects the *eikha* in Deuteronomy describing the degeneration and cynicism of a society to the *eikha* of the destruction of the Temple.

CR CR CR

It's All a Question of Approach

וַתִּקְרְבוּן אֵלַי כֻּלְּכֶם וַתֹּאמְרוּ נִשְׁלְחָה אֲנָשִׁים לְפָנֵינוּ וְיַחְפְּרוּ לָנוּ אֶת הָאָרֶץ וְיָשִׁבוּ אֹתָנוּ דָּבָר אֶת הַדֶּרֶךְ אֲשֶׁר נַעֲלֶה בָּהּ וְאֵת הֶעָרִים אֲשֶׁר נָבֹא אֲלֵיהֶן.

> **And all of you approached me** and said, "Let us send men ahead of us so that they will search out the land for us and bring us back word which route we shall go up, and to which cities we shall come."
>
> (Deut. 1:22)

In his speech, Moses recalls the sin of the spies, but before he even goes into detail regarding the actual sin, he reminds the people how he was approached and asked to send spies to the Land of Israel: "And all of you approached me." Rashi elaborates: "In a state of disorder, children pushing the elderly, and the elderly pushing the heads of the tribes." No wonder that the final outcome of this request was so dismal, when one considers the lack of respect evident right from the start.

Rashi compares this event with a similar yet different event. Describing the scene at Mount Sinai when the people rushed toward him, Moses uses the same words, "and you approached me," but continues, "all the heads of your tribes and your elders." Rashi explains that in this case, they approached Moses in a "proper" manner: "Children respected the elders and let them go ahead, and the elders gave the heads of the tribes the honor of going ahead of them."

The Torah compares the two scenes, one being the peak of greatness and the second the nadir of sin. The lesson is that, even before the curtain rises, the way in which a task is approached is also significant. Good manners and courtesy precede Torah observance. When children disregard the wisdom of the elders in the first act, it is not difficult to guess how things will end up in the final act.

ೞ ೞ ೞ

Crumbs

וְטַפְּכֶם אֲשֶׁר אֲמַרְתֶּם לָבַז יִהְיֶה וּבְנֵיכֶם אֲשֶׁר לֹא יָדְעוּ הַיּוֹם טוֹב וָרָע הֵמָּה יָבֹאוּ שָׁמָּה וְלָהֶם אֶתְּנֶנָּה וְהֵם יִירָשׁוּהָ.

And your little ones, who you said will be prey, and your children, who on that day did not know good and evil, **they will go there and I will give it to them, and they will possess it.**

(Deut. 1:39)

The Lubavitcher Rebbe was childless. Nevertheless, he explains this verse by using imagery that resonates chiefly with parents trying to feed their young children. About to enter the Land of Israel, Moses addresses both the generation of the wilderness, who will all soon die, and their children, who will merit entering the land: "And your little ones…they will go there and I will give it to them, and they will possess it."

Young children play with their food and, if they are given a slice of bread, more crumbs remain on their plate than go into their mouth. Still, the child does eat something. The Lubavitcher Rebbe compares this to the nation's entry into the Land of Israel. The people are compared to a child, and the Torah to bread. In the wilderness, the Torah was whole, perfect, and clean, which made for a comfortable existence. Once they enter the Land of Israel, the Jewish people will have to begin applying it in real life and it will turn into crumbs. They won't have absorbed everything they were taught, and they will not be fully keeping all the commandments in a calm, relaxed manner. After all, their food will no longer fall as manna from the heavens like it did in the wilderness. Now they will have to work hard for their food and worry about their material existence.

Only a small amount of Torah (bread) will actually go into our mouths, and many crumbs will remain on the plate. The Lubavitcher Rebbe explains the parable and says that, nevertheless, this is the right thing to do and the natural course of history. God prefers the child's attempts to eat, our attempts to keep the Torah in the Land of Israel, to the toil of the generation in the wilderness.

Va'ethanan

Managing Our Account

כִּי מִי גוֹי גָּדוֹל אֲשֶׁר לוֹ אֱלֹהִים קְרֹבִים אֵלָיו כַּה' אֱלֹהֵינוּ בְּכָל קָרְאֵנוּ
אֵלָיו.

For what great nation has God so near to it, **like the Lord our
God is at all times, that we call upon Him**?

(Deut. 4:7)

Rabbi Yehuda Amital, the founder of Yeshivat Har Etzion, wrote about
prayer: "Every person has been given a great merit – God allows us to
pray. The human race would be different, it would be sadder and more
desolate, were it not for this great merit given to man."

Throughout the Book of Deuteronomy, Moses repeatedly exhorts
us to turn to God, to connect to Him by praying, begging, and speaking.
Rabbi Amital used to tell the following story in connection with prayer:

> I heard this from the director of a senior citizens' home in Miami.
> Many of the residents' children live far away in places such as New
> York, Washington, and Chicago. The director categorizes the chil-
> dren into three groups. The first is the children who mail a check
> to their parents every month, sometimes, but not always, adding
> a personal note. Thus, the parent knows that his child remembers
> him every month. The second group is the children who mail the

check directly to the office. Although the check isn't sent directly to the parent, at least the child shows that he still remembers him. The third group pay by standing order. The bank clerk sends the check and the child does not even know if his parent is alive or not. Everything works automatically.

What kind of relationship do we want to have with God? The Torah asks us to keep a near and personal relationship and not to sign on a standing order.

CB CB CB

If Not Now, When?

אָז יַבְדִּיל מֹשֶׁה שָׁלֹשׁ עָרִים בְּעֵבֶר הַיַּרְדֵּן מִזְרְחָה שָׁמֶשׁ.

Then Moses separated three cities beyond the Jordan toward the sunrise.

(Deut. 4:41)

When I was a young child and would defer doing something until "later," my mother used to say, "Later means tomorrow." Most of us tend to put off tasks until later on or until tomorrow, and if possible to the day after that. In this *parasha* we read that Moses acted completely differently, even at the end of his life. He was energetic and sprightly and was careful not to put off doing anything to a later date.

Think about the verse, "Then Moses separated three cities beyond the Jordan." Moses designated three cities of refuge (where an accidental murderer would flee and be protected from revenge killings). The commandment to set up these cities would only come into effect when the people of Israel would complete their conquest of the west side of the Jordan River and would set up an additional three cities. Moses knew he would not lead the people into the Land of Israel but, nevertheless, he designated the three cities and marked them out now, ahead of time.

Rashi asks why Moses acted so promptly and gives a simple and famous answer: "Moses said: 'If there is a commandment that can be

fulfilled – I will fulfill it.'" In other words: If not now, when? If I can
do something good here and now, even if I will only be fulfilling half a
commandment, why shouldn't I hurry and do so?

‎CB CB CB

The Moment After

אֶת הַדְּבָרִים הָאֵלֶּה דִּבֶּר הי אֶל כָּל קְהַלְכֶם בָּהָר מִתּוֹךְ הָאֵשׁ הֶעָנָן
וְהָעֲרָפֶל קוֹל גָּדוֹל וְלֹא יָסָף וַיִּכְתְּבֵם עַל שְׁנֵי לֻחֹת אֲבָנִים וַיִּתְּנֵם אֵלָי.

**The Lord spoke these words to your entire assembly at the
mountain** out of the fire, the cloud, and the opaque darkness,
with a great voice, which did not cease. And He inscribed them
on two stone tablets and gave them to me.

(Deut. 5:19)

If we want to know what God said to Moses after the Revelation at
Mount Sinai, we need the perspective of Deuteronomy. In this book,
we find out new facts in Moses' speech and discover new connections
and meanings that can only be understood in retrospect.

For example, Moses relates how the people were frightened by
the majesty of the occasion and wanted to run back, away from the
burning mountain. They wanted to hear the words of God through an
intermediary, through Moses. Now in Deuteronomy, Moses tells them,
"And God listened to your words," and reveals what God said to him
immediately after receiving the Ten Commandments: "Would that their
hearts be like this, to fear Me and to keep all My commandments all the
days, that it might be well with them and with their children forever."

It seems that as soon as the Revelation was over, both sides were
already nostalgic for the event and begging for the relationship to continue. God prays: "If only the feelings at this event could be retained."

At the conclusion of the daily morning services, the siddur has a
small section called "The Six Remembrances," which contains six sections with verses telling us to remember and not to forget certain events.
One of these is the Revelation at Sinai:

But beware and watch yourself very well, that you will not forget the things that your eyes saw, and that these things will not depart from your heart, all the days of your life, and you shall make them known to your children and to your children's children – the day you stood before the Lord your God at Horeb when the Lord said to me, "Assemble the people for Me, and I will let them hear My words, that they may learn to fear Me all the days that they live on the earth, and that they may teach their children."

Ekev

Seared in Our Memory

וְאָמַרְתָּ בִּלְבָבֶךָ כֹּחִי וְעֹצֶם יָדִי עָשָׂה לִי אֶת הַחַיִל הַזֶּה.

And you will say to yourself, "**My strength and the might of my hand** has accumulated this wealth for me."

(Deut. 8:17)

This *parasha* contains the well-known phrase in which we are warned not to enter the land, build houses, amass cattle, silver and gold, and reach the situation in which "You will say to yourself, 'My strength and the might of my hand has accumulated this wealth.'" This describes someone who thinks that he alone is responsible for his success and leaves God out of the equation. Rabbenu Bahya writes about the manner in which wealth and property cause a person to err in this manner: "Pride is what causes a person to forget the most important, because through having plenty and being worry-free, a person's heart becomes proud, and the evil inclination tempts him so that all his possessions become the most important, and that which belongs to Heaven becomes secondary."

The source of this illusion is forgetfulness. We cannot avoid this fact when we read the *parasha* because the importance of remembering and the dangers of forgetting are mentioned at least four times: "Beware that you do not forget," "Your heart grows haughty, and you forget," "But you must remember the Lord your God," and finally, "And it will be, if you forget." We are told to remember that during our sojourn in the wilderness we had no way of taking care of our food, water, and clothing. God took care of all our needs. As we are about to enter the Land of Israel, Moses is trying to sear this historical remembrance in our collective consciousness.

We can avoid the danger of forgetfulness if we make a point of studying our history and the lessons it holds for us. The Baal Shem Tov summed this up succinctly: "In remembrance lies the secret of the redemption."

CB CB CB

Breaking News

וָאֶתְפֹּשׂ בִּשְׁנֵי הַלֻּחֹת וָאַשְׁלִכֵם מֵעַל שְׁתֵּי יָדָי וָאֲשַׁבְּרֵם לְעֵינֵיכֶם.

And I grasped the two tablets, threw them out of my two hands, **and shattered them before your eyes**.

(Deut. 9:17)

As a journalist, I think understand why I like the Book of Deuteronomy so much. Because it contains another version, a different angle, a first-hand account of great events.

Today's scoop: "We present a personal and moving first-hand account. Moses speaks about breaking the tablets." Moses recounts those dramatic moments when he came down from Mount Sinai and saw the people dancing around the Golden Calf. Speaking in the first person, he describes the scene: "And I grasped the two tablets, threw them out of my two hands, and shattered them before your eyes."

The commentators take special note of the last words in this verse, "before your eyes." Moses chose to break the tablets in front of the people, indicating the motive for his action. Moses wanted to shock them and show that there was no inherent holiness in the tablets. After all, we do not worship the tablets, but the One who gave them to us.

Many midrashim describe these dramatic moments. In one of them, the Torah is compared to light: "To what can this be compared?

To a man who is holding a candle which blew out. When he saw that the light had been extinguished, he asked, 'Why am I holding this candle?' and threw it to the ground."

The tablets are just a means, a reminder. If what is written on them has no significance, then they also become worthless.

 G3 G3 G3

We Carry Our Fragments with Us Forever

בָּעֵת הַהִוא אָמַר ה' אֵלַי פְּסָל לְךָ שְׁנֵי לוּחֹת אֲבָנִים כָּרִאשֹׁנִים וַעֲלֵה אֵלַי הָהָרָה וְעָשִׂיתָ לְּךָ אֲרוֹן עֵץ.

At that time, the Lord said to me, "**Carve for yourself two stone tablets like the first ones** and come up to Me onto the mountain, and make a wooden ark for yourself."

(Deut. 10:1)

Imagine this scenario: The Children of Israel continue their wanderings in the wilderness. They carry with them the tablets of stone with the Ten Commandments carved on them, which had been given to them a second time, and also the fragments of the first tablets that had been shattered, as they danced around the Golden Calf. Our sages say, "The tablets and the fragments of the tablets were placed in the Ark." We continually carry around with us both our failures and sins and also our improved selves.

In this *parasha*, Moses describes how the tablets were given a second time. After Moses begs God many times, He forgives us and we are given another chance. Why did the first tablets only last for such a short time, while the second ones are eternal? What is the difference between the first set that was given before the sin of the Golden Calf and the second set that heralded the concept of repentance and forgiveness?

The Midrash talks about one of the major differences: "The first tablets were received with clapping and shouting, so the Evil Eye ruled over them and they were broken. Yet with the second tablets – there is nothing as nice as the modesty in them."

When we talk about the Revelation at Mount Sinai, we think of the thunder and lightning and the "highs" displayed there. However, the bottom line is that the Torah that was given to Moses secretly, without any fanfare or mass celebrations, was the one that ultimately survived.

The true matters, the ones that hold great value, are not the headlines. I am reminded of what a journalist once told me: "If you get married in the gossip columns, don't be surprised if you get divorced there as well."

CB CB CB

Learn the Parents

וְהָיָה אִם שָׁמֹעַ תִּשְׁמְעוּ אֶל מִצְוֹתַי אֲשֶׁר אָנֹכִי מְצַוֶּה אֶתְכֶם הַיּוֹם לְאַהֲבָה אֶת ה' אֱלֹהֵיכֶם וּלְעָבְדוֹ בְּכָל לְבַבְכֶם וּבְכָל נַפְשְׁכֶם.

And it will be, if you hearken to My commandments that I command you this day to love the Lord, your God, and to serve Him with all your heart and with all your soul.

(Deut. 11:13)

Doesn't it feel strange to see something in a different context? We are used to saying the above verse by heart in the daily *Shema* prayer and now we are reading it in the original context in *Parashat Ekev* as part of the Torah and not as part of our prayers.

"And you shall teach them to your sons to speak with them, when you sit in your house and when you walk on the way and when you lie down and when you rise." Rabbi Dudi Braverman offers an explication of the literal meaning of this verse: we are commanded to teach our children Torah and to speak with them about it when we are at home and on the road, when we go to bed and get up in the morning. In other words, we are commanded to constantly teach them the words of the Torah.

Rabbi Braverman expands on this idea with a helpful parenting lesson. The Torah is actually telling us parents that we do not teach our children when we stand in front of them and tell them what to do. We can lecture them about what is permitted and forbidden, we can wag our fingers at them and tell them they are not behaving properly, but the real education occurs when they are with us and observe our actions. They see what we do when we sit at home or are on the road, when we go to bed and when we get up in the morning. The children observe and learn how they ought to behave.

This is especially true during summer vacation. The rigid structure of the school year is absent and the family spends time living together and interacting in ways that are not always possible during the year.

Children do not learn from us, they learn us.

Re'eh

What Is the Blessing?

רְאֵה אָנֹכִי נֹתֵן לִפְנֵיכֶם הַיּוֹם בְּרָכָה וּקְלָלָה.

Behold, I set before you today **a blessing and a curse**.
(Deut. 11:26)

Parashat Re'eh opens with the verses, "Behold, I set before you today a blessing and a curse. The blessing, that you will listen to the commandments of the Lord your God, which I command you today; and the curse, if you will not listen."

These verses are a repetition of the concept of freedom of choice. A person chooses either the blessing or the curse, between good and bad.

However, a careful and literal reading of the verses shows that there is no promise of reward or punishment. Choosing to go along a certain path is in itself the actual blessing and the curse is not going along that path.

The Malbim explains this verse: "If you do so, that you listen to God's commandment, this itself is the blessing." How simple it is to write these words, yet how difficult it is to grasp and absorb them: the mere action of doing the correct thing is in itself the blessing. When you choose, you are blessed.

ଔ ଔ ଔ

Follow in His Footsteps

אַחֲרֵי ה' אֱלֹהֵיכֶם תֵּלֵכוּ וְאֹתוֹ תִירָאוּ וְאֶת מִצְוֹתָיו תִּשְׁמֹרוּ וּבְקֹלוֹ תִשְׁמָעוּ וְאֹתוֹ תַעֲבֹדוּ **וּבוֹ תִדְבָּקוּן.**

You shall follow the Lord, your God, fear Him, keep His commandments, heed His voice, worship Him, and **cleave to Him.**
(Deut. 13:5)

We are told to "cleave to Him." How are we supposed to fulfill this commandment? Do we use fire? A shofar? Grandiose accessories? A dramatic setting? How extreme do we need to be in cleaving to Him? Should we use exceptional means? The Midrash gives us instructions: "Cleave to His ways: be kind, bury the dead, visit the sick, like God Himself did."

How do we know that God did all these good deeds? In the Garden of Eden, He did a good deed by providing clothing for Adam and Eve. He buried Moses and He visited Abraham in his tent after his circumcision.

During a visit to the States, I looked at the schedules of various synagogues and noticed an addition to the schedule of services. On Shabbat afternoon, shortly before the Minha afternoon service, congregants met at the synagogue "to visit the sick." They went on foot to visit housebound and sick people.

Without emphasizing that we are being given a revolutionary idea, the Midrash is teaching us a major life lesson: If you want to get close to the Divine Presence, if you desire to be holy and if you wish to cleave to God, follow in His footsteps.

CS CS CS

What Is a Jew?

כִּי עַם קָדוֹשׁ אַתָּה לַהִ' אֱלֹהֶיךָ וּבְךָ בָּחַר ה' לִהְיוֹת לוֹ לְעַם סְגֻלָּה מִכֹּל הָעַמִּים אֲשֶׁר עַל פְּנֵי הָאֲדָמָה.

For you are a holy people to the Lord, your God, and the Lord has chosen you to be a treasured people for Him, out of all the nations that are upon the earth.

(Deut. 14:2)

Yes, we are the Chosen Nation. In the Book of Deuteronomy, we are repeatedly told about the essence of Jewish faith and its most basic values. Moses conveys to the Children of Israel, and by extension tells us, the most important messages in his final speech: holiness, a sense of purpose, chosenness, and destiny. It is such a pity that the tone and content of contemporary dialogue is going in a completely direction.

I only came across this passage written by Uri Orbach, the well-known writer, journalist, and politician, after he passed away:

> It is too bad to see how, in the Jewish State, any discussion about Judaism is superficial and empty. Those involved in dialogue invariably shout at each other and no one has the patience to actually listen to the other side. Judaism is associated with causes such as a struggle over Shabbat, an immodest advertising billboard, or an uproar in the Knesset about personal status legislation. To the average person, Judaism equals fights about state and religion or the religious/secular divide. It is rare to see a discussion about the relationship between Judaism and the Jews. There is little or no relation to the Jewish experience in Israel when discussing issues such as coalition agreements or in the arguments, curses, brawls, and confrontations between different sectors of Israeli society. It has been so long since I have heard a discussion about how Israelis love their Judaism.

Orbach ends this text with a plea to change Judaism's public agenda. He calls for us to return to dealing with the core issues:

Here is a list of words we hear when talking about Judaism: boycotts, fights, protests, discrimination, coercion, prohibitions, evasion, and the religious establishment.

Now here is a list of words we never knew or have forgotten about when discussing Judaism: feelings, experiences, identification, study, justice, land, memory, yearning, continuity.

Which words do you prefer? How do you like your Judaism?

CB CB CB

A Tenth Is Really the Majority

עַשֵּׂר תְּעַשֵּׂר אֵת כָּל תְּבוּאַת זַרְעֶךָ הַיֹּצֵא הַשָּׂדֶה שָׁנָה שָׁנָה.

You shall tithe all the seed crop that the field gives forth, year by year.
(Deut. 14:22)

We are instructed to "tithe," to take one tenth of all we earn and give it to someone else. This is just one of many monetary commandments in this *parasha* dealing with loans, interest, charity for the poor, and letting the land lie fallow every seven years (*Shemitta*).

The basis of all these commandments is that our money is not our own. Although we worked hard to earn it, we received our money for another purpose and we are a mere conduit through which money passes in this world. The tithe is only one tenth of our earnings, but in essence it is the main part.

I remember paying a babysitter and watching in awe as she automatically took ten percent of what I had given her and put it in another section of her wallet to be used for giving charity.

The Baal HaTanya writes that it is possible for a person to exert himself physically all day at work, such that it is considered to be a sanctification of God's name and the fulfillment of one continuous commandment. How so? If a person thinks about the charity he will give from his earnings, then he is not really working to earn the ninety percent he will keep, but in order to earn the remaining ten percent which he will use to make the world a better place.

Shofetim

Translating Hebrew into Hebrew

שֹׁפְטִים וְשֹׁטְרִים תִּתֶּן לְךָ בְּכָל שְׁעָרֶיךָ אֲשֶׁר ה' אֱלֹהֶיךָ נֹתֵן לְךָ לִשְׁבָטֶיךָ וְשָׁפְטוּ אֶת הָעָם מִשְׁפַּט צֶדֶק.

You shall set up judges and law enforcement officials for your-self in all your cities that the Lord, your God, is giving you, for your tribes, and they shall judge the people with righteous judgment.

(Deut. 16:18)

I vividly recall the scene. I was a fourteen-year-old listening to the rabbi talking in an impassioned voice and I didn't understand a word. He quoted the opening verse of *Parashat Shofetim*, "You shall set up judges and law enforcement officials for yourself in all your cities that the Lord, your God, is giving you," and explained that we must place judges and police officers at the personal gates that God created for each of us. The rabbi told us: "Our eyes, ears, and mouth are the gates of our face and we must place guards at their entrance. We must be careful about what we put into our body and mind, to watch what we eat, hear, and see, and be on guard about what people around us say."

I did not understand a single word he said. The gap between the Hebrew spoken by secular Israelis and the one used in religious conver-sation is very great. Jumping from past to present, skipping between the

Oral and Written Law, was all very confusing to me. I was unaware that an educational lesson can be learned from almost any verse. Sometimes it is obvious and other times we have to read between the lines. There is a purpose in everything we read and even if we don't mention it every time we read it, the lesson hovers around the text.

I sat listening to him, confused and not understanding what he said. The girl sitting next to me whispered an explanation: "The rabbi took the first verse in this *parasha* and explained it using an allegory. The Torah commands us to appoint real guards at the entrance to our cities. However, the rabbi is referring to the 'gates' of a person's body and says that we have to place 'guards' there. I understand what he is trying to tell us. He is telling us to think about the television programs we watch or to be careful not to gossip or talk badly of others."

Since then, when we read *Parashat Shofetim* I am reminded of the scene so many years ago and of the gap between the two Hebrew languages. We need to bridge the gap and make the Torah more accessible.

CR CR CR

In God We Trust

תָּמִים תִּהְיֶה עִם ה' אֱלֹהֶיךָ.

Be wholehearted with the Lord, your God.
(Deut. 18:13)

Rashi explains this command to be wholehearted with God: "Walk with Him wholeheartedly and trust in Him. Do not try to divine the future, but rather accept wholeheartedly everything that befalls you. Then you will be His nation and His portion."

It is not so simple to be a simple Jew. It is not that easy to be naïve in our cynical world. In times of heresy on one hand and mysticism and magic on the other, the Torah demands that we be simple, upright, and faithful. Rabbi Chaim Navon relates that a woman once called him asking that he pray for her good health. He answered, "Both of us will pray," and she replied, "Thanks to both of you." It took him a few seconds to realize that it hadn't even occurred to her that he had invited her to pray for herself. She was convinced that he and another mysterious partner would both pray on her behalf.

The Lubavitcher Rebbe once received a letter from someone telling him about a mystical book of good omens and palm reading. The Rebbe sent him a sharp reply: "Abandon this path. Completely. If you want a book of charms – choose the Torah, and if you are looking for wisdom – choose the Torah. Why am I telling you this? 'Be wholehearted with the Lord your God.'"

In another, no less pointed letter, the Lubavitcher Rebbe replied to someone who had written to him about good luck charms, facial shapes, fortune tellers, and dream interpreters. Here again, the Rebbe gave clear, unequivocal instructions to abandon these practices and quoted the same verse: "Be wholehearted with the Lord your God." Walk along the straight and simple path that has been trodden for generations, choose the path of keeping the Torah and its commandments. You will have enough to keep you busy along this path.

He added another, surprising reason for keeping away from these practices, saying that they are simply a waste of time. They are not only mistaken but also steal away from the time allocated to a person to fulfill his task in life: "Every person is given a fixed time to fulfill the destiny for which God put him in this world. Every hour and every day that a person wastes on matters that are not his, he is also running away from fulfilling his destiny."

CB CB CB

The Yearly Safe Room

שָׁלוֹשׁ עָרִים תַּבְדִּיל לָךְ בְּתוֹךְ אַרְצְךָ אֲשֶׁר ה' אֱלֹהֶיךָ נֹתֵן לְךָ לְרִשְׁתָּהּ.

You shall separate three cities for yourself in the midst of your land, which the Lord, your God, is giving you to inherit.

(Deut. 19:2)

The Torah tells us to designate cities of refuge. If a person commits an accidental murder, he flees to one of these cities where he is afforded protection and undergoes rehabilitation until he returns to society as a new person. This concept is unknown in criminal law. The city of refuge is not like a prison; it is more a place where a person is given the chance for re-education while being protected from revenge killings.

Throughout the generations, commentators have explained these cities of refuge on a personal, existential level. The hasidic approach is that the month of Elul preceding the High Holy Days is compared to a city of refuge. Note also that *Parashat Shofetim* is invariably read in the first week of Elul. A very well-known acronym for the name of the month (spelled *aleph-lamed-vav-lamed*) is "*Ani ledodi vedodi li*," "I am my beloved's and my beloved is mine." A less famous acronym is taken from the verse in Exodus (21:13) which describes an accidental murderer: "*ina leyado vesamti lekha*," "put in his hand and I made a place for you."

Elul is the yearly safe room. It is the appropriate period of introspection and a time to rehabilitate and improve from all the bad things we have "accidentally" done throughout the year and make amends for the things that "slipped out of our hand." We should "flee" to the safe room of Elul once a year.

By the way, commentators note two activities that are compared to the cities for refuge for everyone, every day of the year, even in the eleven months that are not Elul. They are Torah study and prayer.

Ki Tetzeh

You Simply Cannot

וְכֵן תַּעֲשֶׂה לַחֲמֹרוֹ וְכֵן תַּעֲשֶׂה לְשִׂמְלָתוֹ וְכֵן תַּעֲשֶׂה לְכָל אֲבֵדַת אָחִיךָ אֲשֶׁר תֹּאבַד מִמֶּנּוּ וּמְצָאתָהּ לֹא תוּכַל לְהִתְעַלֵּם.

And so shall you do with his garment, and so shall you do with any lost article of your brother which he has lost and you have found. **You cannot ignore it.**

(Deut. 22:3)

Giving us details of the commandment of returning lost property, the Torah declares, "You cannot ignore it." If you see an object that someone else has lost, you have to take it, look for its owner, and go out of your way to return it to him. In other words, it is a moral requirement that if you find an ass or an ox – or a camera – belonging to someone else, you simply cannot ignore it and leave it where it was found. You do not live alone in this world. Even though the prevailing message in society might be "just ignore it," or "live and let live," the Torah gives the opposite message in a few succinct words.

Rashi's comment on this phrase is that you will not be able to "cover your eyes pretending you cannot see it." Even if you convince yourself that it is none of your business, deep down you know that you are purposely avoiding the situation. In psychological terms, note that the Torah does not just say, "Do not ignore it," as if we are being given a sound piece of advice, but it states a fact, "You simply cannot ignore it."

Over time, the commandment of returning lost property has taken on a wider perspective: we are not only told to make great efforts to return a lost item to the person to whom it belongs, but to return a person to himself, to help restore lost souls to the straight and narrow. A person can also be lost, and when we help bring him back to himself, to his self-identity and to sanity, then we have fulfilled the commandment of returning lost property.

ೞ ೞ ೞ

Thou Shalt Install Protective Bars!

כִּי תִבְנֶה בַּיִת חָדָשׁ וְעָשִׂיתָ מַעֲקֶה לְגַגֶּךָ וְלֹא תָשִׂים דָּמִים בְּבֵיתֶךָ כִּי יִפֹּל הַנֹּפֵל מִמֶּנּוּ.

When you build a new house, you shall make a guard rail for your roof, so that **you shall not cause blood [to be spilled] in your house**, if any man should fall from it.

(Deut. 22:8)

When we move into a new home, we are eager to celebrate the fixing a mezuza on each door and consider this to be a commandment. Let us ask ourselves whether we are equally keen to celebrate fulfillment of the commandment to install safety bars on all windows. Have you ever been invited to a party to celebrate the installation of safety bars as commanded in the Torah?

The Torah instructs us: "When you build a new house, you shall make a guard rail for your roof, so that you shall not cause blood [to be spilled] in your house, if any man should fall from it." We are told, in plain language, to put a protective railing on the roof of our house, and if we do not, then we risk that people will fall off the roof. Many halakhic rules concerning safety are derived from this verse, especially from the phrase "you shall not cause blood [to be spilled] in your house."

We are commanded to be vigilant about making our homes as safe as possible to prevent anyone risking bodily harm. For example, if there is a pit in the yard, put a fence around it; make sure your ladder is not shaky; and control your dog so that it doesn't frighten the neighbor's children, etc.

Maimonides has the following to say on the subject: "Similarly, it is a positive commandment to remove any obstacle that could pose a danger to life, and to be very careful regarding these matters, as it is written: 'Take care for yourself; and guard your soul.'"

The commentators have offered many profound explanations to this verse. However, taken at the literal level, the simple meaning of the words may very well be the most difficult to put into practice. The Torah requires us to take safety rules and regulations very seriously, as seriously as any other commandment.

ငဒ ငဒ ငဒ

True Speech

מוֹצָא שְׂפָתֶיךָ תִּשְׁמֹר וְעָשִׂיתָ כַּאֲשֶׁר נָדַרְתָּ לַה' אֱלֹהֶיךָ נְדָבָה אֲשֶׁר דִּבַּרְתָּ בְּפִיךָ.

Observe and do what is emitted from your lips just as you have pledged to the Lord, your God, as a donation, which you have spoken with your mouth.

(Deut. 23:24)

A well-known expression in Israeli politics is "I made a promise, but I never promised to keep it." In the American context, we are familiar with the phrase "Read my lips," as if there is no presumption of truth if what the person says is not prefaced by these three words (and sometimes even when it is).

While discussing the laws of making vows, the Torah tells us, "Observe and do what your lips say," or, in plain language, fulfill the words that leave your mouth, and respect your words and your promises.

Writing about the essence of the power of speech, many commentators expand on what it means to keep what we say. They explain that not only should we guard the words after they have left our mouth, but also before. In other words, think before you speak.

Rabbi Yehuda Aryeh Leib Alter writes in his book *Sefat Emet*, or *True Language*, that most of our speech should be devoted to talking about Torah. He reminds us that although the power of speech may seem to be trivial, it is a very special tool:

> Observing what leaves your mouth means guarding your tongue, because the mouth is an inner organ, and all the breath and internal essence of a person comes out through his mouth, and therefore must be guarded carefully. The root of man's life force is the internal breath and when a person guards the breath leaving his mouth, this is the source of all deeds, because all deeds depend on guarding the mouth. Man is superior to animal because of the power of speech, and the creation of the power of speech is the most wonderful thing of the entire creation, as can be readily seen by those considering this wonder.

Have you ever considered that the words leaving your mouth are "the most wonderful thing of the entire creation"?

CB CB CB

Under Construction

כִּי יִקַּח אִישׁ אִשָּׁה חֲדָשָׁה לֹא יֵצֵא בַּצָּבָא וְלֹא יַעֲבֹר עָלָיו לְכָל דָּבָר נָקִי
יִהְיֶה לְבֵיתוֹ שָׁנָה אֶחָת וְשִׂמַּח אֶת אִשְׁתּוֹ אֲשֶׁר לָקָח.

When a man takes a new wife, he shall not go out in the army, nor shall he be subjected to anything associated with it. **He shall remain free for his home for one year and delight his wife, whom he has taken.**

(Deut. 24:5)

Shortly after we got married, a relative told us that we should put on our front door the same notice that is placed at building sites: "Caution: Under Construction."

A young couple needs time to build their relationship after the wedding without a lot of external disturbances. With today's hectic pace of life, it seems difficult to allocate time to this task, but this is nothing new. Even in the time of the Torah we are told that during the first year of marriage, a man is not sent to war and is basically exempt from all public duty. Why is this so? "He shall remain free for his home for one year and delight his wife, whom he has taken." In the first year of marriage, the young couple should free up their busy schedules so that they have the peace of mind to be happy together. They are exempted from public duty so that they can build up their family home and bond together. They need this time together to lay the foundations for the family unit without any external disturbances.

In one of the seven blessings recited at the wedding ceremony, we ask God, "Grant abundant joy to these loving friends, as You bestowed gladness upon Your creation in the Garden of Eden." We hope that the young couple will be as happy together as Adam and Eve were in the Garden of Eden. The first couple in history were totally absorbed in each other, simply because there were no other people in the world. We bless the bride and groom that, at least at the start of their marriage, they will feel as if they are in Paradise where no one is competing for their attention and there are no external disturbances.

Ki Tavo

The Fig Speech

וְלָקַחְתָּ מֵרֵאשִׁית כָּל פְּרִי הָאֲדָמָה אֲשֶׁר תָּבִיא מֵאַרְצְךָ אֲשֶׁר ה' אֱלֹהֶיךָ
נֹתֵן לָךְ וְשַׂמְתָּ בַטֶּנֶא וְהָלַכְתָּ אֶל הַמָּקוֹם אֲשֶׁר יִבְחַר ה' אֱלֹהֶיךָ לְשַׁכֵּן
שְׁמוֹ שָׁם.

And you shall take of the first fruit of the land, which you will
bring from your land, which the Lord, your God, is giving you.
**And you shall put [them] into a basket and go to the place
which the Lord, your God, will choose** to have His Name
dwell there.

(Deut. 26:2)

Early one morning, you go out to your garden and discover the first fig
of the season growing on the tree. What would be the most natural reaction? To pick it and take a bite of the juicy fruit! However, the Torah has
a completely different idea: tie a string around the fruit to remind you
that this was the first fruit, the *Bikkurim*. Then set off to the Temple in
Jerusalem, carrying a basket of First Fruits, and go to the priest to present him with the fruit. In this presentation ceremony, you give a speech
that goes back to the dawn of Jewish history: "An Aramean [sought
to] destroy my forefather.... And the Egyptians treated us cruelly and
afflicted us, and they imposed hard labor upon us.... And He gave us
this land, a land flowing with milk and honey."

Why is the farmer instructed to deliver a passionate speech about the entire history of the Jewish people while holding his first fig, and what does the Exodus from Egypt have to do with it? Every single detail has a purpose and the fig is meant to serve as a reminder. This ceremony takes us out of our everyday life and reminds us that even this one fruit growing in our garden is part of a much larger, very meaningful story of Jewish history.

CB CB CB

Today Is the Day

הַיּוֹם הַזֶּה ה' אֱלֹהֶיךָ מְצַוְּךָ לַעֲשׂוֹת אֶת הַחֻקִּים הָאֵלֶּה וְאֶת הַמִּשְׁפָּטִים וְשָׁמַרְתָּ וְעָשִׂיתָ אוֹתָם בְּכָל לְבָבְךָ וּבְכָל נַפְשֶׁךָ.

This day, the Lord, your God, is commanding you to fulfill these statutes and ordinances, and you will observe and fulfill them with all your heart and with all your soul.

(Deut. 26:16)

Everything is always so special and fresh for the first few days. At every beginning, anticipation hangs in the air. In this festive atmosphere, we are happier and smile more, and our books and equipment have a new feel to them. But how do we feel a month later, two months later, a whole year later? What happens to the sense of novelty on a routine day when we are deep into our studies, our military service, or our new job?

Parashat Ki Tavo tells us, "This day, the Lord, your God, is commanding you to fulfill these statutes." When we read this verse, thousands of years after the Torah was given on Mount Sinai, how are we meant to understand the words "this day"? Our sages explain, "Every day you shall regard the commandments as if they are brand new, as if you are being commanded them on this very day."

Each day anew, the Torah wants us to feel as if we were standing at the foot of Mount Sinai. We should try to feel that every day is a new beginning. When we are studying, we should not see ourselves as rehashing old material, but that we are learning something new. We are being given a formidable challenge. Let us try to wake up each morning as if it is the first day of the school year, a new job, or our military service. Each day is a chance for change and turning over a new leaf. "Every day they should appear to be brand new."

୧୫ ୧୫ ୧୫

A People Becomes a Nation

וַיְדַבֵּר מֹשֶׁה וְהַכֹּהֲנִים הַלְוִיִּם אֶל כָּל יִשְׂרָאֵל לֵאמֹר הַסְכֵּת וּשְׁמַע יִשְׂרָאֵל הַיּוֹם הַזֶּה נִהְיֵיתָ לְעָם לַה׳ אֱלֹהֶיךָ.

Moses and the Levite priests spoke to all Israel, saying, "Pay attention and listen, O Israel! **This day, you have become a nation** to the Lord, your God."

(Deut. 27:9)

What was so special on this day? What was Moses referring to when he declared, "This day you have become a nation"? He wasn't speaking about the day of the Exodus, nor about the day that the Torah was given. So what transpired on this particular day that transformed us from a people to a nation?

For a behind-the-scenes explanation, let us see what Rashi has to say. Moses was saying his farewells to the people just before his death. He handed over his *sefer Torah* to the tribe of Levi, which caused major discontentment among the people of Israel. They all went to Moses to say that they had also received the Torah at Mount Sinai and that it belonged to them just as much as to the tribe of Levi. They asked Moses why he had only charged the Levites with keeping the Torah after his death. Moses was thrilled with this complaint and reacted by saying, "This day you have become a nation." Rashi explains, "Today I have understood that you really wish to cling to God."

Let us not forget that Moses had heard many complaints from the people of Israel during the forty-year sojourn in the wilderness about food, water, and the route to the Land of Israel. Now they are coming to him with a completely different kind of complaint and he is thrilled. They also want to be a link in the chain of passing the Torah to the next generation. They also want to keep its commandments and be actively involved in the Torah. Moses is so moved by their concern and sense of responsibility to the Torah that he makes his surprising declaration. His actual intent was to tell them, "Now I know, this entire journey has been worthwhile, and we have succeeded. You are now a nation."

CB CB CB

Leave as You Come

בָּרוּךְ אַתָּה בְּבֹאֶךָ וּבָרוּךְ אַתָּה בְּצֵאתֶךָ.

Blessed are you **when you come**, and blessed are you **when you depart**.

(Deut. 28:6)

One of the most famous greetings when two Jews meet is this verse, "Blessed are you when you come, and blessed are you when you depart." In its simplest meaning, we wish that someone be blessed when they leave home in the morning and return in the evening. Our sages give two additional explanations: On the personal level, the verse wishes a blessing upon one who comes to learn Torah in the beit midrash and one who leaves to go to work; on the national level we should be blessed when we enter the Land of Israel, and also when we leave it and go into exile. This is a blessing to the Jewish nation to help it survive all the exiles and diasporas throughout its history.

Rashi gives a different explanation and says that this verse refers to a person's entry into and exit from life. We should try to remain complete throughout the entire journey: "Your exit from the world should be the same as your entry, without sin." Just as an infant is pure and has not sinned, so we should try to keep the slate as clean as possible throughout our lives. We are blessed when we come into the world; let us try to leave in the same manner.

CB CB CB

The Virtue of Happiness

תַּחַת אֲשֶׁר לֹא עָבַדְתָּ אֶת ה' אֱלֹהֶיךָ בְּשִׂמְחָה וּבְטוּב לֵבָב מֵרֹב כֹּל.

Because you did not serve the Lord, your God, **with happiness and with gladness of heart, when [you had an] abundance of everything.**

(Deut. 28:47)

This *parasha* is about the consequences of our deeds and how God might bless or curse the Children of Israel as a result of their behavior. The *parasha* lists the devastating punishments that might befall the people: exile, disease, destruction, fear, and lack of basic security. The physical and emotional sorrows are heartbreaking, almost too much for anyone to bear. And in the middle of all this foreboding, seemingly providing the reason for this unremitting list of tragedies, we read, "because you did not serve the Lord your God with happiness and gladness of heart when you had an abundance of everything." Are you kidding? Just because we weren't happy enough, we were exiled, punished, and murdered? Could it be that because we were not happy enough beforehand, we are condemned to cry afterwards?!

The most common reason given for the destruction of the Temple is baseless hatred, which affects society as a whole. In this verse, the Torah is teaching us that there is also a personal reason, that we were not happy when keeping the commandments, even when our standard of living was comfortable and all was well.

Maimonides writes: "The joy a person has when fulfilling the commandments and loving the God who gave them – is a great religious accomplishment."

Rabbenu Bahya adds: "A person must be happy when fulfilling the commandments. This joy is in itself a commandment."

We learn from the above that joy is not simply an extra aspect of fulfilling commandments, but it stands as a commandment in its own right.

Nitzavim

Each of Our Parts

אַתֶּם נִצָּבִים הַיּוֹם כֻּלְּכֶם לִפְנֵי ה׳ אֱלֹהֵיכֶם רָאשֵׁיכֶם שִׁבְטֵיכֶם זִקְנֵיכֶם
וְשֹׁטְרֵיכֶם כֹּל אִישׁ יִשְׂרָאֵל.

You are all standing this day before the Lord, your God: the
heads of your tribes, your elders, and your officers, every man
of Israel.

(Deut. 29:9)

In the following verse, the Torah spells out all the people who stood
together before God: "Your young children, your women, and your
convert who is within your camp, both your woodcutters and your
water drawers."

Parashat Nitzavim is always read in one of the weeks preceding
Rosh HaShana and the Torah appropriately suggests several ways to
approach the New Year.

The first is that we come together as one: "You are all standing
here today." The power and influence of individuals coming together
to pray is greater than an individual's prayer. At the New Year we join
together many times to fulfill commandments such as blowing the
shofar or saying the *Selihot* penitential prayers. Unity is a popular buzz-
word. However, in this verse the unity we should strive for is "before
the Lord, your God."

Second, all the different sections of the people are included when we come together. The leaders and the woodcutters, the upper echelons of society and the man on the street. We are all in this together and share the same story.

The third approach is based on hasidic thought and explains this verse as speaking to the individual. We are told to bring together all the different parts of our personality, from "the heads of your tribes" to "your woodcutters and your water drawers." These describe the compartments of our soul. During the soon-to-be-finished year, there were periods when we were the "heads" and others when we were "woodcutters." Sometimes we were successful and happy and at other times we sinned, were confused, and missed out on opportunities. As the year draws to a close, we enter the period of the Days of Mercy with the sum of all our parts. Sometimes we felt on top of the world and at other times we were in a downward spiral. In the month of Elul, as we approach Tishrei and the New Year, we bring together all the parts of the past year and pray for a better year ahead.

CB CB CB

Consulting the Past and the Future

וְלֹא אִתְּכֶם לְבַדְּכֶם אָנֹכִי כֹּרֵת אֶת הַבְּרִית הַזֹּאת ...כִּי אֶת אֲשֶׁר יֶשְׁנוֹ פֹּה עִמָּנוּ עֹמֵד הַיּוֹם לִפְנֵי ה' אֱלֹהֵינוּ וְאֵת אֲשֶׁר אֵינֶנּוּ פֹּה עִמָּנוּ הַיּוֹם.

But not only with you am I making this covenant…but with those standing here with us today before the Lord, our God, **and with those who are not here with us, this day.**

(Deut. 29:13–14)

In one of the international discussions about partitioning the Land of Israel, David Ben-Gurion asked advice from Yitzhak Tabenkin, a founder of the Kibbutz Movement. Tabenkin asked for a day in which to consider his response, saying that he wanted to take counsel from two individuals. A day later, Tabenkin urged Ben-Gurion to refuse the offer. Ben Gurion said that he accepted Tabenkin's decision and asked who he discussed it with. Tabenkin answered, "From two people, from my grandfather who died ten years ago, and from my grandson who is not yet born." In his answer, Tabenkin showed that he bears responsibility for the past and the future, even for people who are not physically present.

The opening verses of *Parashat Nitzavim* told us that the covenant is binding on all sections of the people, from the upper echelons of society to the man in the street. Later on in *Nitzavim*, the Torah tells us that this not only applies to the breadth of society, but also to its depth. God made the covenant with all the past and future generations, with the grandfather who is no longer alive and with the grandson who is not yet born: "But with those standing here with us today before the Lord, our God, and with those who are not here with us, this day."

I was unable to find the original source of the story about Ben-Gurion and Tabenkin, but during my research I came across another one of Tabenkin's gems about intergenerational relationships: "If I feel a sense of the miraculous in my life, it is when I see my grandchildren and two great-granddaughters. New worlds are born within us, and they give us the sense of eternity above all of our transient efforts."

଼ଷ ଼ଷ ଼ଷ

Concealment Within Concealment

הַנִּסְתָּרֹת לַה' אֱלֹהֵינוּ וְהַנִּגְלֹת לָנוּ וּלְבָנֵינוּ עַד עוֹלָם לַעֲשׂוֹת אֶת כָּל דִּבְרֵי הַתּוֹרָה הַזֹּאת.

The hidden things belong to the Lord, our God, **and the revealed things apply to us and to our children forever**: that we must fulfill all the words of this Torah.

(Deut. 29:28)

In *Parashat Nitzavim* we are told of hidden things that we will never understand, issues about reward and punishment, God's role in the history of the world, the reasons for the commandments, and other subjects.

Studying Kabbala and the secrets of the universe is clearly a fascinating experience. Some say that we are obligated to study it as far as the human intellect can reach, but there will always be "hidden things" that defy human understanding and will remain as a mystery for us.

If so, what is our role? First, we have to deal with the revealed parts, "And the revealed things apply to us and to our children forever: that we must fulfill all the words of this Torah." Before we study mysticism, before we use our creative powers to their fullest, before we adopt far-reaching innovations, we have to deal first with the revealed Torah. Our task is to pass on the Torah in its plain sense, and ensure continuity for the day-to-day activities of Judaism from one generation to the next.

This verse may also be explained differently, that only God and we know the truth of who we really are, because these matters are "hidden things." You can be a righteous or wicked person on the outside and no one will know your inner self. Yet, sometimes a person's children bear witness to who he really is. "The hidden things belong to the Lord, our God," but "the revealed things apply to us and to our children." Our descendants are the revealed parts, and we can sometimes discover who a person really is by looking at his offspring.

Rabbi Michel Yehuda Lefkowitz made a pithy comment on this verse: "There are only two who know if a man is truly God-fearing – God, and his wife."

ଓ ଓ ଓ

No Further Comment

וּמָל ה' אֱלֹהֶיךָ אֶת לְבָבְךָ וְאֶת לְבַב זַרְעֶךָ לְאַהֲבָה אֶת ה' אֱלֹהֶיךָ בְּכָל לְבָבְךָ וּבְכָל נַפְשְׁךָ לְמַעַן חַיֶּיךָ.

And the Lord, your God, will circumcise your heart and the heart of your offspring, [so that you may] love the Lord your God with all your heart and with all your soul, for the sake of your life.
(Deut. 30:6)

This *parasha* contains some wonderful verses that are completely self-explanatory. I believe it is not coincidental that we read it on the last Shabbat of the year. It reminds us of the most fundamental beliefs of Judaism. Below are six verses from the *parasha* that encapsulate all our history:

> And it will be, when all these things come upon you the blessing and the curse which I have set before you that you will consider in your heart, among all the nations where the Lord your God has banished you. And you will return to the Lord, your God, with all your heart and with all your soul, and you will listen to His voice according to all that I am commanding you this day you and your children. Then, the Lord, your God, will bring back your exiles, and He will have mercy upon you. He will once again gather you from all the nations, where the Lord, your God, had dispersed you. Even if your exiles are at the end of the heavens, the Lord, your God, will gather you from there, and He will take you from there. And the Lord, your God, will bring you to the land which your forefathers possessed, and you [too] will take possession of it, and He will do good to you, and He will make you more numerous than your forefathers. And the Lord, your God, will circumcise your heart and the heart of your offspring, [so that you may] love the Lord your God with all your heart and with all your soul, for the sake of your life.

The themes mentioned in these verses are: exile and redemption; the intertwining of returning to the land and returning to God; the Ingathering of the Exiles from the furthest corners of the earth; a requirement to be of a pure heart; love and life and the obligation to pass all of this on to the coming generations.

No further comment needed.

CB CB CB

What Is the Greatest Sin?

וְאַתָּה תָשׁוּב וְשָׁמַעְתָּ בְּקוֹל ה' וְעָשִׂיתָ אֶת כָּל מִצְוֹתָיו אֲשֶׁר אָנֹכִי מְצַוְּךָ
הַיּוֹם.

And you will return and listen to the voice of the Lord, and
fulfill all His commandments, which I command you this day.
(Deut. 30:8)

Where do we get the strength to erase the past and start all over again?
How can we reboot the entire system? How does one clean the entire
slate? The answer is in the miraculous power of "repentance," although
it may be more fitting to say that "man" is the miracle.

Parashat Nitzavim deals extensively with the topic of repentance:
"And you will return and listen to the voice of the Lord," and "When you
return to the Lord, your God, with all your heart and with all your soul."

The well-known educator Rabbi Shlomo Wolbe claimed that we
do not sufficiently believe in ourselves and do not realize how great the
power to make changes to ourselves really is. He was fond of saying that
the biggest sin is the belief that we are destined to sin. In a conversation with a group of teenagers in the 1970s he made the following very
meaningful comments:

> If I were asked to state my number one belief, it would be "I
> believe in the greatness of man." This greatness enables him to
> correct himself, his surroundings, and the entire world. Many
> people believe in God, it is nothing unusual. But not everyone
> believes in the greatness of man as well. I do. I believe that a per-
> son can reach a true and significant connection with his Creator,
> that he can instigate great changes. These changes are not only
> external, pertaining to the world, but also internal. A person has
> the formidable spiritual strength to control himself.

ca ca ca

It Is Near to You

כִּי הַמִּצְוָה הַזֹּאת אֲשֶׁר אָנֹכִי מְצַוְּךָ הַיּוֹם לֹא נִפְלֵאת הִוא מִמְּךָ וְלֹא
רְחֹקָה הִוא. לֹא בַשָּׁמַיִם הִוא.

For this commandment which I command you this day, **is not
concealed from you, nor is it far away. It is not in heaven.**
(Deut. 30:11–12)

You may be familiar with the expression "it is not up in the sky," meaning that "it is doable, it is not an exaggerated task." It comes from a
section of four momentous verses in this *parasha* as part of Moses'
farewell speech.

> For this commandment which I command you this day, is not
> concealed from you, nor is it far away. It is not in heaven, that
> you should say, "Who will go up to heaven for us and fetch it for
> us, to tell [it] to us, so that we can fulfill it?" Nor is it beyond the
> sea, that you should say, "Who will cross to the other side of the
> sea for us and fetch it for us, to tell [it] to us, so that we can fulfill
> it?" Rather, [this] thing is very close to you; it is in your mouth
> and in your heart, so that you can fulfill it.

Moses is not commanding us to do impossible things. Quite the
contrary! Not only are there no physical obstacles to overcome, the task
is really close. It not in the heavens or sea, and it is not even being kept
by the rabbi or your friend. Moses tells us it is within *you*, in your mouth
and heart. Everything begins with your inner self.

Rabbi Abraham Isaac HaKohen Kook writes about repentance
in his book *Lights of Repentance* (*Orot HaTeshuva*): "The principle of
repentance which immediately illuminates the dark spots is for a person
to return to himself, to the source of his soul, and he will immediately
return to God."

It is not up in the sky.

Vayelekh

As We Approach the Finishing Line

וַיֵּלֶךְ מֹשֶׁה וַיְדַבֵּר אֶת הַדְּבָרִים הָאֵלֶּה אֶל כָּל יִשְׂרָאֵל. וַיֹּאמֶר אֲלֵהֶם בֶּן
מֵאָה וְעֶשְׂרִים שָׁנָה אָנֹכִי הַיּוֹם לֹא אוּכַל עוֹד לָצֵאת וְלָבוֹא וַה' אָמַר אֵלַי
לֹא תַעֲבֹר אֶת הַיַּרְדֵּן הַזֶּה.

**And Moses went, and he spoke the following words to all of
Israel.** And he said to them, "Today I am one hundred and twenty
years old. I can no longer go or come, and the Lord said to me,
'You shall not cross this Jordan.'"

(Deut. 31:1–2)

Vayelekh is the shortest *parasha* in the entire Torah and it is always read
at the end of the year, as we approach Rosh HaShana, the New Year.
Rabbi Berel Wein explains that this is no coincidence. We are not the
only ones who are in an introspective mood at this time; Moses also
reviews his life in his final days. The ends of the year, the Torah, and
Moses' life are all interconnected.

As the year draws to the end and we are engaged in reviewing
our actions, we can look to Moses' speech for guidance in this process.
Moses speaks frankly and expresses his feelings. He talks of his disap-
pointments and successes and calls on the Children of Israel to keep the
Torah and to continually reaccept it.

This is the essence of this time of the year during the months of Elul and Tishrei. It is the annual opportunity for an honest assessment of what is good and bad in our lives. If necessary, it is the chance to turn a new page, to correct, and to refresh. This is not a time to be depressed; rather we should be optimistic and look for our winning and strong points. One of the most positive comments I have heard about the month of Elul tells us, "When you want to correct yourself, it is very important to know what your bad qualities are, but it is far more important to know your positive qualities."

CB CB CB

The Reunion

הַקְהֵל אֶת הָעָם הָאֲנָשִׁים וְהַנָּשִׁים וְהַטַּף וְגֵרְךָ אֲשֶׁר בִּשְׁעָרֶיךָ לְמַעַן יִשְׁמְעוּ וּלְמַעַן יִלְמְדוּ וְיָרְאוּ אֶת ה' אֱלֹהֵיכֶם וְשָׁמְרוּ לַעֲשׂוֹת אֶת כָּל דִּבְרֵי הַתּוֹרָה הַזֹּאת.

Assemble the people: the men, the women, and the children, and your stranger in your cities, in order that they hear, and in order that they learn and fear the Lord, your God, and they will observe to do all the words of this Torah.

(Deut. 31:12)

Moses does not rest for a moment during the last day of his life. He instructs the people about the commandment of *hak'hel*, where the entire nation meets together in Jerusalem once every seven years to listen to the entire Torah. The *Sefer HaHinukh* gives a wonderful description of the *hak'hel* ceremony, of the exceptional ceremony reminiscent of the gathering at Mount Sinai.

> The source of the commandment is that the whole essence of the Jewish nation is the Torah, and this is what separates them from all other nations and languages, and what guarantees them to have eternal life, and the highest form of eternal pleasure. So because everything is contained in the Torah, it is fitting that at

a fixed time they should all gather together to hear the Torah's words. The talk of all the nation – men, women, and children – would then be: "Why have we assembled for this large gathering?" And the answer would be: "To hear the words of the Torah – our essence, glory, and pride!" This would lead them to praise the Torah and speak of its glorious worth, and implant within their hearts a desire and motivation to study and know God. Thus they will merit the ultimate good, and God will rejoice in His creations.

In the final moments of his life, Moses reminds the Children of Israel of their core identity.

C03 C03 C03

Hide and Seek with God

וְאָנֹכִי הַסְתֵּר אַסְתִּיר פָּנַי בַּיּוֹם הַהוּא עַל כָּל הָרָעָה אֲשֶׁר עָשָׂה כִּי פָנָה אֶל אֱלֹהִים אֲחֵרִים.

And I will hide My face on that day, because of all the evil they have committed, when they turned to other gods.

(Deut. 31:18)

God gives Moses a glimpse of what will befall the Jewish nation in the future: they will not follow the straight path and, as a result, their relationship with God will change. The undoing of the natural closeness we once enjoyed with our Creator is one of the future punishments we will be cursed with. God says we will no longer have the close relationship on a daily basis with Him as we had in the wilderness. It will now seemingly be more distant, "And I will hide My face on that day."

The *Netivot Shalom* writes about this:

The biggest trial is when God hides Himself from us. So long as a Jew feels close to God, he has the strength to withstand the trial. However, after a Jew has committed the most serious transgression in the Torah, if he cannot pour out his heart in supplication to God, then he hasn't even stepped on the threshold of Judaism. None of the barricades and fences are as serious as the ones that a Jew himself puts in his heart and distances himself from God. This is the most severe separation. It is known that when the Evil Inclination tempts a Jew to commit a sin, its main purpose is not to cause him to sin, but to do away with the feelings of remorse and despair after he has sinned, causing him to feel distant from God. The distance is worse than the actual sin. When God hides His face, it is a deception and therefore there is a double mention of hiding, "I will surely hide (*haster astir*)." The hiding is because of the sin itself and because the sinner has despaired. As we approach the High Holy Days, the main preparation we ought to do is to believe that the close connection between us and God is an eternal reality.

03 03 03

The Music School

וְעַתָּה כִּתְבוּ לָכֶם אֶת הַשִּׁירָה הַזֹּאת וְלַמְּדָהּ אֶת בְּנֵי יִשְׂרָאֵל שִׂימָהּ
בְּפִיהֶם לְמַעַן תִּהְיֶה לִּי הַשִּׁירָה הַזֹּאת לְעֵד בִּבְנֵי יִשְׂרָאֵל.

And now, write for yourselves this song, and teach it to the Children of Israel. Place it into their mouths, in order that this song will be for Me as a witness for the Children of Israel.

(Deut. 31:19)

The public agenda is full of discussions about religious Jews versus secular Jews. In *Parashat Vayelekh* a completely new topic is introduced, poetry and song. Up to this point, the Torah has been replete with words such as Torah, commandments, and covenant, and now this new word appears: "And now, write for yourselves this song." Moses tells the nation that the Torah is not only a collection of laws, but also song. If the point is not made clearly enough this first time, the word song is mentioned another three times in the *parasha*.

And it will be, when they will encounter many evils and troubles, this song will bear witness against them, for it will not be forgotten from the mouth of their offspring. (Deut. 31:21)

And Moses wrote this song on that day, and taught it to the Children of Israel. (v. 22)

Then, Moses spoke into the ears of the entire assembly of Israel the words of the following song, until their completion. (v. 30)

And the following *parasha, Haazinu,* will indeed bring the full text of this song.

Rabbi Yaakov Moshe Harlap described this song as a complex musical composition in which every individual and every commandment plays a role:

The Torah is described as a song. When we keep the commandments, we strum the chords so that the most beautiful notes will be produced. When we make the effort to keep all their minutiae, when we are eager to promptly fulfill the commandments, when we understand the meaning behind the commandments then we ensure that the entire symphony will be played in all its glory. When a person holds the commandments in disrespect, he is in contempt of the world's orchestra, meddling with the song, and destroying the poetry.

Haazinu

Lessons from My Grandparents

זְכֹר יְמוֹת עוֹלָם בִּינוּ שְׁנוֹת דּוֹר וָדוֹר שְׁאַל אָבִיךָ וְיַגֵּדְךָ זְקֵנֶיךָ וְיֹאמְרוּ לָךְ.

Remember the days of old; reflect upon the years of generations. **Ask your father, and he will tell you; your elders, and they will inform you.**

(Deut. 32:7)

A dog does not have a grandfather, and a mosquito has no grandmother. People have grandparents.

I once heard Rabbi Yeshayahu Steinberger talk about this concept. When a person becomes a grandparent, a great part of his or her humanity is realized, and part of his or her role in life is fulfilled. In the animal kingdom, parents have a relationship with their offspring, but a chain of three or more generations is unique to humans. It is especially meaningful when a parent passes on traditions to a child and then on to a grandchild.

In his farewell song of *Haazinu*, Moses refers to the theme of intergenerational relationships: "Ask your father, and he will tell you; your elders, and they will inform you." The curious child wants answers and asks his father: "Ask your father and he will tell you." The father tells his child to ask his grandfather: "Your elders and they will inform you." Each generation respects the previous one and relies on it to a certain extent. This idea is particularly relevant to the time of year when we read *Parashat Haazinu.* As Yom Kippur approaches, people often recall the customs and style of prayer they grew up with and look to continue them.

Our sages also describe the opposite social structure. When they try to describe a society rife with arguments and unruly behavior they use the imagery of "youths who insult their grandparents, elderly people who have to stand up and give their place to youngsters, a son who curses his father, a daughter fights her mother…a son has no fear of his father, etc."

Moses paints an idyllic picture of family traditions and wisdom being passed down through the generations.

ʻʒ ʻʒ ʻʒ

Think Positive!

צוּר יְלָדְךָ תֶּשִׁי וַתִּשְׁכַּח אֵל מְחֹלְלֶךָ.

You forgot the Rock who bore you; **you forgot the God who delivered you**.

(Deut. 32:18)

Moses talks to the Children of Israel about the time when "Jeshurun became fat and rebelled," or "You forgot the God who delivered you." How can we move on from such a state toward better things? Rabbi Shlomo Wolbe writes that Yom Kippur is the antithesis of such feelings. It is a day intended to prevent us from forgetting who bore us and prevent us from sinking into the heartless situation described in these verses. In a speech given shortly before Yom Kippur he lays out the main purpose of the day:

> Many of us are confused by the idea of repenting and leaving the path of sin. We tell ourselves that, whatever happens, we will anyhow go back to our old ways after Yom Kippur so our repentance

is not honest. This is a mistake, and because of this mistaken thinking we might not repent at all, God forbid. Who can be so certain that we will go back to sinning in the new year? Are we prophets? How can we be so sure? This (dis)belief in ourselves borders on heresy. One of the fundamental beliefs of the Torah is that people are born with freedom of choice. If we believe a person's actions are pre-determined, then the whole belief in Torah falls by the wayside. The influence of modern psychology has caused us to believe this, and we have to stand firmly against that school of thought.... The lowest level of heresy is when one stops believing in freedom of choice because then a person is no different than an animal. We have also been caught up in this school of thought. Do we believe that it is feasible that we will not commit any sins between one Yom Kippur and the next? We surely must believe in the power of choice, that we can be truly righteous in the coming year. All we need is to have a strong will! We must have complete belief in the power of free will. If the very least that we achieve on Yom Kippur is to strengthen our belief in the power of our freedom of choice, then this holy day will have achieved wonders.

CS CS CS

Right Now

רְאוּ עַתָּה כִּי אֲנִי אֲנִי הוּא וְאֵין אֱלֹהִים עִמָּדִי אֲנִי אָמִית וַאֲחַיֶּה מָחַצְתִּי וַאֲנִי אֶרְפָּא וְאֵין מִיָּדִי מַצִּיל.

See now that it is I! I am the One, and there is no god like Me! I cause death and grant life. I strike, but I heal, and no one can rescue from My hand!

(Deut. 32:39)

In the *Song of Haazinu*, Moses describes the entire history and all future events of the Jewish people. In this dramatic sentence, he talks about God's rule over the world: "See now that it is I! I am the One, and there is no god like Me! I cause death and grant life. I strike, but I heal, and no one can rescue from My hand!" Rabbi Nahman of Breslov explains this verse differently and says it refers to a person's self-control. His explanation puts the emphasis on the word "now" in the first part of the verse. This reading is a definite catalyst for implementing decisions and changes, especially since we read this *parasha* during the month of Elul as we approach the New Year.

> Whoever has even a small amount of common sense will understand that time is not anything at all, because the past in no longer, the future has not yet occurred, and the present is like the blink of an eye, so most of a person's time is only the exact moment of the present, because the past has gone, and who knows what the future holds. Thus we can explain the verse, "See now that it is I, I am the One," just "now," because the most important thing is the present, the here and now moment that exists currently. Just skip over what needs to be overlooked, and merit to find the true good that can be found in each and every moment. People make many errors in this aspect and give a lot of thought to what will happen in the future, but we do not know what will be tomorrow. So the best advice is to be fully aware that the only time is the one in which we are right now, and to connect oneself at this moment to God.

C3 C3 C3

Fill the Void

כִּי לֹא דָבָר רֵק הוּא מִכֶּם כִּי הוּא חַיֵּיכֶם וּבַדָּבָר הַזֶּה תַּאֲרִיכוּ יָמִים עַל הָאֲדָמָה אֲשֶׁר אַתֶּם עֹבְרִים אֶת הַיַּרְדֵּן שָׁמָּה לְרִשְׁתָּהּ.

For it is not an empty thing for you, for it is your life, and through this thing, you will lengthen your days upon the land to which you are crossing over the Jordan, to possess it.

(Deut. 32:47)

Rabbi Abraham Isaac HaKohen Kook had a special custom in his home on the festival of Purim. Guests were permitted to ask any question they wished and the rabbi would connect the answer to the festival of Purim and the Book of Esther. As the guests sat at the festive Purim meal, between the drinking and the dancing, they would ask their questions and be awestruck by the rabbi's wisdom and wide-ranging knowledge.

One year a guest named Moshe Bezalel, who was slightly tipsy, chose a verse from Genesis and waited curiously to see how Rabbi Kook would connect it to Purim. The words he chose were, "And the sister of Lotan was called Timna." To his amazement, Rabbi Kook gave a whole sermon explaining that the entire story of Purim has its roots in this very verse.

The details of the sermon can be found in a highly recommended book called *The Festivals of Rabbi Kook* (*Moadei HaRayah*), and we will not discuss them here. I was reminded of this Purim story when I read the last few verses of *Parashat Haazinu*. Moses tells the Children of Israel that the Torah "is not an empty thing for you." It is not empty, it is rich with content. The sages expand on the verse and comment that "it is not an empty thing for you, and if it is empty – it is because of you, because you do not put enough effort into studying the Torah." If you do not find reason in the Torah or if you feel an emptiness within you, it is because you did not delve deeply enough into the Torah. If we do not feel connected to the Torah it is due to us, and it is not the Torah's problem. Even the above verse from Genesis, which may seem "empty" to us, has deep significance. There is no such thing as a superfluous verse; there are only verses which we have not made enough effort to get to the bottom of. If we speak to truly great Torah scholars (such as Rabbi Kook) we may be in for a big surprise when we are told about the meanings of words in the Torah that we hadn't been aware of.

Vezot Haberakha

Only One Blessing

וְזֹאת הַבְּרָכָה אֲשֶׁר בֵּרַךְ מֹשֶׁה אִישׁ הָאֱלֹהִים אֶת בְּנֵי יִשְׂרָאֵל לִפְנֵי מוֹתוֹ.

And this is the blessing with which Moses, the man of God,
blessed the Children of Israel before his death.

(Deut. 33:1)

In one of his interesting comments, Rabbi Menachem Mendel of Kotzk
says that just as you can accept that your friend's nose is not like yours,
you must understand that your friend's views are different from yours.
If we do not get annoyed that other people's nose or eyes do not look
the same as ours, we have to accept that sometimes others don't think
the same way we do.

Moses opens this *parasha* with the words, "And this is the blessing with which Moses, the man of God, blessed the Children of Israel
before his death." He declares that we all share an overall goal: "The
Torah that Moses commanded us is a legacy for the congregation of
Jacob." Moses continues with a series of blessings, varying in content
and purpose, that are tailor-made for each of the Twelve Tribes. Each
one is given a different attribute and different life task.

Take note that although each group is given a different task in life,
the blessings do not commence with the introductory words, "These are
the blessings" in the plural form. The fact that the singular form, "This

317

is the blessing," is used proves that it is one blessing only. We all share a common goal and each tribe has its own way of achieving it. Being different is not a problem. It is an integral part of the blessing.

The kabbalist Rabbi Hayim Vital discusses in his book *Etz Hayim* what his teacher, the Arizal, says about the different styles, customs, and versions of prayers of Jewish communities:

> At the entrance to heaven there are twelve windows corresponding to the Twelve Tribes of Israel, and each tribe's prayers go up to heaven passing through its designated gate. If the prayers of all the tribes were the same, there would be no need for twelve different gates. But since each gate has its own path, therefore it must be that each tribe's prayers are different. Just as the source and root of each tribe's soul is different, so the nature of their prayers is different.

ജ ജ ജ

So Sweet

וּמִמֶּגֶד תְּבוּאֹת שָׁמֶשׁ וּמִמֶּגֶד גֶּרֶשׁ יְרָחִים.

And with the **sweetness** of the produce of the sun, and with the **sweetness** of the moon's yield.

(Deut. 33:14)

One of the most common literary devices taught in high-school literature and Tanakh classes in Israel is the *leitmotif,* a word or idea occurring throughout the text which is meant to teach us something. In the blessing given to Joseph, the word "sweetness" occurs five times. Rashi explains that it denotes "delicacies and sweetness."

Hasidic commentators note that Moses' blessing was that the Torah should not be viewed as a technical list of laws, but that it should fill us with pleasure and sweetness. The five-fold use of the word alludes to the Five Books of the Torah, as the Torah provides not only a set of guidelines for living our lives but also a source of sweetness.

This idea ties in very well with the time of year when *Parashat Vezot Haberakha* is read, immediately after Sukkot, on Simhat Torah. An additional name given to the festival is "The Time of Our Joy," when we are commanded, "And you shall rejoice in your festival … and you will only be happy." While we are observing the commandments of the festival such as the Four Species and dwelling in the sukka, we are given an extra commandment that continues throughout the week-long festival, to be joyous.

CB CB CB

What's the Headline?

וַיָּמָת שָׁם מֹשֶׁה עֶבֶד ה' בְּאֶרֶץ מוֹאָב עַל פִּי ה'.

And Moses, the servant of the Lord, died there, in the land of Moab, by the mouth of the Lord.

(Deut. 34:5)

We have reached the finish line. After an entire year of weekly encounters with the Torah, we have reached the final *parasha* of *Vezot Haberakha*. I would like to end with a discussion among the sages which, in my opinion, sums up what we have learned throughout the entire cycle of Torah learning. A number of sages asked what verse best sums up the whole Torah. In other words, "What headline should be given for the Torah?"

One sage chose the verse which is the most famous declaration of Judaism, "Hear O Israel, the Lord our God, the Lord is one." Another suggested, "Love your neighbor as yourself." The first suggestion relates to our relationship with God, the second encapsulates our dealings with fellow humans. The Midrash continues with another, surprising, suggestion. Shimon ben Pazi declares that he has found a more inclusive commandment which describes the daily *tamid* sacrifice that was brought twice daily: "The one lamb you shall offer up in the morning, and the other lamb you shall offer up in the afternoon." The Midrash's conclusion is that ben Pazi's suggestion is the best of the three and it was chosen as the verse that best sums up the entire Torah.

This verse seems to be telling us a mere technicality about the laws of sacrifices. Why was it preferred to "Hear O Israel…" and "Love your neighbor…"? Persistence. There is no glamor, drama, or heroism in bringing the daily sacrifice, just the daily routine that repeats itself twice a day, every morning and afternoon. This routine is the essence of life itself.

One-time events with their high peaks are wonderful. Who would not want to experience an event like winning the lottery? However, most of our lives are filled with routine tasks like preparing lunch for our children or saying our daily prayers. Carrying out these tasks faithfully is not at all glamorous. The Midrash tells us that it is precisely these moments that are the most important ones in life. The pinnacle of our prayers is not only at the *Ne'ila* service at the end of Yom Kippur but also on any given weekday afternoon. The pinnacle is to continue being faithful to our routine throughout our lives, even when countless nuisances and stumbling blocks threaten to derail us.

CR CR CR

Get on the Field

תּוֹרָה צִוָּה לָנוּ מֹשֶׁה מוֹרָשָׁה קְהִלַּת יַעֲקֹב.

Moses commanded us a law, an inheritance of the congregation of Jacob.

(Deut. 33:4)

In one of the final verses in the Torah, we are told that the Torah is an inheritance belonging to the entire congregation and this treasure is now our responsibility. "Moses commanded us a law, an inheritance of the congregation of Jacob."

When I was growing up, I thought that the Torah only belonged to those annoying religious fanatics, the primitives who went on the rampage during demonstrations, the extremists who were involved in all kind of unclear protests. I was angry at them, I did not understand them, and I was forever criticizing them.

Sometime in my teenage years, I heard an amazing comparison from the world of sports that changed my perspective. In a sports match, there are fans who sit in the stadium and think they run the whole show. They criticize the umpire, the goalkeeper, the coach, and the owner. Throughout the game they shout, curse, and blame everyone for how the game is played and this pattern repeats itself each and every season. They would not consider, for even one second, going onto the field and trying to score a goal, to work hard to be part of the team and join the game. They do not think that the game actually belongs to them, or that they are part of it. These fans are happy to observe from the sidelines, and do no more than criticize.

The same applies to the Torah. We can choose to remain in the stadium and complain non-stop, or we can decide to get on the field and take responsibility. We may then discover that what we thought about the other players is not exactly the truth. It is our choice whether we remain sitting on the sidelines or decide to take the plunge and be part of the team by learning Torah and connecting to our heritage and previous generations. We choose whether we want to look for the relevance and meaning in the Torah in our generation.

As Moses concludes his historic speech, in the moments before he leaves this world, he addresses the entire Jewish nation and tells them, "I am bequeathing an inheritance to you. Take responsibility for it, all of you together."

Glossary of Names

Abrabanel, Rabbi Isaac (1437–1508) – One of the greatest biblical commentators, statesmen, and philosophers in Spain and Portugal and among the most influential Jewish leaders during the Inquisition and exile from Spain. He is known for his commentary on the Torah, and for being secretary of the treasury in Castile and Aragon for eight years.

Alter, Rabbi Yehuda Arye Leib (1847–1905) – The third leader of the Ger hasidic dynasty and one of the leaders of Polish Jewry, he is known by the name of his book, the *Sefat Emet*, which is a collection of sermons about the *parashot* and a commentary on the Talmud.

Amital, Rabbi Yehuda (1924–2010) – Head of the Har Etzion hesder yeshiva in Alon Shvut, and founder of the Meimad political party, he served as a minister in the Israeli government. His many books included *Steps Out of the Depths* and *Jewish Values in a Changing World*.

Arama, Rabbi Isaac (1420–1494) – One of the Torah luminaries during the expulsion from Spain, he wrote a commentary on the Pentateuch entitled *Akeidat Yitzhak*. He also wrote a commentary on the Five Megillot and on the Book of Proverbs called *Yad Avshalom*.

Azoulay, Rabbi Abraham (1570–1643) – Rabbi and kabbalist, a native of Morocco, he moved to Israel and settled in Hebron, where he is buried.

Baal Shem Tov, Rabbi Israel ben Eliezer (1690-1760) – He was the founder of the hasidic movement. Most of his teachings were recorded by his disciples.

Bahya ben Asher, Rabbi (1255–1340) – Biblical commentator and rabbi, he lived in Zaragoza in Muslim-ruled Spain.

Banai, Ehud – Singer, songwriter, and lyricist, he hosts the "Here is the Place" radio show.

Ben Ish Hai, Rabbi Yosef Hayim of Baghdad (1835–1909) – Chief rabbi of Baghdad and a famous halakhic decisor, preacher, and kabbalist, he is known as the *Ben Ish Hai* after his most famous book.

Ben-Attar, Rabbi Hayim (1646–1743) – One of the greatest biblical and talmudic commentators during the era of the *Aharonim*, he was a kabbalist and halakhic arbiter. His most famous work is the *Or HaHayim* and he is commonly known by this name.

Berezovsky, Rabbi Shalom Noah (1911–2000) – The rebbe of Slonim Hasidim, he established and headed the Beit Avraham yeshiva of Slonim. He wrote *Netivot Shalom*, a series of books on the Torah and the festivals, and is commonly known by this name.

Berlin, Rabbi Naphtali Zvi Yehuda (1893–1916) – Known as the Netziv of Volozhin, he was head of the Volozhin yeshiva and one of the greatest Torah leaders in Eastern Europe in the nineteenth century. Rabbi Kook studied in his yeshiva when he was young. He wrote many books, most famously *Haamek Davar*, a commentary on the Torah.

Bernstein, Aharoni – Graduate of the Ramat Gan hesder yeshiva, he edits a popular *parashat hashavua* pamphlet and is author of *Once a Week*.

Bina, Rabbi Aharon – Formerly a rabbi at Yeshivat HaKotel, he founded the Netiv Aryeh yeshiva in the Old City of Jerusalem for students from abroad studying in Israel.

Blumenzweig, Rabbi Eliyahu – Founder and head of the Yeruham hesder yeshiva.

Braverman, Rabbi Dudi – Senior lecturer at the Arachim organization.

Breslov, Rabbi Nahman (of) (1772–1810) – Grandson of the Baal Shem Tov, he founded the Breslov Hasidism but had no successor after his death. His teachings are based on the importance of joy, simplicity, and pure belief in God. He died from tuberculosis at age 38 and was buried in Uman, Ukraine.

Cohen, Rabbi David (1887–1972) – One of the leading disciples of Rabbi Kook who edited most of his writings, he was a philosopher and talmudic scholar and known as the Nazirite Rabbi for his customs of not drinking wine, eating meat, or cutting his hair.

Dessler, Rabbi Eliyahu (1892–1953) – One of the greatest ethicists of the Kelm *Musar* movement in the twentieth century, he served as a rabbi in England and as the *mashgiah ruhani* in charge of the spiritual welfare of students at the Ponevezh yeshiva in Benei Berak. His students collated his writings into a set of books called *Mikhtav MiEliyahu* dealing with faith and ethics.

Edelstein, Rabbi Yaakov (1924–2017) – Rabbi of Ramat HaSharon from 1950 until his death, he was also a *dayan* (rabbinic judge) and rabbi of the Neot Yosef neighborhood in Benei Berak.

Eliyahu, Rabbi Mordechai (1929–2010) – Former Sephardic chief rabbi of Israel, he was a halakhic arbiter, *dayan*, kabbalist, and leader. He was appointed as *dayan* in Be'er Sheva at a young age, and later promoted to the Supreme Rabbinical Court in Israel.

Elyashiv, Rabbi Netanel – Rabbi and educator at the Benei David pre-army academy in Eli and founder of the Binyan HaTorah Institute publishing house.

Firer, Rabbi Benzion (1914–1988) – Rabbi and author of books on Jewish topics and novels, he taught Judaism at the Givat Washington women's seminary, and at the Kerem BeYavneh yeshiva.

Friedlander, Rabbi Chaim (1923–1986) – One of the leaders of the *Musar* movement in Israel and a rabbi and *mashgiah* at Ponevezh and Be'er Yaakov yeshivas, he was an expert in the writings of the Malbim and published new editions of several of his books. His lectures were gathered together in a series of books called *Siftei Hayim*.

Gerondi, Rabbi Yona (1210–1263) – Lived in Spain in the era of the *Rishonim* and wrote many books, most famously *Shaarei Teshuva*, which gives detailed guidance on the various stages of repentance. He was known as Rabbenu Yona the Hasid.

Gordon, Judah Leib (1830–1892) – One of the greatest Jewish poets of the Enlightenment period in Russia, he coined the phrase "Be a man in the street and a Jew in your home," which became the slogan of the *Haskala*.

Hakham, Amos (1921–2012) – The first winner of the Bible Quiz, he was emblematic of broad Tanakh knowledge. He became a biblical scholar and one of the authors of the *Daat Mikra* series, and wrote many of the entries in the *Encyclopedia Hebraica*. In 1984, he was awarded the Rav Kook Prize for Torah Literature.

HaKohen, Rabbi Yisrael Meir (1839–1933) – Known as the Hafetz Hayim of Radin, he was one of the most influential rabbis of pre-war Europe. His many books include the *Mishna Berura* on practical halakha and *Hafetz Hayim* on the laws of "evil speech."

Halberstam, Rabbi Chaim (1797–1876) – Founder of the Sanz hasidic dynasty and one of the greatest leaders of Eastern European Jewry at the time. The most popular book he wrote was the *Divrei Hayim*, and he is commonly known by that name.

HaLevi, Rabbi Judah (1075–1141) – A philosopher, poet, and scholar during Spain's Golden Age and author of the *Kuzari*. He wrote many poems, including lamentations about the destruction of the Temple, and many verses expressing longing for Jerusalem.

Harlap, Rabbi Yaakov Moshe (1882–1951) – Rabbi Kook's leading disciple who replaced him as head of Yeshivat Merkaz Harav after his death, he also headed the Beit Zevul yeshiva and served as rabbi of the Shaarei Hesed neighborhood in Jerusalem.

Hartman, Rabbi Yehoshua – Head of the Beit Midrash program at Hasmonean Grammar School for Boys in London, England, and editor of several books of the Maharal.

Hirsch, Rabbi Samson Raphael (1808–1888) – Appointed rabbi of the K'hal Adath Jerushun congregation in Frankfurt, Germany, during the height of the Enlightenment, he promoted the *Torah im Derekh Eretz* way of life, combining Torah and culture. He wrote a commentary on the Torah as well as books on philosophy, including *Horeb* and *The Nineteen Letters*.

Horowitz, Ariel – Singer, songwriter, and lyricist, he is the son of the songwriter Naomi Shemer and the author and songwriter Mordechai Horowitz.

Jungreis, Rabbanit Esther (1936–2016) – An American rebbetzin and lecturer, founder of the "Hineini" movement, and author of many books.

Kanievski, Rabbi Yaakov Yisrael (1899–1985) – Known as the "Steipler," after the city of his birth, he was one of the leading rabbis of the ultra-Orthodox community in Israel. His most famous book is called *Kehillot Yaakov*.

Katz, Rabbi Yaakov – Former head of Yeshivat HaKotel and now head of the kollel at the Netiv Aryeh yeshiva in the Jewish Quarter of the Old City.

Kook, Rabbi Abraham Isaac HaKohen (1865–1935) – Philosopher, halakhic arbiter, kabbalist and the first Ashkenazi Chief Rabbi of Israel, he was one of the founding fathers of Religious Zionism and established the Merkaz HaRav yeshiva. He wrote books on the entire Torah, both on the revealed and hidden levels, including *Orot, Orot HaKodesh, Ein Ayah*, and *Musar Avikha*.

Kook, Rabbi Zvi Yehuda (1891–1982) – The son and successor of Rabbi Abraham Isaac HaKohen Kook, both as head of the Merkaz HaRav yeshiva and as spiritual leader of the Religious Zionist movement.

Kotzk, Rabbi Menachem Mendel of (1787–1859) – Founder of the Kotzker hasidic dynasty, he was one of the unique personalities in the hasidic movement. He was known for his sharp wit and relentless and uncompromising search for the truth.

Kovner, Abba (1918–1987) – A partisan leader from the Vilna ghetto during the Holocaust, at the conclusion of WWII he joined the "*Nakam*" squad which sought revenge against Nazis. He moved to Israel and was a cultural officer in the IDF in the War of Independence. During the Eichmann trial, he was one of the key witnesses and was later involved in setting up the Diaspora Museum in Tel Aviv. He wrote many books and poems.

Lau-Lavie, Naphtali (1926–2014) – Diplomat, journalist, and public figure, he was the Israeli consul to New York. He was a Holocaust survivor who saved his younger brother, Rabbi Yisrael Meir Lau. His autobiography is titled *Balaam's Prophecy*. He also wrote about the history of his place of birth in *Pietrkow Trybunalski and Its Environs*.

Lefkowitz, Rabbi Michel Yehuda (1913–2011) – Head of the Ponevezh yeshiva for younger students for more than fifty years and one of the leaders of the Lithuanian ultra-Orthodox community in Israel, he wrote many books, including the *Beit Yehuda*.

Leibowitz, Professor Nehama (1905–1997) – Professor and commentator on Tanakh who taught in many different frameworks, she was awarded the Israel Prize for Education in 1956. Her lessons were put together in a series of books called *New Studies in the Weekly Parasha*.

Leiner, Rabbi Mordechai (1800–1854) – Founder of the Izhbitza-Radzin hasidic dynasty, his writings were gathered and published as the *Mei Shiloah*.

Levovitz, Rabbi Yerucham (1873–1936) – The legendary *mashgiah* of the Mir yeshiva who formulated the ethical character of the yeshiva.

Liadi, Rabbi Shneur Zalman of (1745–1812) – A disciple of the Maggid of Mezeritch, he was the founder and first leader of the Chabad dynasty, a position he held for forty years. He wrote the *Tanya* and *Shulhan Arukh HaRav*.

Lizhensk, Rabbi Elimelekh of (1717–1787) – A third-generation hasidic leader, one of the leading disciples of the Maggid of Mezeritch, and the younger brother of Rabbi Zushe of Annipoli. He is known by the name of the book he wrote, *Noam Elimelekh*.

Luntschitz, Rabbi Shlomo Ephraim of (1540–1619) – Chief rabbi of Prague after the Maharal, his most famous work is the *Kli Yakar* and he is known by this name.

Luzzatto, Rabbi Moshe Hayim (1707–1746) – Known by the acronym of his name, Ramhal is most famous for writing *Mesillat Yesharim*, which became the classic book of the *Musar* movement. He was a rabbi and kabbalist and wrote many books. He lived in Italy and is buried in Tiberias.

Luzzatto, Rabbi Shmuel David (1800–1865) – Known by the acronym of his name, Shadal, he was a biblical commentator, poet, linguist, and philosopher who lived in Italy.

Maimonides, Rabbi Moshe ben Maimon (1138–1204) – One of the greatest halakhic writers in Jewish history and also one of the most important philosophers of the Middle Ages. He was a community leader and physician whose most famous books are *Guide of the Perplexed, Mishneh Torah*, and books on healthy living. When he is described in Jewish circles, it is said that "From Moses to Moses there arose none like Moses." Born in Spain, he later moved to Morocco, Israel, and then Egypt.

Malbim, Rabbi Meir Leib ben Yehiel Michel (1809–1889) – A Torah sage and biblical commentator, he held rabbinical positions in many town in Romania, Russia, and Prussia. *Eretz Hemda, Mikra'ei Kodesh*, and *Artzot HaHayim* are some of the books he wrote.

Melamed, Ori – Restaurant critic, standup comic, and musician.

Mizrachi, Rabbanit Yemima – Popular teacher whose talks deal with the connection between the *parasha* and people's lives, and are distributed widely.

Nahmanides, Rabbi Moshe ben Nahman (1194–1270) – One of the greatest Torah leaders of the Golden Age of Spain, he was a halakhic arbiter, kabbalist, and physician who also wrote commentaries on the Torah and the Talmud. He moved to the Land of Israel at the end of his life.

Navon, Rabbi Chaim – Rabbi, author, and publicist. A graduate of the Har Etzion yeshiva, he has edited some of Rabbi Aharon Lichtenstein's writings and published many books of his own about Judaism in modernity.

Nebenzahl, Rabbi Avigdor – Rabbi of the Old City of Jerusalem and son of Dr. Yitzhak Nebenzahl, the second state comptroller of the State of Israel, his talks on the *parasha* were collected together and published in a series of books.

Neriah, Rabbi Moshe Tzvi (1913–1995) – Rabbi, educator, and spiritual leader, he was a pupil of Rabbi Kook and founded the network of Bnei Akiva yeshiva high schools. He was awarded the Israel Prize.

Nordau, Max (1849–1923) – Philosopher, orator, author, and physician, and one of the founders of the Zionist movement, he was a delegate to the Zionist Congresses. He was born in Hungary, passed away when on a visit to Paris, and was buried in Tel Aviv. Many neighborhoods in Israel bear his name.

Orbach, Uri (1960–2015) – Author, satirist, publicist, and one of the most prominent media personalities in the national-religious sector, he entered politics and served as a Member of Knesset in the "Jewish Home" party and was Minister of Pension Affairs.

Peli, Professor Pinchas (1930–1989) – Rabbi, professor of philosophy, and chair of the Jewish Studies department at Ben-Gurion University, he translated and edited some of the writings of Rabbi Abraham Joshua Heschel and Rabbi Joseph B. Soloveitchik.

Porat, Rabbi Hanan (1943–2011) – Educator and thinker, he was one of the founders of renewed settlement in Gush Etzion and a leader of the Gush Emunim settler movement. His writings on the *parashot* were collected into a series of books, *Me'at Min HaOr*.

Radak: Rabbi David ben Yosef Kimhi (1160–1235) – One of the greatest biblical commentators of the medieval era, his commentaries cover most of the books of the Bible. He was also a noted scholar of the Hebrew language, writing a classic book of Hebrew grammar, *Mikhlol*.

Rashbam: Rabbi Shmuel ben Meir (1080–1160) – Rashi's grandson and the brother of Rabbenu Tam. One of the greatest biblical commentators among the Tosafists, he also commented on parts of the Babylonian Talmud. He is known for his style of adhering to the literal meaning of the biblical text.

Rashi: Rabbi Shlomo ben Yitzhaki (1040–1105) – The greatest Jewish commentator, writing seminal, systematic commentaries on the Tanakh and Talmud that are cornerstones of Jewish study to this day. He lived in Troyes in France during the time of the First Crusade.

Razel, Yonatan – Singer, songwriter, lyricist, and musical composer, he has had many hits, including *"VeHi SheAmda"* and *"Katonti."*

Saba, Rabbi Abraham ben Jacob (1440–1508) – A rabbi, kabbalist, and philosopher during the time of the expulsion from Spain, he wrote *Tzror HaMor* and *Eshkol HaKofer* on the books of Esther and Ruth, and *Tzror HaHayim* on Ethics of the Fathers. He passed away on the eve of Yom Kippur on his way to Italy.

Sabato, Rabbi Shabtai – Head of the Netivot Yosef yeshiva high school and the Meor Tuvia post-high school yeshiva, he founded a project to produce a recorded audio commentary on the entire Talmud.

Sacks, Rabbi Lord Jonathan – Former chief rabbi of the United Kingdom, he was made a Life Peer and sits in the House of Lords. He is a philosopher of religion and professor at Kings College, London, New York University, and Yeshiva University.

Salanter, Rabbi Yisrael (1810–1883) – One of the founders of the *Musar* movement, he headed a yeshiva in Vilna and gave many talks about the importance of studying ethics and working on one's character. Many yeshivas were established based on his ethical teachings.

Schneerson, Rabbi Sholom Dovber (1860–1920) – The fifth head of the Lubavitch hasidic dynasty, a position he held for thirty-eight years in Russia. He set up the Tomhei Temimim yeshiva and wrote many essays about the hasidic movement, as well as general halakhic responsa.

Schneerson, Rabbi Yosef Yitzhak (1880–1950) – The sixth head of the Lubavitch hasidic dynasty, a position he held for thirty years, and was succeeded by Rabbi Menachem Mendel Schneerson, the last Lubavitcher Rebbe. He was born in Lubavitch and died in the USA.

Schneerson, Rabbi Menachem Mendel (1902–1994) – Known simply as the Lubavitcher Rebbe, he was the seventh and final head of the Lubavitch hasidic dynasty, a position he held for more than forty years. He developed the concept of sending Lubavitch emissaries all over the world.

Seforno, Rabbi Ovadia (1473–1550) – Biblical commentator, rabbi, physician, and one of the heads of the Jewish community in Rome, Italy.

Shapira, Rabbi Moshe (1935–2017) – Rabbi and expert in Jewish philosophy, especially of the Vilna Gaon and the Maharal of Prague, he headed the Pithei Olam yeshiva for newly religious students.

Sharansky, Natan (Anatoly) – The most famous Prisoner of Zion in the USSR who, upon his release, moved to Israel, he was a Member

of Knesset and Government minister and is currently the head
of the Jewish Agency.

Shemer, Naomi (1930–2004) – A singer, songwriter, and lyricist who
was awarded the Israel Prize for Israeli Song in 1983, she wrote
hundreds of poems which have entered the cultural pantheon,
including *Jerusalem of Gold.*

Singer, Isaac Bashevis (1902–1991) – One of the greatest Yiddish novel-
ists, he won the Nobel Prize for Literature in 1978. He was born
in Poland and lived in the USA. His most famous novels are *The
Slave, The Magician of Lublin,* and *The King of the Fields.*

Sofer, Rabbi Yaakov Hayim (1867–1939) – A rabbi and halakhic decisor,
he wrote many books on halakha and Jewish philosophy, including *Kaf HaHayim* on the *Shulhan Arukh.* In 1904, he made *aliya*
from Baghdad to Israel and settled in Jerusalem.

Steinberger, Rabbi Yeshayahu – A rabbi and teacher at the HaKotel
yeshiva in the Old City of Jerusalem as well as serving as a neighborhood rabbi and the head of the Ziv HaTorah kollel, he has
edited a book on the writings of the Rosh on the Talmud and is
a pupil of Rabbi Yitzhak Hutner.

Tabenkin, Yitzhak (1887–1971) – One of the leaders of socialist Zionism and a delegate to the Zionist Congresses, he later served as
a Member of Knesset representing the Labor party. He was one
of the founders of the United Kibbutz Movement and was a firm
believer in the Greater Land of Israel.

Vilna Gaon: Rabbi Eliyahu of Vilna (1720–1797) – The leading halakhic
and spiritual leader of his time, he is known for his unbelievable
diligence in learning. He refused to accept a rabbinic position.

Vital, Rabbi Hayim (1542–1620) – One of the Safed kabbalists, he was
the leading disciple of Rabbi Yitzhak Luria (the Arizal) and edited
all his writings. He wrote many books on Kabbala and works
on one's character such as *Shaarei Kedusha.* He passed away in
Damascus, Syria.

Wein, Rabbi Berel – Rabbi, historian, author, and lecturer, he founded
many educational institutions in the USA and became rabbi of
the Nassi synagogue in Jerusalem when he moved to Israel. He
has written many books in English and Hebrew.

Wiesel, Elie (1928–2016) – Novelist, philosopher, and journalist, he was a Holocaust survivor who wrote many novels, as well as books on philosophy and history. In 1986 he was awarded the Nobel Peace Prize for his work on human rights.

Wolbe, Rabbi Shlomo (1914–2005) – One of the greatest spiritual guides in Israel in recent times, he set up and served as *mashgiah* in the yeshiva of Be'er Yaakov and Givat Shaul and wrote many books on spiritual self-development in accordance with the principles of the *Musar* movement, including *Planting and Building* and the multi-volume *Alei Shur*.

Yosefi, Rabbi Yehiel Michael (Michi) – A spiritual leader whose teachings are based on Rabbi Nahman of Breslov and the Yemima method, he has lived in India and set up hostels for Israeli and Jewish backpackers. He now lives near Shilo, in the Benjamin region of Israel.

The fonts used in this book are from the Arno family